8.23.17
$26.95
AS-14
8/17

Withdrawn

MORE PRAISE FOR *THE DOGS OF AVALON*

"A self-confessed non-animal lover when her journey begins, Schenone writes with sensitivity and genuine curiosity about the world of greyhounds—inspired by her own beloved amber-eyed rescue dog, Lily. An extraordinary story, told with compassion and grace."

—Christina Baker Kline, *New York Times* best-selling author of *Orphan Train* and *A Piece of the World*

"If you have ever wondered what motivates those who risk their lives to save animals and why their work matters, this book answers those questions. It may even convince you that we become greater human beings when we show compassion to all the earth's creatures. An incredible journey chronicled with journalistic integrity that will resonate with anyone who has ever loved an animal."

—Allen and Linda Anderson, founders of Angel Animals Network and *New York Times* best-selling authors of *A Dog Named Leaf*

"In *Dogs of Avalon*, author Laura Schenone discovers the unique world and dedicated personalities of international greyhound rescues and adoptions. And it's that passionate world that allows Laura to warmly and philosophically explore the bigger world of animals in peril. A wonderful book!"

—Steven Wolf, author of *Comet's Tale*

ALSO BY LAURA SCHENONE

The Lost Ravioli Recipes of Hoboken

A Thousand Years Over a Hot Stove

The Dogs
of
Avalon

The Race to Save Animals in Peril

LAURA SCHENONE

W. W. Norton & Company
Independent Publishers Since 1923
New York • London

For information about permission to reproduce selections from this book,
write to Permissions, W. W. Norton & Company, Inc.,
500 Fifth Avenue, New York, NY 10110

For information about special discounts for bulk purchases, please contact
W. W. Norton Special Sales at specialsales@wwnorton.com or 800-233-4830

Manufacturing by LSC Communications, Harrisonburg, VA
Book design by Dana Sloan
Production manager: Anna Oler

ISBN 978-0-393-07358-4

W. W. Norton & Company, Inc.
500 Fifth Avenue, New York, N.Y. 10110
www.wwnorton.com

W. W. Norton & Company Ltd.
15 Carlisle Street, London W1D 3BS

1 2 3 4 5 6 7 8 9 0

For my mother, Marcia Schenone,
and my friend, Elizabeth Rush Marsden

CONTENTS

PART III

PART IV

AUTHOR'S NOTE

The story I set out to write includes many events that occurred decades prior to the time when they were recounted to me. My reconstruction of dialogue, where it occurs in the book, is based on interviews with individuals having knowledge of these conversations; I also referred to published articles reporting on the events concerned. Dialogue and facts from Marion Fitzgibbon's childhood are based on her recollections and my own research into the history of post–World War II Ireland. Dialogue and facts for Beverly Wolf's early life are based on her memories, supplemented by press reports. No dialogue was invented in service of the plot.

PART I

PROLOGUE

A flash of fur and bones. She flung the car door open and, without a moment's hesitation, was running across the fields, dressed in evening clothes and high-heeled shoes. They'd been on their way out to dinner with friends—but there was no choice, no choice at all but for her to run across the field, around the farmhouse, past bales of hay stacked like a wall. Perhaps she paused for a moment to call out to some farmer's wife standing there, "Did you see the dog? Did you see the dog?" (Of course she hadn't.) She ran across a cattle guard, and into tall grass. Everything else disappeared: the friends waiting at the restaurant, the husband aggravated in the car . . . Everything disappeared except for the animal in the field, running in the half-light. It was as if she and the creature were somehow one—the chased and the chaser. The only thing that existed was the sound of her own panting and the pace of her legs in sync with those of the animal.

Later—how much later, she couldn't say—she returned to the car with the mutt in her arms. And what a filthy, ragged one it was, a cowering mess of bones. There was always a leash and a blanket in the back seat. Her husband gave a loud sigh, but otherwise was silent as he turned the car around and headed back home.

Years later, Marion told me this story early on so that I would understand how it worked—that it was like a big wave that comes and carries you off, then you're gone.

1

—

WILD

1993

M arion stood in the hallway in a hospital gown, phone to her ear, trying to ignore the other cancer patients waiting in line behind her. The phone constantly rang for Marion, and by the time she'd gathered herself up from the bed and hauled her IV down the hall, a queue would already be forming. Cancer was hard enough without standing in line to make a phone call. The other patients had long ago lost patience with her.

This was the early 1990s, when Ireland was a poor nation; some people were fond of calling it the last Third World country of western Europe. They had a point, when you looked at the hospitals. Marion's room had five beds in it, and more than a dozen patients shared a single toilet. There was one phone for the entire floor.

"Marion Fitzgibbon! It's for you . . . again!"

It seemed like she got a dozen calls a day. Finally, someone asked, "Why in the world are you on the phone all day?"

Others were listening now, waiting for her to explain herself.

"Animals," she said. And then, "Animal *welfare*"—as if this would clarify her answer.

Dumbfounded silence.

"You mean to say that here you are really sick with cancer and you're standing there talking about animals all day? Are you mad?"

This time, the voice on the other end of the line belonged to Marion Webb, Yes, there were two Marions—Fitzgibbon, the one with cancer, and Webb, the healthy one. They both worked at the Irish Society for Prevention of Cruelty to Animals (the ISPCA) in Dublin, though "worked" was not quite the right word because it suggested a salary, and of course there was none; everyone was a volunteer. Webb was the chairperson in charge. Fitzgibbon was the vice chair, her number two.

Webb politely asked about Marion's health, then seamlessly shifted to business.

"I've got news."

Marion turned her head toward the hospital wall to shut out the glaring faces behind her. She wanted to concentrate on the voice coming through the receiver.

"My husband is being transferred to Scotland," Webb announced, and paused a moment to let it sink in. "The company is quite eager to get us there quickly. They're even selling the house for us."

A gurney rolled by. Heart monitors beeped. The nurses' station hummed along unperturbed.

"When?" Marion asked.

"Three weeks."

Webb's British accent was perfect for this sort of stoic we-must-carry-on message.

"Look, I know you're sick right now. But you're going to have to take over. You're the vice chair. It's your time."

Silence.

"I don't know . . . The doctor wants me to rest at home for six weeks. Then they're sending me to the radiation hospital in Dublin."

She felt like she was halfway dead. (In a day or two she'd be diagnosed with an MRSA infection in the wound.)

"Yes, and then it will be over . . . I know. It's very hard. A very hard
time, indeed. But the surgery went well. You're going to get better, and
I'll make sure there's help for you. You won't have to do it all alone."

There it was, the inevitable. Even as Marion stood leaning against
the wall for support, with her armpit feeling like it had been hacked
with a machete. Even with a lump and twenty-four lymph nodes
gone . . . She knew she'd do it. She would because that was what she
always did.

"It's your time," repeated Webb. "And you are going to get well."

A couple of days later, Webb arrived at the hospital with a large stack
of folders. She handed them over one by one, explaining each.

"Here are the files for each shelter. This is the file for farm animals. Here's the folder for exotics." Webb had them all organized:
Fundraising. Budgets. Financial projections. Legislation.

When they got to the last folder, Webb paused and took a breath.
"This is the greyhound situation," she said, holding up a thick file
bursting with papers.

Webb was unusual. She kept a greyhound herself as a pet, but that
was because she was British, and British people were in general more
advanced when it came to animal welfare, a fact that pained Marion.
In Ireland, greyhounds were working animals and not considered suitable as pets. Out in the countryside, you'd see dogmen walking their
greyhounds muzzled so they looked like criminals, like savages. They
were creatures of the track. A greyhound in the house? Never. The
slow, the injured, the aging who could no longer race or breed, for the
most part quietly disappeared. Did anyone know where they went?

Yes, it was a terrible situation, Marion agreed, accepting the folder
and thinking, Yes of course, someday, but not now. Soon even—but
not now. Christ, a year earlier they'd rescued a greyhound from a gar-

bage dump, the sweetest little bitch ever; she walked with a beautiful prance. They'd fed her, vaccinated her, put up posters all over the city trying to find her a good home. But no one called or came forth—not one person. People didn't care about greyhounds.

Marion thanked Webb with sincerity and put the greyhound folder at the bottom of the stack. They wished each other good luck and said goodbye.

Several months later—after finishing her radiation and inching up to 110 pounds on her five-foot-seven-inch frame, and after Marion Webb was resettled in Scotland—Marion put on what clothes she could find that didn't hang off her too terribly and set off in her car to deal with a situation that had been plaguing her for years.

She had no particular plan.

She just knew she had to drive about twenty miles and knock on the door. Her husband, John, had suggested more than once that she was always on the lookout for trouble. Sometimes, when they walked out the front door, he made a public service announcement that all the hurt and needy animals of Ireland should come forth and show themselves to Marion Fitzgibbon. "She's coming out now. Here's your chance!" Marion strenuously protested. She'd tried in vain again and again to explain to him that, in fact, she was most often trying to keep her head down so she would *not* see animals. Now, as she drove along the scruffy fields beneath the thick grey sky of autumn, she caught sight of the low-slung stone bungalow with turf smoke coming from the chimney. Up the long narrow driveway, careful not to get her car wheels stuck in the mud. It took but a moment to catch sight of what she'd come for. The creature was chained to a tree, lying in the grass, a leather collar around its neck.

"Jesus," she whispered, then parked the car and headed toward the front door of the farmhouse, her eyes all the while on the orange and black stripes down the long back, and the large head lying on the ground.

She took a breath and knocked.

A tall, middle-aged man opened the door and looked at her with no expression at all.

Marion introduced herself and gave her title.

"I hear you're keeping tigers."

It's a pet, he said, looking at her with big grey eyes. He seemed only slightly antagonistic and perhaps a bit weary, too. He'd been fighting for a long time and probably had expected someone like Marion to come along eventually. Now she was here.

She peered discreetly behind him. It was a modern-looking bungalow, with curtains and carpets and paintings on the walls, on a small farm. His name was Stafford Taylor and he lived there with his family. She assumed he was a circus buff; traveling circuses found such people who would accept castoffs. Tigers and bears could only learn to do so many tricks, and if they made the same rounds year after year doing the same performances, the crowds became bored. It was not unusual for a circus to offer a pair of animals to a fan in return for the offspring, which they'd pick up the following summer when they made their rounds again. Owning a dog required a license, but you needed nothing to own a tiger. Some years earlier, the *Limerick Leader* had done a feature on Taylor and his tigers—a story of fatherly love. He'd had a dream of building a menagerie circus for his twelve-year-old daughter.

"Mind if I have a look?"

Without waiting for his reply, Marion walked toward the yard.

The baby tiger was about six months old and far too thin. He lay in the dirt, chained to a tree in front of the house. When he saw Marion, he tried to pull himself up, as if to greet her. But that's when things went terribly wrong. His knees buckled and he collapsed to the ground. Getting closer, Marion could see that the lower part of his back was deformed. He looked something like a seal, his feet useless as flippers for standing. After several more failed attempts to get up, the tiger began to drag himself toward her with his two front legs. (Later, a vet would call it cage paralysis, an affliction of wild animals kept in captivity.)

"Where does this tiger stay at night?" Marion asked.

Taylor pointed across the way at his garage. Based on the pressure sores on his joints, Marion could tell that he slept on a concrete floor.

She glanced around and saw a low shed across the yard with a wood door bolted shut. What horror was inside? A post-cancer wooziness rolled over her. Her legs began to falter, so she looked away from Taylor and out at the road to steady herself. Just then a giant truck passed by, stacked with cages of tightly packed chickens on their way to slaughter. (She later learned that there was a chicken factory just down the road, and this accounted for the acrid smell in the air, which was making her queasy.)

"Mr. Taylor, you can't keep these animals here anymore." Her voice rose more than she intended. She was fully aware that her emotions were getting away from her, and yet she couldn't help it.

"We've had complaints from your neighbors. You can't continue. This baby tiger is in terrible health. Look at its legs. They're ulcerated from sleeping on a concrete floor. It's tied to a tree and can't move. It can't stand. This is all wrong."

She pointed at the calf house. "Should I understand that you have two more tigers in there right now? A mother and father, yes?"

He told her that they'd been way worse off before he took them. Then he nodded toward the yard, where he had built a little circus ring and several pallets made of slatted timbers. He'd had big plans to build a proper enclosure, but his neighbors fought it. What was he to do? His tone was righteous.

Why he had not anticipated that the council would refuse to allow such plans was anyone's guess. His farm was near an elementary school. Marion could just imagine the gruesome possibilities if a tiger got loose.

Of course the council was not going to endorse Mr. Taylor's dreams of a circus compound for his daughter. His neighbors did not help, but rasther ridiculed and reviled him: Irish small-townism at its worst.

He insisted that he'd rescued them and saved their lives.

"Look, Mr. Taylor. This is totally unacceptable. How many babies have there been before this one? And I hear you've got a bear. And two baboons."

Taylor's weathered face clenched tighter, turning red. He turned his back and stomped off to his house, slamming the door shut. Marion stood in place, waiting, not sure what to do next. A minute later, the door opened and he emerged once again, this time carrying a rifle. He marched straight toward Marion and cocked it. Then he tossed the gun toward her.

With an unexpected reflex, her arms reached out and caught it. She was surprised at the sudden cold weight of it in her hands.

She looked up at him. "What do you want me to do?"

Go ahead, he told her. Shoot him.

Up until then, it had not been the ISPCA's policy to take on the cause of exotic and wild animals. At that point in Ireland, the Animal Protection Law of 1911 had been applied only to farm animals and domestic creatures. Nor did the ISPCA *want* to start reaching out to exotics, as they already had their hands full with tens of thousands of stray dogs and cats and barely any funding. Just the same, Marion argued relentlessly at ISPCA council meetings, until she got them finally to agree to take Stafford Taylor to court.

After many months of effort, the ISPCA won the case and won custody of the circus animals, setting a new precedent. For a moment, Marion was overjoyed, but then she realized there was serious work to do. The judge had set a two-month deadline for the ISPCA to find an appropriate home for the menagerie, which totaled two baboons, one Canadian black bear, and the two Siberian tigers, plus their poor deformed baby. If appropriate homes were not found within sixty days, the animals would be destroyed. It was November. They had till just past Christmas.

This was before the Internet, which meant days and days on the phone with every animal welfare organization in Europe, begging for help. The local television news did a feature on the plight of Taylor's circus animals, and the newspapers did stories too. Yet no one came forward.

Marion questioned herself: had she made a mistake? When she went to court, she had hardly understood the gravity of finding new homes for tigers and bears. Who would even know how to sedate them properly, or transport them? Every vet she called refused, saying the same thing: "Tigers? Baboons? Bears? We have no experience with exotics. Sorry." The vet world in Ireland was a small club that tended to agree on most issues. Only one vet on the entire island was trained for such things, and he was at the Dublin Zoo and unable to leave. Who would mind his bears and tigers if something should go wrong while he was gone?

In the meantime, the animals needed care, as they were all starving and malnourished. How in the world to feed three Siberian tigers? How to pay for it? Marion's only idea was to go to the nearest meat factory—twenty-six miles away—and ask for help.

A man in a blood-speckled white apron and hat squinted at her, unsure of what she was saying. Marion told him about the tigers from the circus, how they were being kept in terrible conditions, starving and thin, one paralyzed from the waist down. They needed food. It was a desperate situation. Had he heard about it on the news? Was there anything they could offer?

What could he say to a frighteningly thin lady who was feeding tigers, claiming to be chair of the ISPCA?

He told her to meet him round the back. Marion drove her car around to the loading bay, where the big doors opened to a rack of cows hanging from their hooves. A small crew of men emerged in their blood-spattered uniforms carrying crates of raw meat, which they loaded into the boot of her car. Meat ends and offal, and even a bit of rump or shoulder as well—all of it smelling of blood and death. The factory gave her enough to last a week. Driving back to Taylor's, she tried not to think of the flesh and organs in the car, telling herself all the while, *Tigers need meat.*

The disgusting odor of chicken processing hung over Taylor's land, and again nausea mixed with Marion's post-radiation fatigue. She presented the meat to Taylor, who, along with his wife, was cooperative. Taylor had known for a long time that he was in over his head and now he saw an end. They did not discuss that the animals had been living imprisoned in darkness and half-starved. Taylor unloaded the meat and walked to the calf house. He opened the doors and threw the meat inside.

The bear, on the other hand, was a vegetarian. Though she was female, for some odd reason her stage name was Clyde. Taylor had bought a circus ring for her, but she didn't use the space. Instead, she stayed huddled inside a hut he'd built out of flimsy wood, which gave her little protection from the endless rain and damp of the Irish weather. Her fur was matted and full of parasites, and she continually scratched herself, rocking back and forth with the repetitious rhythms that animals adopt when under great stress. She was extremely thin. Marion brought Clyde fruit and nuts, which she left at the door of her hut.

"Here you go," said Marion. The bear lumbered out on four legs, snatched up the food, and raced back to her corner. This Canadian black bear—a species that evolved over millions of years to wander across acres of woods—had been so conditioned to confinement that she now feared open space.

Marion gave in to her temptation and stepped to the edge of the hut to look inside. Clyde raised her head and looked back blankly at Marion.

The funny thing about black bears is how they can look at you and seem like dogs, their intelligent eyes peering over gold-colored snouts. You might feel like you could have a conversation with the bear, and possibly pet it. The fact that they can stand on their hind legs only adds to the illusion that they might be friendly to humans. In fact, Marion felt a desire to step inside and pet the bear and console her. Of course she knew better and never would. She'd heard that circus bears were trained to dance by being forced to stand on hot plates. She hummed a tune, "The Blue Danube." To her shock, after the first few notes, Clyde dropped her fruit on the muddy ground and stood upright, then began to turn in circles. Marion's heart lurched, and she began slowly backing away. But instead of approaching her, the bear continued to dance. Clyde lifted her forelegs as though making a circle above her head as she did a pirouette, like a doll whose dancing button had been pressed. Then, after a few minutes of this humiliation, she went back to eating her fruit.

~

BRENDAN PRICE was at home in Dublin when he saw the story on the evening news. He greatly respected Marion Fitzgibbon, but knew immediately that she was out of her depth. How would she find sanctuaries for tigers, a bear, and two baboons, and then get them off the farm safely? A tiger could take off your arm in a heartbeat. He'd seen it happen.

Brendan specialized in handling wildlife and exotics. He had been a keeper at the Dublin Zoo for nine years. He'd also founded, along with his wife, Mary, the Irish Seal Sanctuary, which focused on rescuing and rehabilitating grey seal pups that were frequently orphaned on Irish beaches after storms. He collected them, fed them, and gave them time to learn to swim in pools he'd built in his backyard. When they were ready, he released them back into the ocean.

He had never planned to get involved in animal welfare work. Ensuring the good health of the animals in his care was not an emotional matter. It had simply been part of his job. But during those years at the zoo, he had witnessed things that changed him. Two polar bears swam like zombies, back and forth in the same loop in the same tiny pool year after year. A pair of hippos lived in a pool hardly bigger than themselves, with a trickle of water in which to bathe. Sea lions spent their lives in a pool so heavily chlorinated that the water burned their eyes. For years, Brendan had tried to highlight problems and seek solutions, from the inside, but he was frustrated with management's indifference. Then two elephants, Judy and Debbie, pushed him to his limit. They were in terrible condition and no one at the zoo knew what to do, nor did they seek appropriate help. When Brendan arrived in the mornings, he often found them swiveling on their bottoms, unable to get up. When one died, he was devastated. Without permission from the director, he invited a world-renowned elephant expert to come to the zoo and inspect the remaining elephant, then advise on her care. It was a marvelous meeting. The famous vet was full of ideas on how they could work together, and finally Brendan felt hopeful. The next day, he was cleaning the bat house and got word that the director wanted to see him. He was sacked on the spot.

This marked the beginning of his transformation. Brendan spoke out to the media, exposing the wrongs he'd seen. He made trouble at the meetings of the national zoological society, demanding transparency and data on animal births and deaths. (His protests ultimately contributed to a government inquiry and investment of 15 million pounds for zoo improvements.) He attended ISPCA meetings, too, where he sometimes got carried away, pounding his hand on the table and asking why the ISPCA wasn't doing something for exotic animals.

As vice chair, and later as chair, Marion respected Brendan and understood that he was an exceptional hands-on animal man, who put welfare first. He'd figured out things about marine animals that no one else yet knew—like how to keep grey seal pups alive by feeding them liquidized fish. She always tried to support him and found a little bit in her budget for his seal sanctuary. When no one would give him a job, she invited him to join the ISPCA governing council to advise them on exotics. In short, she believed in him. She brought him in from the shadowlands, the place where all whistleblowers go.

That's why when Brendan Price saw Marion on the evening news with Stafford Taylor's circus animals, there was no question in his mind that he would be getting himself on a train to Limerick.

After several weeks of despair, Marion felt joy at the sight of Brendan at her door with a rucksack on his back, ready to serve.

Soon he was calling sanctuaries all over the world in search of a place that would accept tigers or bears. He also set about finding a vet who was qualified to sedate the large exotics for transport, whenever (and to wherever) that would be. He reached out to Samantha Lindsey, a young vet in England who was then just emerging as an advocate for elephants and other animals who were abused and abandoned by traveling circuses. Lindsey agreed to come and help. Next, Brendan persuaded a particularly humane member of the Garda—the Irish police—to help, and this was essential, because without police support, they would not have the authority to set foot on Taylor's land. Also, Brendan wanted Taylor to see he was serious: that a prosecution was coming and the game was up.

An unexpected complication emerged when they learned that the mother tiger was pregnant.

"Pregnant?" Marion gasped.

Taylor insisted that Marion couldn't take the new baby because he owed it to the circus.

It was true: they didn't have the right to the baby. The ISPCA had to go back to court, and Marion had to testify once more about how inhumane it was to keep tigers in such poor conditions and in such a dangerously insufficient enclosure on a farm in Limerick, locked up in the dark. The judge extended custody of all the offspring of the captive animals to the ISPCA, and from that point forward, Taylor and his wife were cooperative. Brendan let them know that he under-stood their good intentions toward the animals, but also helped them understand that they needed expert help. It was the only way to get out of the mess they'd created.

Stafford Taylor wasn't cruel. In fact, he'd probably acquired the animals in the first place because he was an animal lover. Price had seen this sort of thing before. The traveling circus needed to unload some tigers, so they set up a ruse, perhaps in a pub, asking if anyone wanted to take a tiger—because, if not, the poor thing would have to be shot that night. It was usually the softest-hearted animal lover who stood up and said, "Me! Yes, I'll take him." Somehow it got worked out that there would be *two* tigers who would breed, and the circus would come back the following season for the babies. It wasn't long before the whole thing got out of control. The tigers were locked up in the dark, and yes, when the baby was born it was cute. But then it grew up and ate the dog. Next, it started eyeing the children. Then it was sent to the garage. The expense, and the isolation—it all got too much for the tiger keeper. Neighbors who used to love the baby tiger started making terrified complaints about the roaring. Before you knew it, the kind-hearted one, the very same animal lover who saved a life in the first place, was accused of abuse.

Marion found one local vet who agreed to handle the deformed baby tiger—and only the baby tiger. Because of his size, he was much less of a threat than his parents. She was not surprised when the vet told her that the only compassionate thing was to put the animal down, as he could not stand or walk and no one in the world would take a disabled, misshapen baby tiger. The humane method was a two-step process: first a barbiturate to sedate, then an intravenous injection to bring cardiac arrest. If you skipped the first step, the animal might have seizures and suffer while dying.

While the vet assembled his syringe, he and Marion discussed the safest way to approach the tiger. They planned to come from behind and quickly inject the tranquilizer into his back hip.

Taylor intervened. This wasn't necessary, he said, because the tiger was tame. They should just go up and give it the needle.

"We're taking precautions, Mr. Taylor," Marion answered in her case-is-closed voice. "The ISPCA has already put me on notice that we aren't insured for putting down a tiger—not even a baby. We can't have any accidents."

It was raining hard. Yet the baby lay chained to the tree, looking peacefully toward them without an inkling of suspicion, his face almost puppy-like. When the syringe sank into his thigh, he barely flinched at the insult. The vet, who had never put down a tiger before, had started with a small dose. It wasn't enough, so after a wait he administered another shot. Marion moved to approach him.

"Stay back," the vet ordered. "You think the creature is asleep, and then it opens its eyes and takes a piece out of you."

Sure enough, when the vet tapped the tiger's front leg with a long pole, his claws shot out like long spears. He loaded another syringe. It took several more injections to knock him out. The rain poured down harder and harder. Finally, after two hours, the tiger was fully sedated and his paws remained still.

With the big orange head lying heavily on the muddy grass beneath the tree, long whiskers shooting out, it was hard not to feel pity. The vet picked up a paw, while Marion circled the tiger from a distance and admired his magnificent orange-and-black stripes and long black-ringed tail.

Next came the final act. The vet shaved away a patch of fur on the front leg so he could find a vein, and placed the needle carefully. They sat still a few moments in silence: the baby tiger, the vet, Marion, and even Stafford Taylor, who had moved a bit closer. The vet raised a stethoscope to the tiger's heart, his eyes downcast as he listened. When he looked up and nodded to Marion, she knew the cub was peaceful and quiet. Thank God, she thought.

⟞⟝

IT WAS December, and the days were shortening. In only a few weeks, the animals would be destroyed. So far, they'd come up empty-handed, despite weeks of calls and pleas for help.

"What sort of cages will we need to take these animals on a plane or a boat?" she asked Brendan.

"Haven't a clue. Do you?"

"No. But these animals will be leaving here soon so we'd better get their transport cages ready."

Brendan called the airlines and ferries and got specifications for the incredibly secure, huge, reinforced cages they required. He could find none available for purchase, so he contacted a carriage man who said he could build them, but the price was ridiculous: 3,000 pounds of ISPCA money, all a waste if the animals would ultimately be destroyed. Marion urged the ISPCA council to support the rescue to the end. There were doubters, for sure, but ultimately they agreed.

"Go ahead," Marion told Brendan. "Have them built and delivered, so we will be ready to go."

In the week before Christmas, an unusually bitter wind blew across Taylor's farm. The reinforced crates were delivered, but no destination was yet secured. There were mere days left before the animals would have to be killed because of the court order. Marion was nearly at breaking point when, one evening, her phone rang.

"May I speak with Mrs. Fitzgibbon?" It was a female voice, American. "My name is Martine Colette, and I'm calling from Wildlife

Waystation in California. I hear you've got some tigers needing a home. We have space in our sanctuary that was set up for tigers by some very devoted philanthropists. It's empty now. If you can get your tigers here, we'd be happy to take them."

A few days later, Brendan told Marion he'd found a sanctuary in Canada that had agreed to take Clyde. It was called Bear With Us, and it specialized in returning Canadian black bears to the wilderness after they'd been freed from circus life, and also took cubs who had been orphaned after the spring bear hunts.

Marion wasn't sure if all this was a dream or a miracle.

Though Samantha Lindsey was credentialed to tranquilize the animals for transport, it was a complicated situation. The animals were extremely thin and in very poor health—the male tiger especially. The female had just given birth to not one but two babies inside the calf shed. Lindsey asked Simon Adams to join her; he was an English vet well known for his welfare work with circus and zoo animals. The two of them had collaborated before. He had hands-on wildlife experience, while Lindsey specialized in the behavioral and legal side of exotic animal welfare. They had made a good team in prosecutions. He was in his thirties and exuded confidence.

Adams and Marion discussed particulars by phone. Would she kindly gather the pipe and darts and other supplies? "Of course," she agreed, and he gave her an exact list.

More challenges came: it was Christmastime, and flights to the U.S. were booked.

"Try the U.S. Air Force," Marion told Brendan. "They take mail back and forth all the time." It was a good idea, but it didn't succeed either. Finally, miraculously, Brendan found a flight for the tigers from Ireland to Los Angeles with two stops, in New York and Chicago. The airline's one stipulation was that the tigers could not travel alone. Simon Adams agreed to make the trip.

The baboons, meanwhile, had been relatively easy to place. A primate sanctuary in Yorkshire agreed to take them, and because they weighed only about fifty pounds each, transport was easy. All that was needed was a van and a volunteer driver for the eight- or nine-hour trip, including a ferry across the Irish Sea, to the sanctuary's door. But the bear, who would be rechristened Molly, faced a far more difficult journey. She weighed at least two hundred pounds and would be in a heavy crate reinforced by steel bars, which would have to be put into a lorry, driven across Ireland and onto the ferry, and once in England driven a few hundred more miles to Heathrow Airport. Finally she would be put on a flight to Canada. Mr. Taylor's animals were now the subject of an international rescue effort involving four nations.

Two days before the big day, the four decided to meet in a pub to go over their final plans. Lindsey and Adams had just arrived from England. They took a table and went through all the details of tranquilizers, trucks, and transport routes. Everything was settled except for one detail. The hut Taylor had built for Molly was in a quarry-like pit. How would they lift her out? They brainstormed for a while, but no one had a good suggestion. Then Marion had a crazy idea. It came in a single word: rugby.

On the big day, Marion got up early to head for Taylor's farm. John made tea and, as usual when she had a big event, he helped make sure she had everything she needed by running through the list: medicine, tickets, itineraries, contact phone numbers for the volunteer drivers who were coming with the lorries, vet certificates. Yes, yes. She had it all, but she was terribly nervous. If the plan didn't work, the animals would be killed. Adding complication, a cold front had arrived, bringing a fast and thick snow that rarely came to Limerick.

Brendan Price and the two British vets were already there. After a few pleasantries and a review of supplies, Marion and Brendan followed Adams and Lindsey across Stafford Taylor's field to the old stone calf shed. Taylor opened it, and for the first time, Marion could look inside. For a moment, it seemed as though she'd glimpsed a portal to hell's darkness and suffering. The smell of excrement and the vision of two half-dead adult tigers and their babies behind bars was just too much. All about the shed were scattered chicken parts that had been cast off from the factory down the road and used by Taylor as food. Marion stepped aside to vomit, while Adams and Lindsey paused only a moment in horror before stepping inside. Quickly they got the tranquilizer darts into the animals and soon the tigers were unconscious. Taylor stepped in and unlocked their iron cages, one on each side of the low building, then Adams and Lindsey bent down and reached in to check each animal's vital signs. The plan was for the men to carry the animals one at a time onto a tarp, which they'd lift into the lorry that had been parked adjacent. The male came out first: skeletally thin, the notches of his spine protruding under his fur. Adams and Lindsey lifted him into the custom-made reinforced cage, lined with blankets and straw, which was already inside the lorry. Next came the female, who was put into a second cage. Each of the tiny tiger cubs was settled into a small, handheld carrier.

They slammed the door shut, and exhaled great sighs of sadness and relief. The tigers were ready to make their trip to San Diego.

Finally, it was Molly's turn, and they all walked down to the quarry. Molly saw them and for a moment Marion believed she could read the animal's mind: she imagined that Molly was expecting the worst. Adams tranquilized her, and the bear gave them all one last blank look before she slumped into a heap. It was a long way uphill carrying a bear, but by this time Marion's solution had arrived, in the form of five strapping lads. Limerick was a famous rugby town, and Marion had convinced the coach to lend her a few of his boys for a couple of hours. It was freezing, but they were good-natured, though clearly frightened that the bear might wake up. With difficulty, they

Simon Adams tranquilizes the male tiger, which was "thin as a rasher," according to Marion. (Courtesy Press 22)

heave-hoed and got Molly into the lorry and into her cage, safe and sound.

She would not be traveling alone. The previous day, Heathrow Airport had informed them that it would not accept an unaccompanied bear. Brendan, after a quick call to his wife, traveled with Molly through the night to the ferry, which made a nauseating journey across choppy, freezing waters, then finally on to Heathrow, where he bade farewell to Molly and watched as she was loaded into the bottom of the plane.

When she arrived in Canada, it was immediately clear to the people at Bear With Us that she could never be released into the wild. She'd spent her life around people and never learned survival skills. Instead, they arranged for her to live with another bear in a four-acre enclosure with a lake. Years later, Brendan Price was visiting the United States and made a detour north to see Molly. She was roaming over the scrub with her companion, a male named Yogi, and she seemed happy and at ease. From a distance, he watched with deep satisfaction as she and Yogi waded into the lake.

Meanwhile, at Shannon Airport near Limerick, Simon Adams had to deal with a vet from the Irish Department of Agriculture who wouldn't approve the tigers' travel because he could feel a tumor on the male's side. He suggested euthanasia. Vet to vet, Adams managed to convince him that the tumor was not serious and could be easily removed at the other end of the journey.

The itinerary was punishing, with two connections between Shannon and Los Angeles, but it was all the harder because Adams had an ambitious plan. He wanted to keep the babies with their parents once they arrived in California. This was more difficult than it sounds: if cubs are away from their mother for more than a few hours, she may instinctively reject or kill them. But Adams had seen all too often that once you separated a baby tiger from its mother, you put the animal at high risk of exploitation. Baby tigers brought in big bucks in advertising, circuses, and other schemes such as selling people a

Molly in 2016, age thirty-one, living at Bear With Us sanctuary in Canada. (Courtesy Bear With Us)

chance to cuddle or take a picture with one. If Adams wanted to keep the family intact, he would have to anesthetize the mother so well that she'd believe she'd gone to sleep in Ireland and woken up in the California hills with little time having passed. And he intended to keep the babies with him every moment until they reached the safety of the sanctuary.

When they arrived in Chicago, a heavy snowstorm had blanketed the region and their connecting flight to Los Angeles was canceled. The airline offered an alternative flight, but the tigers' crates were too large to fit in that plane. Adams stood in the airport with two adult tigers in their crates and the babies in hand carriers realizing that, even if he could get himself to the Chicago zoo, he did not have the required permits to stay overnight. He woke the tigers, let them drink, and then knocked them out again with more tranquilizer. Meanwhile, he noticed that an American Airlines flight was headed to Los Angeles that same night, but they refused to put him on it because the cargo compartment was already full, with a transport of U.S. mail.

That's when he got out his video camera and turned it on.

"You mean to tell me that I have come all this way to euthanize these tigers because you can't move the mail onto a flight tomorrow?"

They made room on the plane.

Adams and the tigers were met upon arrival in L.A. by Martine Colette and her staff. After loading the tigers onto her truck, they drove to her sanctuary in the hills outside San Diego, where more than two hundred volunteers happened to be having their holiday party. When the truck pulled in, the crowd sent up a jubilant cheer.

Adams was impressed by the space that Colette had built for the animals. The next step was to attach the transport boxes to the enclosure and wait for the tigers to wake up. The male emerged right away, but the female did not come out at first. Everyone at the sanctuary was worried. It was dark by then, and Adams carried the cubs to the outside of the enclosure, ensuring that he was covered in the scent of their bedding. They both chirruped, calling for their mother. Immediately she appeared and came over to lick the cubs through the wire. That's when they knew it would be okay. Martine opened the door and popped the cubs inside. The female tiger carried them one by one back to the safety of her crate and began to nurse them. For a week she remained inside her crate with her babies. Finally they stepped outside, into the warm hills of Southern California.

Marion heard the whole story later, and Martine Colette sent her a video. There, in her living room in Limerick, she watched the mother tiger and babies emerge from the crate and, after a life in darkness, look up for the first time at the bright blue San Diego sky. She heard the birdsong and watched the tigers blink with astonishment.

2

—

GYPSY DOG

2007

Perhaps it's best that I say up front that I have never been a big animal lover, and I get bored by long conversations about pets. I have never been an animal rights activist. I have never given money to the ASPCA or the Humane Society because I generally prefer people to animals. When I donate time or money to a charitable cause, it is usually to reduce the suffering of humans, especially children; in fact, I spent many years working with an organization dedicated to saving children from poverty and abuse. I respected those who worked on behalf of hurt or abused animals, and I wished them well; it's just that they didn't interest me.

In fact, I'd always been afraid of most animals. They are too unpredictable for my quick-trigger startle reflex. Cats make me nervous, the way they can lunge and scratch with no warning, and though many dogs are wonderful, you never can be sure. I really really, really disliked the savage squirrels outside my kitchen, because they gnawed through the plastic of the garbage cans and the wood in our soffits,

trying to get into our house. I was sure they could get into my bedroom at night if they really wanted to. I am quite afraid of mice,
because even though I know they are harmless and scared little creatures, they remind me of you-know-what. And I have a serious you-
know-what phobia, and it is so bad I'd rather not discuss it.

I'd been fortunate to have a wonderful dog in my childhood, a
Doberman named Charade. Everyone thinks their childhood dog was
wonderful, and maybe they all were, but Charade was exceptional
because she was so smart that she could read your mind and telepath
back to you. My parents made arrangements—through channels I
couldn't fathom—to breed her to another pedigree-perfect Doberman
named Postmaster General, who was a virile-looking guy, according to
his photo, standing in the AKA power pose with the choke collar high
on his neck. The process fascinated my on-the-brink-of-adolescence
mind—here they were packing up our dog and driving her four hours to
Baltimore to have sex with another dog. This odd manipulation of nature
seemed to me both absurd and thrilling, as well as a bit embarrassing.
Whatever happened down in Baltimore was successful, because Charade's belly grew and grew. She had thirteen puppies in a whelping box
my father built in our basement—one of the brightest moments of my
childhood. We kept one of her pups, a red Doberman named Cognac.

I loved those puppies, but it wouldn't be accurate to say I was
a dog lover simply because I loved *our* dogs. You wouldn't say that
people "love children" if they love their own and have little concern
for other people's children. And I had good reason to be afraid of
dogs: twice in my childhood I was bitten. The first time I was quite
young and taking horseback riding lessons at the county park. When I
walked into the office at the stable to deliver an envelope with my tui-
tion fee, I was greeted by a German shepherd that sank his teeth into
my thigh. The second time was far worse. I was thirteen years old, in
my Catholic-school plaid skirt and knee socks, delivering newspapers
after school. At one particular house on my route whenever I came to

the door to collect, one family member paid me while another used great strength to hold back a dog, who barked and foamed and snarled and nearly choked himself trying to break free so he could kill me.

One day I walked around the back of the house to deliver the paper to its appointed spot and found the dog off-leash waiting for me. The dog and I looked at each other for a moment, and time stood still. We both knew full well what was going to happen.

I turned and ran for my life, and he was right behind me. It was winter, with ice and snow on the ground. I made it as far as the front yard, but then slipped on the snow and fell face down. He sank his teeth deep into my calf and mangled it badly before his owners pulled him off. In the hospital, when I dared to look at what lay beneath the sheet, I saw inside parts of the leg hanging outside where they weren't supposed to be. (I recovered fully, with only a couple of mild, permanent dents.)

But, anyway, didn't this fear of unknown animals, whether wild or domestic, make perfect sense? Aren't we *supposed* to be afraid of them? Aren't we *supposed* to keep our distance?

For many years I wrote about food and cooking. Animals for the most part meant meat, milk, cheese, eggs, fish. I believed they should be treated humanely, but they were food, nonetheless. I marveled over artisan prosciutto that my friend Lou made in his garage, and rhapsodized over perfectly braised meat. I spent years hunting down and perfecting a family recipe that contained both pork and beef. I believed, and still do, that the capture, cooking, and eating of animals was fundamental to the rise of human civilization. I was more sympathetic to Indians wanting to kill a whale to continue their tradition than to the whale. Traditions were important when they served people and bonded them to one another. I suppose we all have a circle of concern, and only so much could fit into mine.

Then I met an animal rescuer named Elizabeth. Of course, I didn't know this about her at first. I was selling an old appliance—a vintage 1920s stove, to be precise—and I'd taken out an ad. Elizabeth was the only person to answer it, which tells you something about both her and me.

One winter day, she showed up at my door to have a look at the stove. She was well into middle age, dressed in an unremarkable parka and snow boots. She had a big head of curly hair and piercingly serious eyes. In this simple transaction, when most people say as little as possible, Elizabeth communicated quite a bit. I learned that her husband had recently left her for a younger woman, that she'd lost a magnificent home and a career as a music agent, that she'd survived illnesses and at least one near-death experience after being hit by a truck while walking on a road in Ireland. Well, at least she still had the cottage in Ireland. Anyway, back to the old stove . . . she'd recently returned to New Jersey and was starting all over, a new life, a new little house not far from mine. She'd left everything behind and was buying furniture second-hand. She thought the stove would be perfect. She loved cast-off and vintage things that no one wanted. I got the feeling that this dark, edgy performance was not intended to entertain me, but to entertain herself, and I couldn't help but like that. She took the stove and we exchanged an email or two and eventually met for coffee.

Early on, Elizabeth told me she had a special dog that my boys (then five and ten years old) should meet. I said sure, and we put it on the calendar.

When the day arrived and the doorbell rang, we found her standing on the step with Daisy. We were a bit stunned. We'd never seen anything like this animal before. It was unclear that she was even a dog. She was tall and thin and wearing a sweater, and for a confused moment I thought "racehorse," imagining it was a saddle blanket on her back. Elizabeth stepped forward, leash in hand, and put the matter to rest. "Daisy is a greyhound," she announced, and from the exalted tone in her voice we were to understand that "greyhound" meant something better than a mere dog. Elizabeth then pulled a big cushion from her satchel and tossed it onto our living room floor, and

Daisy, on cue, cantered over to the soft spot then, bone by bone, lowered herself into a lying position with her long front legs outstretched and her rear knees hitched up high. She looked like an Egyptian sphinx. Elizabeth explained that she had found Daisy many years earlier, on a street in Ballycotton, Ireland, pregnant, with her head in a garbage can looking for food. We didn't know that she was dying.

My sons approached cautiously, and Daisy gently bowed her head to accept their petting. It didn't take long for her to fall over on her side and thoroughly surrender. She was a gentle, sweet creature and our friendship was immediate.

"The greyhound is the fastest dog on earth, and the second fastest mammal," said Elizabeth. "Only the cheetah is faster." My sons stared at Daisy, incredulous. They could not understand how such a still creature could possibly be a superhero.

This was the beginning of my greyhound education, and Elizabeth continued in a slow, calm voice, like Scheherazade settling into a long, wonderful story. Indeed, that's what it was, because thousands of years of breeding and history were writ upon Daisy's aerodynamic body—the powerful legs and deep chest that arced up to the sculpted narrow waist, the head, feet, and pointy snout all slender and narrow, to suit the single purpose of speed—and to use that speed to hunt.

After Elizabeth lost her beloved Daisy, I didn't see her for a long while. A year or so later, she showed up again at my house with a new dog. He, too, was a greyhound—kind of: wider and sturdier, his back thicker, his face less pointy. As he flew around our backyard tearing up the lawn, she explained that he was a lurcher, which meant a kind of mixed-breed sight hound made up of a greyhound plus something else. Lurchers were a specialty of the Irish gypsies.

"Irish gypsies?"

"Yes, but they don't like to be called that—and you shouldn't call them tinkers either. Today, they prefer 'Travellers.' They're not the same as the Romany gypsies of Europe. They've been in Ireland forever.

Some still live in camps and move around the country. They used to live in painted wagons drawn by horses, but now they've got campers."

Each time Elizabeth came back from her annual visit to Ireland she brought back lurchers, because they needed homes and no one there wanted them. It seemed utterly ludicrous to me that anyone would be flying dogs from Ireland to the U.S., as there were millions of abandoned dogs here. I said nothing, though, as it meant so much to her and I didn't want to offend. Elizabeth put me on her list of potential lurcher adopters. Before or after each trip, I received an email advertising the most recent Irish lurcher needing a home.

"We're not ready for a dog."

She ignored my words and kept sending emails.

And I kept deleting them.

⁓

ULTIMATELY, I got a dog for one reason and one reason only: my older son needed one. I delayed—first with a tank of fish and then with a couple of gerbils, as silly parents often do. Some time later, when the pressure was closing in, a big, thick dog encyclopedia found its way into our home, and I patronized my son and told him to study it and research breeds so that maybe, at some point in the future, when we were seriously considering getting an animal, we could make a good decision.

Whether it was the universal loneliness of childhood or his own particular version, I cannot say. But this quiet, dark-eyed boy of mine was the seven-, eight-, and then nine-year-old who did not find much fun in playing sports and games. He loved books but despised school. All too often he seemed to be standing at the gates of childhood, not going in. A sage person told my husband and me that childhood wasn't for everybody. "Some kids just don't make good kids. It will get better in time." And it did, though of course back then we couldn't have known.

One thing we knew for sure was that in the presence of animals, our son was happy and at ease. He seemed to know intuitively how to approach and speak to them, and whether a creature was stressed and needed space. He was one of those people who from the beginning of life have an eye toward the creatures of the world. He was a kid who could hold lizards and snakes without flinching, and he protested when other boys took frogs from the creek. He pitied my fear of small furry things, such as mice (which remind me of you-know-what). Once, when a mouse scuttled across my kitchen floor and I screamed and shrieked like an idiot, a friend who happened to be there captured it in a bag, then let it loose in the backyard. Gabriel came to see what all the noise was about and shook his head, clearly disgusted, then went outside to see about the mouse. The tiny thing was so stunned by the screaming and capturing and tossing out that it stood frozen by the backyard fence. He bent down and looked the creature in the eye, able to see instantly what I did not—that a house mouse might not survive in the outside world during the depth of winter. Ignoring me entirely, he came back inside and made the mouse a bed of cardboard and tissues for warmth, with a bit of food, then returned to the yard and set the mouse shelter outside by the fence, where he hoped the mouse would find it.

I saw my own selfishness at that moment. And I also saw it when he looked at me with his big black eyes and said, "I'm not looking in this dog encyclopedia anymore. Don't lie to me. You're never going to get me a dog."

I was running out of time.

Not long after this, an email arrived from Elizabeth, who was about to go to Ireland. The subject line read: "Lily our beautiful Lurcher: How is she still alive?"

Underneath were horrifying photos of a dog skinny as death, bent over, scratching herself. She had barely any fur; her raw skin was pink and bloody. One of her eyes was infected so badly it was nearly sealed shut. The email explained that Lily had been found abandoned in this terrible condition. She looked like a greyhound, but slightly smaller and with floppier ears.

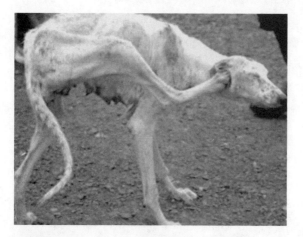

Lily, as she was found abandoned in County Cork in 2006, and her progress over the following three months. (Courtesy Limerick Animal Welfare)

This time, it was hard to click delete. There was something about the dog's face. Her expression went beyond pain and hunger and had the odd quality I'd seen during my Catholic girlhood in the images of martyred saints who'd been humiliated and tortured, burned at the stake, yet looked outward beyond the physical world, enduring the wrongdoings of humanity with resignation.

The email took the form of a success story. Further down were photos taken three weeks later, at an animal shelter in Cork. The bleeding had stopped, and Lily's fur was growing back snow white, dotted with black. Her expression was calmer and happier. A caption told of her sweet nature and constantly wagging tail. I scrolled down. More photos—taken two months later—revealed a breathtaking transformation. She was an exquisite animal, with the most feminine face a dog could have. Her eyes appeared to be lined with black kohl eyeliner, one side smeared. She was a small, more delicate version of a greyhound. In the final photo, one of her ears was flipped back, like hair swept glamorously over her head. Her face toward the camera, she had the eyes of a doe.

I knew this was no way to choose a dog. What kind of sucker was I? But when I read the phrase "Lily is a real miracle dog," I knew she was our dog. I called my husband to come and see.

A few weeks later we were at Elizabeth's house, looking down at Lily sprawled out on the bed, more beautiful and weirdly leggy and thin than in the photos. She was jet-lagged and lying very still, having only arrived the night before after a long trip from Shannon Airport. I leaned close to her, and with some effort Lily lifted her head and looked at me. We held a glance for a moment, her amber eyes and mine, and then she lay back down in sleepy submission. In this way, we came into possession of Lily the lurcher.

Lily was a ballerina dog who pranced rather than walked and carried herself regally aloof. It was hard to imagine that she'd been born in the shadows of campsites and campfires and caravans, an outcast among outcasts. Someone had found her by the side of the road in Ireland and taken her to an animal sanctuary, where they had bathed her, fed her, put ointment on her skin and got her veterinary attention, then arranged to get her out of the country because people in Ireland didn't want greyhounds as pets, and especially not mongrel versions of greyhounds. Elizabeth told us there were women in Ireland who devoted their lives to saving thousands of cast-off dogs like Lily.

Even stranger: now here she was with us, living in a New York suburb where many people venerated dogs. Though she was feared and unwanted at home, here she was seen as an exotic beauty. When we went out walking, cars would slow and heads turned to stare at her slim form and unusually elegant bearing. Everyone wanted to know what kind of dog she was.

"Oh, so regal!"

"Look at that beautiful creature!"

"Did she race at the track?"

During her first weeks with us, Lily maintained a blank-faced caution. She flinched when we came close, and, when in doubt, she immediately dropped to the floor, one cheek down, waiting to be beaten. She seemed afraid of her food and crept toward her bowl cautiously, lest another dog might race in snarling and push her aside.

It wasn't until we let her run that we understood her true nature. There was a double tennis court around the corner from our house, and the first time we snuck her in there and clinked the gate shut, everything changed. We took off her leash and watched Lily tear forth with a speed and form that astonished us. She was a cheetah dog and galloped in a broad circle around the courts, using a special mechanism for running known as the double suspension gallop, which meant she held herself in the air twice as long as other dogs, pumping her rear legs forward and then extending them back behind her, all in a single stride. The overwhelming effect was nothing short of flight. I understood then that she was more bird than dog, more air than earth.

3

—

DOMESTIC

1945–65

She had been a fragile wisp of a girl with pale blue eyes and skin so delicate that you could almost see through to her veins and bones. The adults in the family fretted endlessly about her being so thin and schemed up tricks to put more flesh on her body. Great-Aunt Mary made up games to get her to drink milk. They gave her Guinness, too (its fortifying properties were highly thought of at the time), and sometimes they even gave her Guinness mixed with milk. This was the most odious of all.

They lived in a tiny village called Patrickswell, eight miles outside of Limerick. Three men were most important in that village: the priest, the doctor, and the headmaster. Marion's father was the headmaster, and his family got to live in the headmaster's house. The school was ten minutes down the road, a damp and drafty place that froze them in wintertime. They'd even seen a rat or two inside. But this was poor, rural Ireland in the 1940s, when many people still lit their homes with candles and some children came to school in bare feet. The headmaster's home, however, was luxurious because it had running water, a flush toilet, and a sitting room with a piano. They even had a maid. When Marion was about six, the headmaster's house got electricity, another luxury. People from the village came to the back door to listen to the news on her father's radio.

Her father taught the country boys chess and had them chanting hymns in Latin, even though those things were of no obvious use to their future lives as farmers or shopkeepers. Later, Marion would reflect on how unusual a man he was. He'd never had a music lesson, but sat down and taught himself to play Chopin. He even had a motorcar at a time when most people were using bicycles.

Considering his background, simply managing to become a schoolteacher would have been amazing enough. He'd come from the city of Limerick, where tuberculosis blew through the poor neighborhoods, wiping out entire families. When he was a child, he, too, came down with the glassy eyes and flushed cheeks, the bloody cough. But he was one of the lucky ones who survived. He returned to school, where he did so well that he won a full scholarship to teachers' college. That he became a headmaster—even just of a small rural schoolhouse—was extraordinary.

Marion's mother—also a teacher thanks to a scholarship—became his number two teacher in Patrickswell. (He taught the older children and she taught the younger ones, because she was a woman.) She too had come from a cursed childhood: mother dead when she was just two years old, father gone to the pub all the time. Yet despite the hardship, Marion's mother became a third-generation teacher. The lifeline of education pulled her above the sea of ordinary Irish poverty.

When Marion was about six years old, the family went out for a drive in the new motorcar, Marion next to her sister in the back seat. It was pouring buckets. While the two girls looked out at the blurry, rain-soaked world, a horse came up behind them, collared and harnessed, pulling a heavy load. He was close enough to the car that Marion could see the wind whip at his face and the rain pelt into his eyes. He blinked and stamped his feet, trying to endure. Something happened then that she'd never be able to explain. For a flicker of an instant, some unnamed force yanked Marion out of the car. Suddenly, she was being pounded by the storm, feeling the weight of a wagon harnessed to her shoulders, while the wind and rain assaulted her head and soaked her mane and the wet and cold froze her four legs. She stayed just as long as she could bear it, and then, as quickly as she'd left, she was back in the car again, restored to her identity as Marion the little girl, with little arms, legs, and body, sitting next to her sister in the shelter of a shiny new car, warm and dry.

The experience shattered her.

"Give me an umbrella! I need an umbrella." She tried to explain to her parents that she wanted to hold it over the horse. She needed to at least try to protect him. When her bewildered parents said no, we don't hold umbrellas over horses, she began to sob. They tried to comfort her by explaining that a horse in the rain was perfectly normal because that's what a horse's life is. Animals don't feel things as we do. They're different from humans. She only cried harder because she knew her parents were lying. Of course, the sheep and cows and pigs and horses felt pain and misery if they stood out in the fields in cold and rain—just as we would. Wasn't it obvious?

She also knew for certain that animals felt fear.

The farmer who lived behind their house sent all the pigs away to die, except one that he held back each year for the family's eating. On butchering day, the pig's screeches would rise up across the fields, sounding like a terrified baby. Marion ran and hid in the orchard and pulled her sweater up over her ears to keep from hearing the moment of death and the terror just before.

⌒

WHEN HER father got sick, it seemed like a cold, perhaps, with a cough. But instead of getting better, he got worse, his breathing became painful, and he took to his bed. He went to the hospital, and Great-Aunt Mary from Kerry moved in to help.

"Nothing to fear," the adults said. "He's getting proper care and getting well."

Perhaps it was true. One day, Marion's mother announced that she'd hired a car and was heading to the hospital to bring him home. They were joyful and ready to celebrate.

Then came a knock at the door—a telegram boy, extending an envelope toward Aunt Mary, who stepped outside, shutting the door. From the window Marion and her sister could see her in the garden, holding the telegram toward the sky, her lips repeating again and again, "No, no, no."

The relatives blamed childhood tuberculosis for scarring his lungs and weakening his heart. Marion's mother took little interest in these medical theories. As far as she was concerned, the rural schoolhouse had killed her thirty-eight-year-old husband; the damp, drafty classrooms had destroyed his lungs.

Marion was eight and still a country sprite of a child. The death of her father ensured that her childhood ended with a sledgehammer blow, to be replaced by a dark hole into which her father disappeared.

Shortly after her father was buried and the funeral over, Marion's mother took the girls out of the country school. Now, every morning, they found themselves on a bus to Limerick wearing itchy woolen uniforms, on their way to be educated by the Faithful Companions of Jesus.

Aunt Mary stayed on more or less permanently, while Marion's mother continued at Patrickswell as a teacher of the younger grades. The school would not consider her for the headmaster's job because she was a woman. They brought in a new one instead, and Marion's family had to leave the headmaster's house. They moved to a house in Limerick, and Marion's mother bicycled eight miles back to Patrickswell each day to teach. Meanwhile, the nuns made sure that

Marion and her sister knew their lives were worth very little in the face of God's greatness, and that all life on earth—as if they needed reminding—was tenuous, subject to God's mercy.

During these dreary years, the first one found her. He was a high-legged terrier, and came up to her at school during lunch. She gave him some of her sandwich. Later that day, she looked over her shoulder and saw him trotting along behind her as she rode her bike home from school. At first he lived in the shed in the back garden, which had a broken door, so he could come and go as he wished. When she came home from school, he celebrated her return. She fed him, then took him to the empty racetrack nearby where she threw a ball, which he expertly caught and delivered to her feet. Marion called him Sparkie because he was the bright spot in her life.

For several months she got away with it, until the dog became so bold that instead of hiding in the shed, he waited for her at the gate pillar, then raced out to meet her.

"I see Marion has a new dog," said a neighbor, loud enough for her mother to hear.

And that was that.

A man arrived to collect the dog and take him, she was told, to a teacher who lived out in the country where he could have a lovely life. Marion cried and cried. Nobody took any notice. Animals had no place in a home. They carried dirt and disease, which reminded Marion's mother of the countryside, which reminded her of the rural schoolhouse that had killed her husband.

A year later a classmate's dog had a litter of pups, and Marion took one and named her Bonnie. This time, she secreted her in her bedroom.

Bonnie was a pretty white spaniel with black markings and long ears. When Marion's mother discovered her, it seemed for a miraculous moment or two that she might be allowed to keep her. But then

Marion's mother realized that Bonnie was female and would be having pups. There was no way in a month of Sundays that they'd pay good money for neutering. Another teacher from the country came to collect the dog, though this one was very sorry and tried to comfort Marion as she cried on the porch.

When she was around twelve, Marion's uncle spoke to her mother and said he would give her "a good clean pup." Miraculously, she agreed, and he arrived one day with a puppy, fawn-colored and shaggy, small enough to hold in her lap. She named him Bruno, and she brushed and bathed him constantly to keep him clean and not annoy her mother. She fed him and walked him and washed her hands a hundred times a day and swept the house of every hair.

But Bruno did not last long. One day, when he was seven months old, she was walking him when a cat darted across the road. Bruno lurched so suddenly that Marion dropped the leash as a car was passing. There was death once again.

No amount of crying or apologizing to her mother, to her uncle, or to poor Bruno's little lost soul could ever make it better.

~

WHEN MARION finished secondary school in the late 1950s, Limerick was a gritty port city closed up tight as a fist. The church seemed to control everything. The national censor purified the people's desires by ridding their films and books of sex, especially sex outside of marriage. On the occasions when they failed and babies were born to unwed mothers, those babies quickly disappeared—taken away by nuns and sent to good families in undisclosed locations.

All Marion wanted to do was leave Ireland. Desperately.

She had the grades for college, but not the money. After a predictable secretarial course, she landed in an insurance company behind a typewriter. Each morning, she wondered how people could do the exact same thing day after day, taking the same bus, seeing the same faces, doing the same boring tasks. Could you die from boredom? If so, Marion was at risk.

It was because of the insurance company, however, that she met John. The girls she worked with signed her up for a music club, which was held in the basement of a church. After rehearsal, there was tea, and that was when she first saw him: tall and slim, well-spoken, with an elegant manner and looking a bit like Cary Grant. Eventually, after a few false starts, they went out on a date. She liked him very much. He was whip-smart, dry-witted, and, yes, very handsome. But there was a restlessness inside her, a fast river whooshing past, muting the outer world.

She needed to go.

Her first escape was Spain. She got a job in Seville, living with a doctor and his family, teaching English to him and his two daughters— a job she'd heard about from the nuns, which lent a certain propriety to the whole thing. She had nine glorious months of Mediterranean sun and heat and freedom, all of which abruptly ended when her sister wrote her to say that she was getting married that fall. Would Marion please come home and be a bridesmaid? Marion had no choice, and no money for a ticket back to Spain. She returned to Ireland the day before the wedding, weeping on the plane. At the church, people looked at her strangely and whispered about her being gone nine months. Marion ignored them. At the reception, in a daze, she saw a familiar face in the crowd. It was John. Her sister had invited him, for her, and though Marion was glad to see him, she'd already made up her mind that she had to find another escape.

This time it was even better. She got a job working for a travel agent in New York City. She was twenty years old and marveled at how much there was to do in New York, even on the pittance she earned. She saw the Rockettes and went to the opera, shopped for silk blouses in bargain basements, went to bookstores and marveled that she could buy any book she wanted—nothing was censored or banned! What twenty-year-old wouldn't have loved New York?

Unfortunately, it didn't take her long to figure out that her boss was a bankrupt alcoholic and his business was sinking. When her six-month visa was up, Mr. Travel Agent said, "Ah, maybe just as well. Business a bit slow and all." He gave her a ticket back to Ireland, and that was the end of that.

John had sent letters to Marion when she was in New York, but she'd been so preoccupied with her new life that she'd written back only brief replies. After she returned, he showed up at her door. This time, when he hugged her, she felt a warm tide pulling her in. The relationship became serious, and he asked her to marry him. Marion slowed down long enough to see him for the excellent human being he was. She knew she wanted to be with him.

"Let's get out of here together," she said. "Come with me to the States."

In another life, he would have said yes. But in this particular one—born in a place and time of so few prospects—John was lucky in having a good job at Texaco Oil. What if he couldn't find a job in New York? What if his parents needed him back home? The answer was no.

"You'll lose that boy if you leave again," Marion's mother warned.

4

—

THE DOGS OF LIMERICK

1965–80

They lived in Dublin for the first twelve years of their marriage, a period that would later be described as the Normal Period. Marion discovered that she loved Dublin. She loved that people didn't watch what she was doing and gossip about her; she loved that she could hear different accents in the street. Dublin was a place where people willingly went to visit and live—not like Limerick, which was a place to leave. Those were grand years, when Marion and John lived as happily and in love as two young people could. They had a modern house with central heating in a stylish neighborhood just outside the city center. They went to the cinema, took holidays, and did normal things like going out to restaurants with friends.

Their first child was a boy they named Joseph. A few years later they had a baby girl, Aideen. Marion gave the first two children all of her attention (as a Normal Mother would), and when they were babies, she'd get up as many times as necessary in the middle of the

Young Marion and John. (Courtesy Joe Fitzgibbon)

night. She ferried them to school, did the daily shopping, helped with homework, and cooked the family meals. John got up early and went off to work for the oil company. He arrived home on time at night, regular as clockwork, often with a little toy or gift for the children.

One evening, he showed up at the door acting strangely. He stood still, waiting for someone to notice that something was hidden inside his coat—something wriggling. Ahem. Slowly he opened it to reveal a spaniel puppy, small enough to fit in the palm of his hand as he held it toward Marion, relishing each second as he watched her face move from confusion to shock, and then to a gasping joy.

These were the many pleasures of the Normal Period, which lasted so long that there was every reason to believe it would go on forever. Except it didn't.

After those first dozen years, the company offered John a significant promotion and raise—wonderful news, of course—but with one hitch: they would have to move back to Limerick. They'd have more money, a better life. Their two children were growing up, now aged eight and six, and there was a third child on the way. The grandparents and family lived in Limerick, and things were better now in Ire-land. They could bury the hatchet with their hometown.

They bought a rambling house five miles outside the city in an undeveloped area, populated mostly by farmers. There were no street-lights, no place to get a newspaper. All around them were fields and farmhouses and little else—a far cry from the neat, urban terraced houses they'd left behind in Dublin. The wilderness—that's what Marion's mother called it. Why in the world would you buy a house in the wilderness?

On the day they arrived, their new baby, James, was just eleven days old.

The gravity of their decision became suddenly clear when they got a look at the farm behind their new house. The farmer was deaf in both ears and had a house of broken furniture and more kids than they could count. When it rained, his cattle were up to their bellies in a sea of mud. They had forgotten this kind of poverty.

Years later, it would be tempting to consider that if they had not moved back, if they had stayed in Dublin, they might have remained normal.

They arrived in the middle of the school year. Aideen adapted easily to her new school, but with Joe it was a different story. When he came home on his first day and Marion asked him how it had gone, he told her that he'd been locked in a cupboard for not doing his homework. She went ballistic on the phone with the headmaster. She then calmly informed Joe he wouldn't be going back to that school the next day, or ever again. Oh, Limerick. What had they done by coming back?

The church ran all the schools back then. Marion found one that seemed more civilized—well, at least not harmful—on the other side of Limerick. That meant a half-hour drive across the city each morn-ing, to the other side of the river Shannon, when the shops had not yet opened for the day.

It was during those drives that the change in her began (though perhaps it was not a change, really, so much as an awakening). Almost immediately, she noticed the stray dogs and found herself looking out of the car window aghast.

They were everywhere.

Every shop had an open alcove by the front door, and it was there that they curled themselves into tight balls or huddled in groups to keep warm. Five, six, seven, eight . . . They were filthy and skinny and matted, many looking to be on the verge of death. A feral cat might flash into view for a moment, then vanish again beneath a car. But mostly she saw the dogs—dogs were everywhere. In downtown Limerick, you could fill a bus with stray dogs and come back the next day for more.

Sleep deprivation comes with a new baby and does things to the mind. A floating feeling came over Marion. Pieces of her seemed to break apart and shift around, like furniture getting rearranged in a room. Items that had been shoved into the corners suddenly moved front and center. And this is how the change began.

Marion went ahead and unpacked the boxes and set up the new house. She fed and rocked and tended her new baby. She made sure the two older children had what they needed and did their lessons. But each time she drove into the city and saw all those animals, her sense of emergency grew.

⁓

IN THE Limerick of the 1970s—and many rural and developing places then and now—dogs could generally be divided into two basic categories: those that worked and those that did not. The first category herded sheep, hunted game, sniffed out bombs, defended property, guided the blind, and so on. The second category—nonworking dogs—was far larger and quite a bit more complicated, ranging from feral dogs that lived on the edge of town and were seldom seen by people to the purebred Jack Russells that sat on laps and jumped for treats. The modern idea of pets—neutered, obedient, leash-walked, a warm body at the foot of the bed at night—was a relatively new proposition, which could only occur in a society that had a middle class and disposable income. And so, modern pet ownership was still quite rare. Ordinary families kept dogs, sure, but usually in the shed or the barn, feeding them household scraps and letting them wander where they wished all day long, begging, scrounging, going into heat, and bringing forth litter upon litter of puppies. These were community dogs. No one owned them. They wore no collars and knew nothing about a leash. They were not family members, but rather sponsored by families whose scraps kept them alive. Taking a dog to the vet to get it stitched up after an accident? To get vaccinated? Or spayed? Are you joking? That was for the wealthy, or the British. In order to afford pets, people had to have jobs and money, and those were still in extremely short supply. Ireland barely had highways.

The dogs Marion saw in the mornings were street dogs that provided for themselves. Every night, after the sun went down and the humans headed home for tea, the dogs emerged from the shadows, a ragged and wounded army that trotted or limped in after the day's battle for food and survival. They were a second civilization surviving upon the first civilization's garbage. At this hour of the morning, they remained under the awnings and arcades on O'Connell Street, yet to be roused and shooed away by the shopkeepers. They had relationships with one another, adventures, and freedom, but they also regularly got diseases and parasites, ripped one another up in fights, starved, led short lives, and disappeared when it was time to die.

Marion called the city to ask if anything was being done about the enormous street dog population. There was no dog warden. The city told her about a sort of dog shelter at the edge of town; it wasn't really a shelter, but the home of a couple paid by the county to take in strays. It was a relief to Marion to find out that there was at least someone to help.

One day, when she saw a black Labrador lying on the sidewalk in awful shape, she stopped her car. He was just ribs, hips, and back-bone. When she offered him a treat and a ride in her car, he looked up from the sidewalk, confused by her kindness. Whether out of depression or sickness, he could barely move.

"Come on, fella. We're going to take care of you. Come on."

Only after many offers of treats and cajoling did he slowly, very slowly, come toward her. He was so far gone he had given up hope. As they drove, Marion kept turning to look back, afraid he might die on her back seat. But he was stable, curled in a ball, one eye open and ready to endure whatever came next.

Marion found her way to the "shelter," which turned out to be a small bungalow with a big garden at the edge of town.

"He needs to see a vet right away," said Marion to a middle-aged woman who answered the door. She wore a look of weary irritation.

"Yes, yes," the shelter lady said, then shook her head with no further response and took the dog to a pen out back. Marion gave her a couple of pounds as a donation. But as soon as Marion left, the dog was put down.

"Better off to get it done straight away," the shelter lady later explained. "No one wants big black dogs. I can't afford to feed something that I'm only going to put down a week later anyway." Her method was to put a needle of barbiturate straight into the heart.

Marion could barely speak for a week. When she closed her eyes at night, she could see the dog's face. She'd led him to his death. She wrote a small bit of verse for him and put it in her drawer so she'd remember him. It was the least she could do. That Lab haunted her for a very long time.

The only other option was the local SPCA, which Marion joined early on. She attended the monthly meetings and helped them raise money, but the meetings came and went and no one ever said what they were doing about the epic stray dog problem. When Marion finally asked, they told her that they couldn't do anything. It was awful, they all agreed. But they couldn't go and pick up dogs because they had no facility to handle them. That's why so much of the fundraising went toward a bank account; they were saving to build a sanctuary someday. Until someday, they did education, visiting elementary schools and giving talks about the importance of animals and their well-being. They strongly discouraged her from getting involved with the strays, which is why, when Marion asked them for twelve pounds to spay a little terrier she'd picked up (such a sweet little white dog, young, and very home-able), they'd said no. They didn't do street dogs.

You are the Limerick SPCA and you won't pay twelve pounds to spay a dog? Are you joking? She got a bit out of control then. She carried on and stormed out, and that was the end of that.

⟡

A CLATTERING in the kitchen, the sound of spoons stirring and things being poured, pots scraped dry, the refrigerator open and shut. Footsteps with a sense of mission. John walked in to see his wife taking a pot of rice off the stove and pouring it into a large container, along with bits of leftover meat and potatoes he recognized from dinner.

"What, may I ask, is this?"

John Fitzgibbon had watched his wife's growing derangement over the street dogs with some concern. It's not that he didn't appreciate his wife's compassion. He did. There was something about Marion that made you want to be a better person, which was one of the reasons he'd fallen in love with her. But he was not a great animal lover and, when he learned that she intended to wrap up food to take into Limerick that night, he began to seriously wonder if she were going mad.

"You mean to tell me that you intend to feed this food to stray dogs on the sidewalk in the dark in the city?"

She answered as though it were the most reasonable and normal thing to do, explaining merely the when, not the why.

"Yes, I know it's nighttime. I tried feeding them in the morning, but they were so frozen from sleeping on cement that they could barely move. I was thinking that maybe if they ate at night, it would help keep them warm and alive until morning."

John might have pointed out many logical facts at this moment— that if there were a thousand stray dogs, feeding just a few accomplished little. Or he could have told her that she was putting herself in danger. He might have suggested that she check on the children's lessons rather than run off into town. He took a breath and told himself that this crazy endeavor would pass. He was a patient man by nature. The best course of action, he reasoned, was to ride it out.

And so it became a routine that on certain nights (especially the coldest), after she'd made sure the children were settled and the dishes were finished (and sometimes when neither of the above conditions were met), Marion went into the kitchen and prepared a big container of whatever scraps she could put together, then made the five-mile drive into the city. Even when they had the fourth baby, sweet little Louise, Marion gave her a bath in the evening, fed her, sang to her, held her, then put her in a crib and left the house to tend to the dogs. She was thirty-eight, full of energy, and unafraid.

She got down on the ground at dog level and approached them gently. When she uncovered the food, their noses sniffed the air and their eyes opened wide, alert. Some were cautious. Others dove in furiously when she put the bowls down on the sidewalk. She made sure all of them got some. Within seconds they slurped up all she had, then lifted their muzzles, looking drunk or, as if awaking from a dream, confused and yet delighted about what kind of world this was after all. They were dogs and it was their nature to grab onto whatever scrap of hope life gave them, then wag their tails full of gratitude. She stayed, petting and talking to them a while before going home.

One evening when she was sitting on the sidewalk opening up her containers of food, a stranger stopped.

"There's a woman who's doing the same thing up the street. You know that, right?"

No. She didn't know that at all.

Rita O'Halloran remembers it like this: She was at the vet, when the door opened and suddenly this woman entered—a tall, pretty blonde in her thirties, wearing a lovely coat and scarf—carrying a filthy dog that smelled like a urinal. The woman sat down and began talking about the dog crisis in a way that Rita had never heard anyone talk about animals before. She was so well-spoken and convincing. When she said something had got to be done, you *wanted* to do it. When, finally, Marion suggested, "Wouldn't it be great if we could work together to get these dogs off the streets into homes?" there was no way Rita could say anything but yes.

In Marion's version, she went looking for Rita, who was known as "the stray dog lady"—an unassuming woman who'd been running a small operation for ten years. The shoe shop where she worked had a huge alcove in front, a magnet for four or five dogs at night. Rita fed them when she arrived every morning, and most trotted off. But the dogs that were in a really bad way—those that were too starving or sick to move—well, she took those to the vet, and sometimes even let them sleep in the empty storage room above the shop. She got in early the next morning to get them out before the owner came, though once she nearly had a heart attack when he called her up to the third floor to discuss inventory, sitting on the single chair in the room. He was wearing a beautiful navy suit and when he stood, his back was covered with dog hair. If he knew, he didn't let on. The worst was when she got a call that the auditors were coming. They'd need to use the upstairs and would be arriving in only an hour. Rita sent out a panicked alert to all her friends to come quickly and collect the dogs, the food, the water, and make them all disappear.

Marion listened to Rita's stories with astonishment. Here was this woman who was taking care of the dogs, and she was doing it out of a shoe shop.

In fact, Rita had a small team of comrades who worked with her. There was Mary Cooke, a housewife whom she'd found on the streets feeding a dog, and there was Irene at the dress shop a few doors down, also feeding street dogs. Rita's neighbor had a daughter named Anne Kelley who was mad about animals, and she pitched in too. They were women you might never notice, those who blended into the background of husbands and children, salesladies. They took as many dogs as they could into their homes. They'd asked no one for permission, but just dove in and appointed themselves. They didn't have meetings. They didn't talk much about it. They just went about doing what they could. Rita had even found a kind-hearted taxi driver to act as her ambulance. He'd pull up at the shop and she'd run out front and put a dog in the back seat for him to deliver to the vet. A couple of times a year, she collected and sold secondhand items to raise money for the dogs.

Not long after meeting Rita, Marion was downtown at lunchtime when she spotted another member of this odd tribe, a young woman walking along the sidewalk peeking into alleys and alcoves with a leash in her hand.

"Excuse me, is it a dog you're looking for?" Marion asked.

"Yes, the dog was here yesterday. I hate it when they disappear."

She was Anne Dynan, barely thirty, and she had been feeding street dogs since she was a teenager. She was a tiny woman, perhaps not even five feet tall, unmarried, and all energy. She was financially-minded, a bookkeeper by profession. She would become the group's treasurer.

And so it all began, a few women doing the ridiculous: feeding animals on the streets, taking them in, getting them fixed, and finding them homes. Marion learned that they'd all tried the Limerick SPCA first and they'd all left in disappointment for the same reason that Marion had—there was a crisis in their midst and something had to be done.

Marion was the most relentless—the talker and convincer, the one with the ideas who got people to do things they'd never dreamed they would, the one who always took it furthest. Feeding street dogs wasn't enough, she said. They had to do more. Someday, somehow, they would build a sanctuary, but for now they would find volunteers to provide temporary homes until permanent ones could be found. People would take dogs in if they got paid for the cost of the food and the vet care, plus a tiny bit extra to cover their time and trouble.

The women held their first fundraiser at a church. For an Irish pound, you could come in for a cup of coffee, and buy the cakes and biscuits they'd baked. The next time they held a rummage sale. After that came a Flag Day, which meant they'd gotten a permit to stand out on the streets with open buckets; in other words, they begged. Everyone who donated got a sticker on their coat that said "Limerick Animal Welfare." That's what they had decided to call themselves. Pensioners rooted around in pockets; old ladies reached into the bottom of their purses. One time, a woman came up to Marion on the street and presented her with a crumpled brown bag containing little bits of change she'd saved. Another day, she got a phone call from a woman whose mother had died and left instructions that whatever was left over after the funeral would go to help animals. It was only ninety pounds. Where could she send it?

They'd got permission from the parish to stand outside the church with their collection buckets after Mass, hoping to catch people who might be feeling grateful and generous. Christmas Eve and the feast of St. Francis were naturally quite lucrative; otherwise it was slow.

When Marion took her turn, standing outside at 8:30 in the morning getting a few dirty pennies in the rain and a bucket mostly full of water, she'd feel despair every time she saw a churchgoer spot her, then swiftly make for the unmanned gate.

Later, she called Anne. "I'll tell you what. Next time, I'm going to stay home in bed and just give you twenty pounds."

Anne said the same thing she would say for the next thirty years:

"Now, Marion, you know that it all adds up. Little by little, it all adds up."

They needed every bit. As their reputation grew, so did the number of animals. And it wasn't only dogs, but cats and the occasional horse or hurt fox, squirrel, or bird. The vet bills frightened them all, but thank God they found John Carroll, a gentlemanly old vet who shook his head at the women each time they came in, but when Marion asked, "How much do I owe you, John?" he replied, "What can you spare?"

They brought him everything—whatever dog or cat was bloody, broken, distempered, smelly, and infected, even a swan with a broken wing, found on the banks of the Shannon. Marion was able to catch it by putting a blanket over it and carrying it to the car, where she'd laid newspaper down to protect the back seat from bird shit (she did not succeed). The vet set the wing, and a couple of weeks later, she returned the swan to the spot where she'd found it. Almost instantly another swan appeared, as though it had been waiting the whole two weeks. (In fact, this may have been so, because swans mate for life.)

Sometimes John Carroll would look at an animal at the edge of death and do them the favor of saying, "This one isn't for ye," sparing them the decision.

After five years, they had about a dozen households they could count on to foster dogs. Meanwhile, the search for people to adopt the dogs never ceased. Marion got the newspaper to run ads. The women put up signs around town and went to fairs and events carrying dogs and posters of animals needing a good home. Anne always tried to keep a small secret reserve of money and learned soon enough to never let Marion know the location of the checkbook, because there was no end to the amount Marion would spend on the animals.

What kept the group together from the beginning was that they all believed the same thing. Without ever having to justify it, put it down on paper, or take an oath, all the women agreed that each animal was important. Simple as that: each was a living, breathing life. They wouldn't say, okay, after three months if it doesn't get adopted we'll put it down. You just wouldn't do that to lives that are important. Who were they to decide who lived and who died?

The Fitzgibbon family telephone number became a de facto animal help hotline for Limerick, though most callers had no idea they were calling a private home. If Marion was out, a child might answer the phone, leading to some rather bizarre conversations.

"No, this isn't the government. It's just my mum and some other ladies. She's not here right now. May I give you another lady's number?"

Stuttering. Confusion, then, "Yes, thank you."

But some people became irate. Why should they have to make two calls? Hadn't they done their part?

"Listen, I have a dog. I don't want it. Who's going to come and take it?" And if the right answer didn't come quickly enough: "All right. Don't worry, I'll just put it out." Or, "All right, I'll just shoot it."

People came to the Fitzgibbon front door, too, with animals they'd found on the street. John went out one morning and found two dogs tied to a tree in front of the house. No word, no note.

For a long time, they'd had a single telephone, located in the hallway by the front door—a rotary phone on one of those 1960s telephone tables with a small cushioned seat. Marion could be seen frequently running to the front hall to answer it, literally keeping her animal business at the outer edge of her home. Soon the phone was ringing so often, that became impractical. She had the phone company install a wall phone in the kitchen, rigged with the longest possible cord so she could be in constant motion—cooking, cleaning up, and folding laundry—while talking. The new phone seemed to sense that it was the focus of her attention and began to ring all the more.

The Normal Period was definitely over.

By the time baby Louise was five or six years old, there were usually ten to fifteen dogs living in the house. About seven or eight of them were regulars; they'd gained permanent status because they were either too beloved to part with or because they had nowhere else to go. At night, they slept in the hallway and the sitting room, on the kitchen floor, in Marion and John's room. Sometimes a puppy was in someone's bed.

Of all those that passed through, the most beloved was probably Sarah the German shepherd. She had arrived with her ribs kicked in and needed an operation. (Somehow they managed to pay for many operations.) On a soft pad on Marion's kitchen floor, she convalesced, bones and organs healing, thick brown fur growing back over her incision. At some point, her amber eyes came into eerily sharp focus, and she reincarnated into her second life—watching, listening, studying each movement of the household, memorizing each member of the family, their faces and voices, each person's way of moving and their footsteps. They started to think she could read their minds. She nosed open doors before they knew they wanted to go through them, and she didn't fully rest until the children were in bed. No matter how many dogs came or went, no matter how big or small, Sarah kept them all in line, living her life with one eye perpetually trained on her human family and the other eye on her ragtag bunch of canine siblings. In the evenings, Marion and Joe sometimes took them all to a nearby rugby field to run. As soon as the car doors opened, the dogs shot off in twelve different directions—all but Sarah, who took a lap around the field and returned to check on Marion, then went back out into the field to patrol the perimeter to make sure all were safe. When it was time to go home, she rounded up the dogs and helped get them back to the car.

Even John loved Sarah, and that was saying a lot.

By contrast, there was Eli, a Pyrenean mountain dog that Rita had found sleeping in front of the shoe shop one morning. He had no teeth or fur, and his 110-pound body was covered in motor oil that some idiot had thrown on him to cure his mange. After they fed and healed him, his fur grew back into a dense mass of long white fluff with a thick downy undercoat. Miraculously, Marion found a priest who agreed to adopt him—no small feat. Everything was set until the priest's mother interceded. "He'll eat too much! You can't do it!" she said. The priest shrank in pathetic obedience. Marion never found a prospect for Eli again. He became one of the permanents simply because no one else would have him. He left big clumps of hair everywhere. His slobber dripped onto the kitchen floor. He killed one of her trees by urinating on it repeatedly. Sometimes he seemed more like a donkey than a dog, like when he would try to jump the garden fence and knock it down instead. He would then climb over it and walk around to the front of the house, patiently waiting until someone called, "Eli's at the front door again!" He lived with them until he became an old man, first deaf, then senile.

One evening at supper, John looked up from his plate and said simply, "When is he going to die?"

Silence. There was little doubt about whom he was referring to.

But Eli would not die, it seemed. He lingered on with them for eight years, every night sleeping on Marion and John's bedroom floor.

Many others came and went. They arrived bloody, broken-boned, emaciated, smelling of their own feces, full of worms or parasites, distempered. Marion regularly turned their bathroom into an emergency room, shutting the door, bathing the new arrivals, putting ointment on wounds, cleaning pus out of eyes. Then came food and medical care and the endless phone calls to find suitable homes. She tried to save every one, but some were too far gone. In these cases, she cleaned them up and provided a soft bed, food, and kindness, even if only for a day or two, so that the animal wouldn't leave the world having known only misery and cruelty. She realized that she could be deluding herself that a few comfortable moments would make any difference to the dog or to the universe. She wondered if the only wretched purpose of these last rites of kindness might be to make herself feel better. On the other hand, what if it did matter?

What if every creature had a right to live and die with dignity?

The house got wrecked. The furniture legs were chewed, the upholstery worn to a nub. Accidents of poo and pee. Barking. And all those phone calls: the bills were obscene. Many times she had to run down to the telephone company with half the money in her hand, begging them not to turn her phone off.

The two oldest kids, Joe and Aideen, teenagers by then, had grown up mainly in the Normal Period, with years of regular meals and the full attention of their mother. Joe was the least intruded upon. In fact, he was the child most like Marion and most willing to share her calling. If she needed help picking up a big dog and lifting it into the car, she could count on Joe. When Marion started to take in cats, Joe was the one who climbed up on the garage roof with hammer and nails and built little houses where they could retreat from the threat of the dogs. Aideen, too, shared her mother's concern, though to what degree it was hard to know for sure because she was quiet and self-contained, good in school, and patient like her father. She realized early on that there would be no stopping Marion, and stepped out of the way.

The younger two, James and Louise, had it the worst. It's not that their mother didn't look after them and make sure they had all they needed and a bit more too. It's not that their father wasn't there every evening and on weekends, attentive and caring. All those things were covered. But children cannot help but observe and compare. Why was their family so different? Why did their mother have this other priority? They all endured car rides to pick up dogs, or sudden diversions on their way home—"Oh, no, did you see that?" and suddenly their mother was off running for a stray. Marion would go out in the morning saying she'd be back in a couple of hours, but not get home until evening. And when she was home, she was on the phone.

James started to become sick, with continually itchy eyes and a runny nose. He was allergic to the animals.

When Marion was off, a hyper-focus took over everything, and the adrenaline that came with it created an all-powerful and encompassing present. But in the moments when it cracked open and she thought of the five of them together without her, a sad kind of thud landed. Then she might go home early, or just push it aside and keep going to the next emergency. Every animal presented another chance of salvation.

John was a rare kind of husband. He made all her work possible by covering for her at home. The other women were in awe: "Such a wonderful man. So patient!" They laughed at the way he answered the phone:

"Hello, John. May I speak with Marion?"

"Marion who? What does she look like?"

Or, "Ah, she left this morning and went to the pub all day."

Or, "I don't know where she is. She only talks to animals and God."

There was no such thing as divorce in Ireland back then, but still, many people wondered how John could possibly put up with it.

"Shouldn't ye be home looking after your family, rather than out on the streets chasing dogs?"

"Is John getting enough cooked meals?"

"Is it even healthy for the children with all these dogs in the house?"

John reflected on the spaniel he'd gotten for Marion those many years ago, and he would say, "Look what I did! It was all my fault."

And she would say, "No, John. I was born this way. Why else would I have cried so hard about the horse in the rain when I was only six years old?"

When John came home from work one night, his wife and four children were nowhere to be found. He walked through the living room calling and calling and then entered the kitchen to find blood spattered everywhere, including on the walls and cabinets. Dishes and half-full teacups were abandoned on the table.

He couldn't know it, but Marion had picked up a bleeding dog in the street and every time the thing shook its head, blood splattered all over. The dog had a broken artery and was bleeding to death before their eyes. Joe, only twelve, ran and grabbed a bath towel and wrapped it tightly around the dog's head, while Marion threw the other three kids in the car, then sped to the vet, who cauterized the artery. The dog fully recovered.

When Marion walked in the door later that night, she saw John's bewildered face and realized what she'd put him through, how wrong she'd been. The problem was that when she was in it—really in it— she was at her best and therefore felt she could not stop or even slow down. She didn't write notes. She just went. When it happened, it was like a wave knocked her off her feet, swept her along, and she was gone.

Most of the time, she believed she was doing some good. But

there was a dark shadow lurking in her, which came and went. Here it was again—that question of whether or not, at the bottom of it all, she was quite selfish.

She knew it for sure when James said to her, "When I want your attention, I'll bark."

Lily and Simon, not long after she arrived in the United States. (Author's collection)

5

—

LILY IN THE SUBURBS

2007

During her initial days with us, Lily ran nervously from one window to the next, as though she were waiting for Elizabeth to come back and rescue her. She'd never been a pet before, and she didn't seem particularly happy about it.

Having come from the survival-of-the-fittest world of the Irish Travellers, who set up camps in designated sites or just on the roadside, she had lived in a community of other dogs and had struggled for her basic needs. Travellers generally kept multiple dogs to trade, sell, and use for hunting. Lily was fed and kept on so long as she could provide value. The biggest and fastest got the best, and Lily was more omega than alpha. Surely she'd had her fights, and had a scar on her leg to prove it. Surely she'd had to fend off aggressive males who'd chased and fought over her when she came into season.

Now, after all that in her young life, she'd been airlifted to a new universe, held captive by four new human beings, and kept indoors much of the time. While I imagine that the soft bed, food, water, and petting were quite pleasant for her, the fact that she was expected to politely and quietly walk down the street among so many unknown dogs, all the while constrained at the neck by a collar and leash, must have seemed not only terrifying but also insanely unfair. It must have felt like being sent into a boxing ring with a blindfold on.

And yet, here she was in a New York City suburb where well-off humans treasured and even fetishized their dogs, treating them like children. I've come to think of it as the Golden Age of Dogdom. Everyone wanted a dog. Five other canines lived in our immediate three-block neighborhood when Lily first arrived. The number clicked up month by month, and to date has reached a peak of thirteen. Lily stationed herself on our porch to keep watch as one dog after the next walked across her territory. She exploded into barking as each one passed. It drove me nuts, and I complained about the noise until one day my sister-in-law, an animal behavior scientist, told me that a) the barking wasn't *that* bad, implying that I could just chill out about it, and b) dogs need jobs. Sprinting and hunting were no longer an option for Lily, so she'd taken on the only assignment available, which was to guard the street. She was doing the best job she could by barking from our enclosed front porch. Her other job took place on her morning walk, when she patrolled the neighborhood, sniffing out the comings and goings of other dogs, then adding her mark.

I was chagrined at my lack of understanding. Over the years, I would become ever more aware of how little I knew about dogs. After that, when Lily barked on the porch, I tried to observe her behavior, thank her, acknowledge her work, and *then* ask her to quiet down. This was slightly more effective. She seemed to appreciate the acknowledgment.

All sight hounds (greyhounds, whippets, deerhounds, wolfhounds, and about ten other related breeds) have been bred for centuries to have exceptionally keen vision over long distances. A glimpse of prey triggers a heart-pounding drive to capture and kill. I'd be out walking with Lily on the lead, and she'd be prancing along as Lily the balle-rina girl. Then in a moment beauty would become beast. She zoomed ahead, nearly pulling me off my feet, fangs at the ready. Every muscle in her body on alert, ears up, eyes in focus, legs slightly bent, ready to lunge. She'd been born knowing how to hunt. When I looked through her sight hound eyes, I saw that small prey lurked everywhere—not just rabbits and squirrels, but also much beloved bichon frises, minia-ture poodles, Chihuahuas, tiny terriers, and cats.

We learned this the hard way, when my husband took Lily out for a run. He is a very early riser, and on weekends, when the streets were still quiet and I was still in bed, it was his habit to let her off lead at the immense athletic field behind our house—flagrantly passing the sign that said, "No Dogs." I knew this crime went on, but rather than argue, I chose to believe him when he said (as hus-bands do) not to worry, that it was harmless because everyone was still asleep and all Lily did was take two or three full-speed gorgeous laps around the field, after which she always returned and lay down, satisfied and panting, near his feet. Happy dog. The whole thing took five minutes.

One winter morning their routine went awry. According to my husband's version of events, Lily had finished her second circuit of the athletic field, but instead of lying down on the grass, she started sniffing around and followed a scent along the back fence, up a little hill, toward an open gate. She must have looked up and seen some-thing because, in a flash, she was gone.

To say that my husband or any human would not be able to catch up with her would be an absurd understatement. When Herb finally made his way to the top of the slope, Lily was a block away, standing in the middle of a busy road by our house. She was interacting with a man—backing away from him nervously. The man appeared hostile as he stood there holding something in his arms that looked like a roll of paper towels. As my husband got closer, it became clear that it was a tiny dog in the man's arms. Herb ran toward them and called Lily to come, but she paid no attention.

In the midst of this altercation, a car suddenly slowed at Herb's side and a woman with a deeply concerned face rolled down her window, eager to insert herself into the situation, perhaps heroically.

"I saw him kick your dog. He kicked your dog. I told him to stop!" And then she added, "I rescue dogs! Do you need help?"

"It's okay," my husband said. "Thanks. I've got her. This is our street. It's okay now."

But the rescue lady was intent.

"Really," Herb told her. "It's okay."

At that moment, Lily saw her favorite neighbors and began wagging and prancing toward them. They quickly surmised that she was up to no good and held her until Herb arrived and clicked the leash on her collar. Thank God, the incident was over.

When Herb got home, he recounted everything. "Never, never again. I will never let her off leash again."

Apparently we did not have the whole story. A half hour later, the doorbell rang. Through the glass of the door I saw a man on our front step. It was clear from many paces away that something was wrong. He was a tough-looking dude with a shaved head, wearing a black puffy jacket. His middle-aged face was agitated, and his entire being had a rock-hard look that exuded hostility. No one had to say that this was the owner of the paper towel dog. Together Herb and I went to the door.

"Does a black-and-white dog live here?" His tone was accusatory.

"Yes," we answered in unison.

"Her name is Lily, right?" And then, as if on cue, Lily stepped timidly onto the porch at our heels. He nodded at her with disdain, then looked back at us.

"Your dog just tried to kill my dog."

He paused for it to sink in.

"She ran across the street and attacked her. Picked her up in her jaws and shook her. Your dog tried to break my dog's neck."

It was a fragile moment. It felt like anything could happen with an angry stranger on our doorstep, a stranger with the hard bone of his skull exposed in the January air.

"What kind of dog?" I asked stupidly.

"A shih tzu. She's only four pounds."

I was trying to fathom a four-pound dog when Herb began to apologize, and then I joined in. "We are so sorry. So sorry." We did not stop. "No, it's terrible. We hate dogs off leashes." (What idiots we sounded like!)

Then we began to explain the small-prey instinct of greyhounds.

"Oh. She's a greyhound?" Eyebrow raised in surprise.

We nodded.

"Oh, she's a hunting dog?" As though gathering evidence against her. He might just as well have said, "Oh, so she's a killer."

"She's totally sweet," I went on to explain how she loved people and was very gentle. It was just small dogs that she wanted to . . . um, um . . . His jaw hardened.

"She ran across the street, you know. She could have been hit by a car."

All we could do was nod and repeat that we were very, *very* sorry.

"I kicked her, you know."

"Well, you had to save your dog."

"I called the police, you know."

"Yes, we understand. We're very sorry."

"What happened? Did she slip out of the house through an open door or something?"

Then Herb had to admit that he had voluntarily let his killer dog off the leash to take a quick run, but that he hardly ever did this (a lie). He faltered as he explained.

"How is your dog?" I interrupted.

"She's still shaking." Suddenly the man's face transformed from tough guy to worried father. "She might have puncture wounds from your dog's teeth."

I began to feel ill. "If you take her to the vet, please bring us the bill."

His face softened, but only a tiny bit. "I have to see what my wife says."

I scrawled our names, address, and phone number on a piece of paper. He seemed only slightly satisfied, but left.

For the rest of the day, I kept seeing a little shih tzu before my eyes with shaken baby syndrome, brain damage, and internal bleeding. I envisioned the owners crying over the furry corpse. *We killed somebody's family member. All because we let Lily off leash.*

Lily, meanwhile, was curled up in a ball on her cushion, oblivious.

At that moment, I saw her predicament.

Dogs are in a prison of our making. We bred them so that they would gladly be our servants in specialized jobs. Now we expect them to suddenly switch jobs and go against their genetic raison d'être so they can be our companions, therapists, teachers, and healers. Okay, maybe any of those is an easier gig than, say, dogfighting or scientific experimentation. In exchange for food and shelter, the modern dog simply has to lie around all day (mainly inside), master a few tricks such as sit, stay, shake hands, and jump, and become addicted like a love slave to the sensation of being stroked on the back or head or belly—and, of course, be collared and leashed.

Since Lily had to work, I suspected she would have been happier in some other life in which she was assigned the job she was born and bred for and good at, one in which she could run free and hunt and be herself and live with other dogs of her own kind. This idea would nag at me for the rest of her life with us.

Unfortunately, it wasn't only Lily's attitude to small dogs that kept her socially isolated. She didn't get along with too many dogs of any size—though she loved puppies, and a friend suggested that perhaps they reminded her of the ones she had birthed and lost. She wanted to make friends, but her social skills were a disaster. Time and again, I watched the sadly predictable script as she signaled to Elizabeth's lurchers with a play bow, wagging tail, and "can you catch me?" sprint. At least half of the time, this promising beginning would culminate in Lily snarling and nipping at the other dog's neck, and that would be the end of that. I shut down the play date. I wasn't willing to test her limits of friendliness by trials on other dogs.

To improve her sociability with other canines, she needed more exposure and practice. I did one of the stupidest moves possible and tried her out in one of those fenced-in dog playgrounds—which I later learned was, from her point of view, like a gladiator pit. Lily quickly retreated to a corner and cowered, foaming at the mouth. She was the kid sitting alone at the lunch table. I am embarrassed to admit that I gave it another two tries. Meanwhile, in a parallel dynamic, I noticed that my son Gabriel liked it there quite a lot. He perked up among the animals and struck up conversations with the humans. "Hey, nice dog you have there. What breed?" Nonetheless, we were there for Lily, who was no more comfortable on the third visit than she had been on the first, so we bagged it. I found a compromise at a different local park where a group of humans walked each morning on a loop, and Lily could be on a leash and still participate, as some dogs were on leash as well. After a while, she did improve her comfort level with other dogs, and I could tell that she genuinely enjoyed it because when we were out walking, she often tried to tug me in the direction of that park.

Over the years to come, each member of my family developed their own relationship with Lily. Gabriel did not follow the script of the child who begs for the dog, promises to care for the dog, then forgets all promises once said dog arrives. He was thrilled to have her, and although he was only eleven, he took care of Lily exactly as he'd promised. He walked her each day after school, fed her many nights, and brushed her when we asked him. He used his animal awareness to advocate for her best interest if the rest of us were not paying attention. ("Stop, you're crowding her.") He was a stellar caretaker, and Lily, who seemed to understand, gave him a certain deference in return.

Simon, on the other hand, was six when she arrived, and for the first couple of years could not safely walk Lily or do much caretaking except to fill her water bowl and occasionally brush her while we held her lead. Lily knew he was a little one. She would not listen to a single thing Simon asked her to do. Not one.

"Lily gives me no respect," he cried.

"She sees you as a brother," said Gabriel. "You're a little wolf, like her. You're a pack mate."

"I want my own pet," he sulked. "I want a bunny. Or a skink. Something I can be in charge of."

One night, I gave Lily a new job of helping me put six-year-old Simon to bed. After he got under the covers, I called her to his room and patted the comforter. She leapt up by his feet while I read to him. Sometimes she climbed up on his body and stretched out over him, belly to belly. After this, it became her ritual to eagerly run up two flights and get into position. When we were done and the lights went out, she sometimes stayed there for a couple of hours until we went to bed, then came to our room and slept on the floor near us.

My husband took the weekend shift. He gave Lily her early morn-ing Saturday walks—though, after the shih tzu incident, he kept her on a leash or sought out fenced-in places.

My role with Lily turned out to be the biggest. I was the work-at-home parent and therefore had to train her and care for her Monday through Friday while everyone else was at school or work. We spent a lot of time together, and as a result she became most attuned to me. I woke up each morning to find her wagging her tail at my bedside. She followed me from to room—never cloying or demanding, just wanting to be near.

My only experiences with dogs had come from the two Dobermans of my childhood, several decades earlier in a galaxy far, far away. Back then, back there, all dogs and other animals were unequivocally stationed below humans, a message reinforced by our Catholic faith.

It was a time of space missions and the first successful Apollo flight to the moon. Sister Theresa, the fifth grade teacher at Holy Trinity, gave my sister's class a special assignment: "Imagine you are going to the moon and you can only bring seven books and seven people. What would they be?"

My sister didn't hesitate. Our immediate family of five humans plus the two Dobermans as numbers six and seven. It was a no-brainer. Sister Theresa, who was especially well known for corporal punishment, was not at all pleased. She flicked the assignment back at my sister, who surely flinched in fear. "Unacceptable," Sister Theresa said. "A *dog* over a human? You would *never* take a dog over a human. Dogs don't have souls. Why didn't you put a priest on your spaceship? Who else would be able to deliver the sacraments?"

Shortly after the first Doberman puppy arrived, my parents hired a trainer and spent countless hours practicing the lessons of hard-core obedience. They saw it as their obligation to ensure that the dog would not be destructive or intimidating to others. Most dog trainers of that era embraced dominance theory. Good behavior brought praise, petting, and love. Bad behavior brought consequences such as a hit on the snout, shaming, rejection, or banishment to the basement. They used a choke collar to teach the dog to heel. The premise was that dogs, like their ancestor wolves, naturally organized themselves in packs based on hierarchy. Therefore, a pet needed to know who was in charge, and a responsible human owner would take the role of the alpha. Otherwise, the dog wouldn't know his place. He would be a lifelong menace who could become destructive and harm others. It was a serious issue, justifying harsh tactics if necessary, not just for the good of the humans but for the good of the dog.

After being schooled in this training, my parents were fond of saying that commands should be only one or two words, because (wasn't it obvious?) dogs can't comprehend sentences and paragraphs. As a child I understood this to mean that they were foreigners among us who did not speak English. You should never say a command more than once— otherwise you teach the animal that it has multiple chances to obey besides right now. Whenever the doorbell rang, my mother calmly said, "Go upstairs," and the dogs instantly clambered up to the landing, where they remained until released. "Heel," and they were instantly at your side, head next to your knee. Even if they weren't wearing a leash, they just walked at your side like a buddy. No one could believe it. I recall being proud of my parents' high standards and that they'd done such a good job.

By the end of puppyhood, our dogs were exceptionally well behaved and remained so for the rest of their lives. They were also sweet, smart, affectionate, loyal, true, and tolerant of us. We loved them. We treasured them. They became a part of the family. But there was no doubt that my father saw them as property to be controlled if necessary. And my mother went along. So did we children.

When we got Lily, I began by using the lessons that had seemed to work so well in my childhood. When Lily stole a ham off the counter, I held her snout and gave a threatening deep-throated "Noooo," according to dominance theory. When she figured out how to push the back door open and went on a racing spree through the neighborhood, I grabbed her by the collar and got in her face, then told her she was a Very Bad Girl. On a walk when she surged ahead for a squirrel, I gave the leash a sharp yank and commanded her to heel.

At these moments she froze in place and squinted her eyes, stunned. She was a statue. I felt bad, but I thought she'd get the idea and we'd be done quickly with this painful yet necessary process. And then, once she learned, we'd have a good life together.

Nothing changed, except that she'd lunge for the squirrel or bark ferociously at a small dog, then look at me with fear of being punished. I told a friend about her reaction.

"You have to go slowly with a rescued dog," she said. "You have to be gentle. Think of what she's been through."

My vet was clearer.

"You have a sensitive soul here," he said, and we both looked at Lily on the examination table. She was clearly not just sensitive but terrified, as always, to be there, beginning to tremble, tail tucked so far under her legs that it nearly touched her belly.

"It's *your* job to make sure she can't get food," he said with disapproval. "*You* have to get it off the counters and tie up the garbage tight. And it's *your* job to fix your doors so she cannot get out and run away. She's a *greyhound*. It's her nature to chase a squirrel or rabbit. When she's gone after one, she cannot hear you no matter how loudly you tell her to come. If you'd had her since she was a puppy, that would be one thing. Maybe you could have trained her to come no matter what. But this dog is nearly two years old."

In other words, Lily was not at fault. I was.

I took his words to heart. I searched online and learned that over the last twenty years, a growing body of research has shown dominance training to be harmful and ineffective. When it comes to addressing dogs' behavioral problems—such as fear, anxiety, and aggression—punishment is not a good solution. In fact, some experts believe it can make a fearful and aggressive dog even worse. The American Veterinary Society of Animal Behavior (AVSAB) states that the use of dominance training should be avoided because it leads to antagonistic relationships between owners and their pets. In its position statement, the AVSAB writes:

> *the standard of care for veterinarians specializing in behavior is that dominance theory should not be used as a general guide for behavior modification. Instead, the AVSAB emphasizes that behavior modification and training should focus on reinforcing desirable behaviors, avoiding the reinforcement of undesirable behaviors, and striving to address the underlying emotional state and motivations, including medical and genetic factors, that are driving the undesirable behavior.*

Even my oldest son brought to my attention that the dominant wolf idea might be a questionable notion for humans to apply to dogs. He found a copy of *Animals Make Us Human* by Temple Grandin, the famous animal scientist, then disappeared to his bedroom and read nearly the whole thing in a night. Next morning, he descended ready for school with his newest hairstyle, a mohawk plastered straight up. He sat himself down beside Lily on her cushion.

"You know," he began, while scratching her head, "dogs may not need us to act as an alpha after all."

"Oh yeah? What do you mean?"

"Well, Temple Grandin says that a lot of the ideas about dogs are wrong because scientists studied wolves in forced packs—not natural ones. It turns out that in the wild, wolves really live a lot in family groups. So it's really not that crazy that we should treat our pets like children."

With a sick feeling in my gut, I got down by Lily on her bed, where she was sitting sphinx-style, and I petted her soft white fur. As she stared into the distance, I looked at all of her parts. Her floppy ears. Her whiskery muzzle and small black nose. Her long swan neck and her strange tail. Her extra-long legs and pointed feet with calloused foot pads, and her belly moving in a steady rhythm, in and out.

Somewhere inside of her was a mange-ridden abandoned dog with bleeding skin left on the side of the road. Somewhere in her was a mother who saw her pups die or be stolen.

I was sad, and told her I was very sorry that I'd been hard on her.

She made no visible response that day. From all I could see, she forgave me for my faults and mistakes, and she did so continually. She forgave because she was a dog and forgiveness was her nature.

⌒

OVER THE first few months, I learned to read Lily. When she needed to eat or go out, she simply wagged her tail and stared at you with laser-beam eyes and her ears up. If you didn't get the message, she'd give one sharp bark and put a paw on your lap.

Otherwise, she was a timid dog who asked very little of humans. Though she loved to be petted, she was never pushy about it.

Like most greyhounds, she spent a lot of time lying around—a trademark of the breed. But when she was happy she could be exuberantly so, and for these moments, she had several dances. The mildest was a simple tap dance, but she could turn that up a notch by adding a leap or two. When she was really happy and celebratory, she added a dramatic side-to-side head toss or a circular motion we called the head whip. Sometimes she'd perform a ridiculously exaggerated single gallop and land two feet from me. There would be a pause while we contemplated the distance between us, and she'd creep forward on her belly another foot in my direction. After all of this display, I would finally lean forward and pet her. She'd look away as if the encounter had been all my idea and she was merely tolerating it. In fact, she often looked away, out of deference and submission, but I did not understand jack shit about dogs. So, instead, I found it amusing that, with her greyhound bearing and refusal to look at me, she looked like a regal snob. I was clueless.

She never lowered herself to lick you. My disappointed younger son once rubbed bacon on his cheek to see if it would do the trick. (It did, but only when you were perfumed with bacon.) If you embraced her too aggressively, she could only take so much before she'd get up and move away a couple of feet. In these and other ways, she sometimes seemed more like a cat than a dog. "She's a dat," my husband declared. Often, though, she seemed as mysterious and ethereal as a thoroughbred.

Lily was extraordinary with children and didn't mind five or six little kids from the block crowding around her, all petting her at once. I could have left a naked baby on the floor alone with her, and that baby would have been safe (though I never tested this). She especially loved women and wagged energetically when they came to the door, did her prancing dance and leaped. Perhaps it was because the Irish women had saved her and nursed her to health. When Elizabeth visited, Lily could barely contain her joy and once fell down a flight of stairs because she running too fast to meet her at the door. (She was fine.) In contrast, when men approached her, she backed up, turned away, and generally ignored their existence. With the exception of the three guys in our household, her discrimination against the male gender was profound. As far as she was concerned, men would always have more to prove.

She didn't know how to play with humans, and this was another thing we had to teach her. We tossed a squeaky toy and she would catch it and take it back to her bed to chew on, and that was the end of that. It took at least six months for her to bring it back to me and insinuate that I should throw it again. I learned how to draw out her athletic skills so that she would rise up from a down position into a spiraling leap and catch the toy on the fly, then pounce down softly, victorious, her eyes reflecting like mirrors.

The boys had to adjust their expectations. They'd thought they were getting a real dog, not a dat. And though they loved Lily and checked themselves from dissing her, they each mentioned at some point that some day they hoped to have a *real* . . . a more extroverted canine who would roughhouse and play catch for hours. This actually hurt me. I thought Lily was the most perfect dog in the world. I was busy, and Lily was not needy. Plus, she was exquisitely beautiful, and I've always been a sucker for beauty.

Soon, I was becoming like the other dog people—wanting the best for my own, searching for fenced-in places where she could run safely off lead. I found a tennis court that had a grass rim around it, which was soft on her paws, and we became regulars at a nearby park where a little island was set off beyond a gate. There, Lily was safe to go off lead and run. The island was the size of a large backyard, but big enough that she could let loose. Always, I felt a thrill as I saw her go. I noticed that as she ran, she looked over her shoulder at me, as though to check that I was watching. When I gave her applause or encouragement, I swore she pushed on faster for my benefit, though Herb told me that was ridiculous.

It took years, but Lily became a more confident dog. She became less afraid of men (though she still strongly preferred women) and stopped trying to bolt out of the door to escape. If I warned her in advance not to bark when we saw a dog heading our way, she did reasonably well.

One day when my husband took Lily out for a weekend walk, he stepped on a wasps' nest, and they were swarmed by attacking wasps that chased them—and stung them—as they ran. They finally made it home, both of them burning from multiple stings. They sat on the porch panting with adrenaline. After a while, Lily went up to my husband's legs, sniffed his wounds, then licked each one. It was the first time she'd ever licked any of us, and she never did it again.

6

—

DIGNITY

2007

Not long after we adopted Lily, Elizabeth called to ask if I was interested in meeting Marion Fitzgibbon, president of the ISPCA, as she was in the States for a week visiting her son Joe, who, it turned out, lived only a half hour away from me. I knew little about Marion other than that she'd somehow been involved with Lily's rescue and recovery, so I said yes. I was curious.

I must have expected some kind of folksy animal person, perhaps an eccentric grandmother, all warm and lovey-dovey. But instead I was introduced to a tall woman with a straight bearing and a manner that reminded me more of a diplomat than a cat lady. Marion was in her late sixties by then. She had short blond hair and a pretty face covered in wrinkles. When she spoke about animals, she sounded like she was addressing the General Assembly of the U.N. describing children caught in a genocide. There was an implicit assumption that animals were important to the well-being of everyone. She wasn't going to explain it if you didn't get it.

I'd brought Lily with me because I thought Marion would be happy to see her. Lily went trotting up to present herself. At first, Marion bent down with a serious face, scanning over Lily almost as if to inspect her. Satisfied, she smiled and put a hand on Lily's back to pet her, but only for a moment, before she looked up and turned her attention away. The brevity of this gesture surprised me. I thought Marion would have been happier to see how well things had turned out. Later I would learn that for Marion, once an animal was saved, she had to move on to the next and the next. An infinity of animals in need were waiting for her attention, and she couldn't linger.

"A man came to the door with Lily," Marion began. "It was a Saturday. She was screaming and crying. Rosie put cortisone cream on her, but she'd keep scratching on the spot. She was in such bad shape. The mange was so bad her eyes were shut. And her skin was bloody. A group of Travellers had been parked in the area for three months or so. They'd just picked up and left the day before. I'm sure Lily was a Travellers' dog. When one of their dogs is sick, they often just leave it behind.

"Lurchers are the lowest dogs on the social ladder. They're known as gypsy dogs. You don't see anyone walking around with them as pets."

We spoke for about two hours, though mostly it was Marion who did the talking, weaving one story into the next while we drank tea at her son's table. She told me about the horse in the rain when she was six, about how she'd gotten started feeding dogs on the streets, and about the women of Limerick Animal Welfare.

"How did you manage all this raising four children?" I asked.

"Badly," she replied, without a flicker of hesitation.

"And the greyhounds?"

"Ireland is the foremost breeder of greyhounds in Europe. Greyhound racing started in the 1920s, and it's a big industry, a great provider of jobs . . . For some it's a hobby. For others it's business; they breed and sell. It's seen to be part of our culture.

"In America and England, the tracks are closing down because of the huge groundswell of people protesting against them. But that's not what's happening in Ireland."

Then she rattled off numbers. "They overbreed far more than they can use. Between 22,000 and 24,000 are registered each year. We estimate that four or five 'saplings' in every litter are not going to make the grade. About 6,000 to 8,000 die of 'natural wastage.' That's what they call it. About 10,000 of those go to England. Then maybe another 1,500 to the coursing pool."

"Coursing?" I asked. She explained that it was another sport, which set two greyhounds on a race to chase a large hare.

"And the rest of the greyhounds?"

"We don't know. There are some kept back for breeding. But they can't possibly absorb all the rest into the Irish racing pool," she said. "A lot of dogs fail their trials."

She told me then about how, a few months earlier, a mass grave had been discovered in England behind a construction worker's house. It was one acre and contained the remains of 10,000 greyhounds in various states of decomposition. Three-quarters of them were identified as Irish dogs. The builder had shot each one for about ten British pounds per dog (not even twenty bucks), a substantial discount from a vet's fee. He said he shot them humanely in the head, but some corpses suggested otherwise.

We paused.

While she was talking, I thought to myself, *What kind of person is this? What kind of person appoints herself to do this?* I asked her as much.

"I was born that way. I cannot walk past a hurt animal. I am physically not capable."

She called it an affliction.

"You think that maybe with the next one we will make a difference. Or the next hundred. But of course, there are only more and more."

"Why animals? Why not suffering children? Why not people in crisis?"

"Oh, we help people too. We would never walk into a place to help an animal and pass by people who needed help. We get to know the families in the public housing estates. We fought to get Traveller kids in school. We also helped them get toilets and running water and land. There was a time once when I got a call about a dog out on a pier. When I went out there I found a prostitute instead, and she was in such bad shape, I took her in my car and got her something to eat and tried to help her find a place where she could get a shower and rest . . . These things are a social service. But our focus is always on the animals."

She could tell that I still didn't understand how animals would be a priority.

"Every living creature has the right to live and die with dignity," she said in a softer, almost reverent tone. I could tell that she'd long ago settled upon this as her religious creed.

It was a beautiful idea then and now. I doubted how such a thing could possibly work. And yet I wanted to believe it was true.

Marion told me I'd be welcome to come to Ireland and see the sanctuary she was trying to build before she died. I told her that maybe someday I would.

7

—

CELTIC HOUNDS

We cannot be sure when or where the dog first emerged as a separate species from its wolf ancestor. Some scientists say it happened 15,000 years ago, in Europe. Others say it happened more than 30,000 years ago, in Asia. In either case, this epic event occurred at a time when humans were still nomadic hunter-gatherers, moving across the land in search of food, much like other animals, leaving little imprint on the natural ecology of the earth.

The old story was that humans, in our infinite foresight, chose to breed wolves into dogs. Now we know that it's far more likely that the wolves chose us. Probably they smelled meat cooking and trailed along behind our camps at a safe distance, hoping to find leftovers. Then, some outliers among them—probably those who were genetically wired to have friendlier temperaments—came in closer. They might have been afraid, but the food was the stronger pull. These bold dogs thrived and opportunistically stayed on. They produced offspring who inherited the friendly temperaments of their parents and were raised around humans. Eventually humans inserted themselves into the reproduction process, matching up this male with that female, in the hope of breeding wolves that would work in exchange for free food. The experiment was a spectacular success. The result was the dog, our first domesticated animal.

When you consider that, later, humans would take these breeding skills and move on to domesticate sheep, pigs, goats, and crops that would make it possible for us to settle down in villages, you start to get an idea of just how stupendous the human–dog alliance really was. The mutual benefit helped both humans and dogs become the most successful two mammals on the planet. But even more than that, dogs were our first step toward civilization.

For thousands of years we refined the first great breeding experiment, developing dogs with traits to match certain jobs. Strong dogs to pull our sleds, good swimmers to work with fishermen, fierce small dogs to hunt vermin in crevices underground, bossy dogs to herd livestock, territorial dogs to guard homes, and, of course, dogs with great speed, sight, and smell to hunt down dinner. You wouldn't keep a dog around and feed it if it couldn't do work for you. And yet the relationship was not merely transactional—work in exchange for food. If you look at ancient art and stories from around the globe, it's obvious that early on humans developed deep emotional and spiritual bonds to dogs. In certain mythologies and creation myths they took on key roles as fire-bringers, loyal friends, monsters, guardians of virtue, tricksters, and quite frequently as spiritual guides to the afterlife.

⌒

IMAGES OF greyhound-like dogs—with their deep-chested, slim-waisted, long-legged forms—appear in Western art going back thousands of years. They race and hunt and pose on Egyptian pottery and tombs, and on ancient Greek and Roman sculptures. They show up in illuminated manuscripts, medieval frescoes, tapestries of the hunt,

The Townley Greyhounds. Marble, Roman, first or second century CE. (Courtesy British Museum)

and Renaissance paintings. It's no wonder that, for a long time, people believed greyhounds were one of the oldest dog breeds in the world. But that turned out not to be true. In 2004, the Dog Genome Project delivered the shocking news that greyhounds did not trace back to Egypt. They were old, yes, but probably northern European, descended from herding stock. The ancient dogs of Egypt represented on pharaohs' tombs were probably salukis, which are long and slender sight hounds that look like—but are not—cousins to the greyhound.

More likely, greyhounds are connected to the Celtic people who made westward migrations from central Europe all the way to Spain, France, England, Wales, and, of course, Ireland. Those who settled in Ireland brought a version of Celtic culture and language that would ultimately become Gaelic. They also seem to have brought a unique dog with them called the Celtic hound, which would revolutionize hunting with their exceptional vision and speed.

Two fascinating documents describe the state of things before and after the arrival of the Celtic hound. In the 300s BC, the Greek philosopher and former military man Xenophon wrote a field guide titled *On Hunting,* for aristocrats like himself who found great pleasure in the pursuit of hare, stag, and boar. His book addressed almost every aspect of the hunt and did so in loving detail, including a lengthy description of the ideal hunting dog: a strong and spirited mastiff with an unstoppable nose and a great work ethic, even in the Mediterranean heat. Much of Xenophon's hunting advice would sound familiar to hunters today—except for one thing. His central technique relied on a complex system of nets set up in advance by slaves, something like fishing seines or traps. The hounds' job was to follow scent lines to find the prey then drive it into those nets. Then, the hunter (who was on foot) would use a javelin, rocks, or a spear to kill the captured animal.

About five hundred years later, in 150 AD, a Greek historian and philosopher named Arrian produced an updated version of *On Hunting,* in which he respectfully noted that a new edition was necessary because so much had changed. The biggest change of all was the arrival of a new kind of hound whose prey instincts were triggered by vision, not scent. Arrian describes these hounds with reverence: "In figure, the most high-bred are a prodigy of beauty; their eyes, their hair, their colour, and bodily shape throughout." He notes that the Celtic hound was so fast and strong that it could easily take down large animals such as deer and boar, then wait for the hunter to arrive, or in the case of small game, deliver it to the master's feet.

Arrian tells us that if Xenophon had known of Celtic hounds, he never would have needed all those complicated nets!

In fact, a whole new hunting method arrived along with these fast-running dogs. Arrian describes a ritual in which two Celtic hounds were set up to compete against one another in pursuit of a hare. Basically, it was a race to see which hound would stop the hare first. By nature, the hounds had more stamina, but the hare was more agile and would weave about to evade capture. The hound won when it "turned" the hare and pounced on the creature, usually shaking or tearing it to death. This type of competition was called *coursing*, and like all coursing men, Arrian defended the sport by reframing its purpose and intention as something other than what it appears to be. "The true Sportsman does not take out his dogs to destroy the Hares but for the sake of the course, and the contest between the dogs and the Hares, and is glad if the hare escapes."

On a personal note, Arrian wrote lovingly of his own Celtic hound, which "had the greyest of grey eyes, who was fast and a hard worker, spirited and agile, so that when she was young she once could get four hares in a day." She was also "most gentle and most fond of humans." If Arrian went away, even for a brief separation, she was full of joy, jumping in the air, when he returned. He described her physical beauty and elegance, the hollow belly and thin long tail, big hind legs, broad chest, long neck. I am struck by his emotion and how much the description of his dog sounds like Lily.

⟨

THE GREYHOUND continued its climb in status during the Middle Ages, when the kings and noblemen of Europe hunted with ritual and pageantry for the sake of sport. Riding horseback at high speed after a stag, in a chase led by dogs, showed off a man's greatness. Greyhounds were the most valued hunting dog and the most elite because of their speed and skills. Queens and kings sent greyhounds to one another as a gesture of friendship and alliance. Evidently, the more dogs you had the better. In 1212, King John traveled with three hundred greyhounds on a hunting expedition.

Starting with the Norman Conquest of 1066, a succession of English monarchs established large preserves as "royal forests," where big tracts of land were set aside for their exclusive hunting pleasure. These were not forests per se, but vast territories that encompassed woodlands, pastures, farms, and villages where peasants had long extracted their livelihoods from commonly held land. Now, every twig, blade of grass, and animal belonged to the king. If you were caught hunting without a permit—whether for the sport of a showy stag or for the smallest hare for dinner—it meant you were stealing the king's property and you could be slapped with a hefty fine. In 1389, Richard II's game law forbade anyone who didn't own at least forty shillings' worth of land to own "hunting hounds." In this way, greyhounds became an enduring symbol of the landowning class and aristocracy. Previously, hunting had been a universal right. Peasants who had always hunted hare and other small game—both for food and to reduce the damage they did to crops—now suffered a great loss. They expressed their resentment and need by poaching.

According to a good deal of unproven legend and lore, peasants and gypsies secretly "borrowed" the greyhounds of the nobility long enough to breed them with their bitches so as to produce mongrels known as lurchers. The term "lurcher" first appeared in a 1668 essay by Anglican clergyman John Wilkins, who describes the dog as a "Lesser Beast" compared to the greyhound (which was a "Greater Beast"). And yet, there were benefits to the lowly lurcher. Full-bred greyhounds were pure speed, but they had little stamina. A good lurcher, on the other hand, was plenty fast, but sturdier. Plus, some lurchers didn't look like greyhounds at first glance. This may have been an advantage for the enterprising peasant, who could slide by under the radar and catch game. "What, us keeping greyhounds? Does this look like a greyhound to you?"

The laws were continually flouted, and a new game law in 1671 brought a severe crackdown. Now, you had to own land worth at least one hundred pounds per year in order to hunt, or be the oldest son of an esquire, knight, or noble (or one of their gamekeepers). Unqualified persons were also prohibited from keeping "any 'engines' that might be used to hunt game, as well as the keeping of greyhounds, setting dogs, ferrets, coney dogs, and lurchers."

Despite the best efforts of Parliament to preserve wild game for the top one percent, widespread hunting and poaching continued, sometimes with violent clashes, writes Emma Griffin in her book *Blood Sport*. The population of large game began to decline in the royal forests and acreage owned by wealthy landowners. Hunters needed to find something else to hunt. Fox were still considered unworthy, but the hare had always been a respected creature because it can run so fast and so far. By the eighteenth century, hare-hunting across open land rapidly gained in popularity, notes Griffin. The hare was also perfect for that very particular type of coursing, described by Arrian, in which two greyhounds compete to take down an animal. Coursing had been popular in England long before, in pursuit of stag as well as hare. In fact, during the sixteenth century, Queen Elizabeth I had been a great fan of blood sports, meaning those that pitted one animal against another. She was a hunter and excellent horsewoman, not the least bit squeamish about slitting an animal's throat.

On the Queen's command, the Duke of Norfolk developed official rules for hare coursing. No more than a pair of greyhounds could chase at one time, and, at the outset of the race, they were to be held on a single leash with side-by-side collars (the slip). A "hare finder" was sent out to scare up hares in advance. When all was ready, the hares were given a head start of "twelve score yards." Then the dogs were loosed. With their muscular force, they rapidly closed the distance. The hare, feeling them closing in, pulled out its single advantage: agility. It weaved and bobbed and made tight, quick turns in a desperate attempt to live. The dog scored points by the number of times it "turned" the hare. If the hare could get itself to the trees or hedges, it stood a chance of escape.

It was a perfect pastime for aristocratic men who had large estates and could follow on horseback while hare and hounds ran for miles. By

1800, *The Sportsman's Dictionary* described coursing as a "recreation in great esteem with many gentlemen." In fact, they loved it so much that they organized clubs to hold meets that were open to the public. In 1836, the owner of the Waterloo Hotel held such an event on the plains of Altcar in Lancashire. The Waterloo Cup became the most important coursing event in English history, an annual three-day competition involving sixty-four greyhounds from Britain and Ireland. After each match, the winning dog went on to the next round. By the end of the century, tens of thousands of people attended each year, standing and sitting on the sidelines, wagering, cheering, and lamenting.

The most heroic Waterloo dog was an Irish greyhound named Master McGrath. His repeated triumph over British dogs made him a national hero while also providing a jab of revenge for seven hundred years of colonization. His story is filled with the magical lore of the underdog. Born weak and small, the pup was about to be drowned when a young boy successfully pleaded for his life. Master McGrath won at Waterloo in 1868, 1869, and 1871, bringing much glory to Ireland. Even Queen Victoria asked to meet him.

Coursing came to the U.S., making it to the American West as early as 1866, by way of Irish and British immigrants. As noted in a 1902 article in the *San Francisco Call*, "The coursing men brought their love of the pastime from Ireland . . . Hardly an English ship arrived in the harbor that did not bring a greyhound." An annual meet took place for decades on the open fields around San Francisco where there were "an abundance of hares."

Not everyone appreciated the ritualistic killing at the center of the sport. The jackrabbit did not go quietly to its death. When mauled by the greyhound, it let out a haunting scream. In 1905, a *Los Angeles Times* article described how "the rabbit was ground to death amid shrieks of agony," with cries that sounded "appallingly like those of a tortured little child."

In 1905, in South Dakota, Owen Patrick Smith, a thirty-eight-year-old engineer and businessman, witnessed his first coursing meet and felt a similar disgust at the sight of a rabbit being torn to shreds for no purpose other than human amusement. Most people who felt this way simply stayed away from coursing meets, but Smith was captivated (as engineers often are) by the idea of designing something that would solve this problem of cruelty. He dedicated the remaining twenty-two years of his life to developing a humane alternative based on the premise that the dogs would chase any small thing that moved—it didn't have to be a living creature. After demonstration races involving the likes of a motorcycle engine pulling a taxidermy rabbit, Smith eventually developed a viable mechanical lure. He was not the first to experiment with this kind of alternative—there had been previous efforts in England to invent something similar—but Smith was the first to get financial backing and a facility where dogs could race. The world's first greyhound race on an oval track took place in Emeryville, California, in 1919. Admission cost ninety-nine cents, the equivalent of about fourteen bucks today. The track closed right away, but it showed enough promise for others to take notice.

For the next few years, dog tracks opened and closed quickly in the States, while Smith struggled to establish his idea despite low attendance and the police breathing down his neck over illegal betting. A core group of dogmen persisted, loading up their greyhounds and traveling long distances on rough, narrow roads in an era before big interstate highways. When, in 1922, the Miami Kennel Club Park opened its doors, fate changed. Florida's warm weather gave the industry a winter venue as well as a steady tourist market and a sense of tropical high style. In Florida, greyhound racing found its center of gravity. In her book *Going to the Dogs,* historian Gwyneth Anne Thayer describes how images of the palm trees, bathing beauties, and art deco swank gave promoters the cachet they needed to portray greyhound racing as glamorous and akin to horse racing. When electric lights arrived a few years later, events were held at night, adding to the glamour. What a thrill it must have been to sit outside in the stands beneath miraculous electric stars! Word spread and people came. Baseball players in Florida for winter training visited the track, bringing their star power with them, and so did entertainers from nearby resorts. Babe Ruth and, later, Joe DiMaggio and Frank Sinatra all posed for photos with winning dogs. The slim greyhound (or two or three) became a signature accessory in 1920s flapper-style fashion ads.

"It's hard to know which came first, the greyhound or the concept of elegance," says Gary Tinterow, a curator at the Metropolitan Museum in New York. "People began trying to look like greyhounds . . . Attenuation became synonymous with elegance."

During the Twenties and Thirties, greyhound tracks successfully opened in St. Louis, Atlantic City, Chicago, New Orleans, and elsewhere, although big horse racing states such as Kentucky succeeded in keeping dog racing out. Some dog tracks were rumored to attract illegal betting and organized crime, and that made the argument against them easier. Though Smith had wanted a clean sport that would make a profit on admissions collected at the gate, he was a businessman and not to be deterred from selling his new brand of entertainment. Sure, some patrons enjoyed watching the dogs race, but gambling gave the sport drama and the power of its own addictive quality. With gambling, the dog races offered the thrill of escape and a dream of hitting it big. Maybe it was hard for an ordinary spectator to identify with a four-legged athlete that dashed by in thirty seconds, but as a bettor you had skin in the game. He was *your* dog.

In 1931, gambling became legal at the Florida dog tracks, and then in other states. Even during the depths of the Great Depression, five thousand people came to Wonderland, a stadium just outside Boston, and bet over $50,000 in a single month.

As the novelty of greyhound racing wore off, the movie stars and wealthy people moved on to other pursuits. The dog track became a workingman's entertainment, and a cheaper alternative to horse racing for men who wanted to own and profit from racing animals. Also, it was cheaper for patrons, who could put down a bet in cents rather than in dollars.

In a parallel timeline, greyhound racing took a feverish hold in England, Ireland, and Australia. In 1926, Britain's first greyhound race, held in Manchester, attracted between two and three thousand people. Soon, the nightly average approached ten thousand. The next year, Ireland and Australia opened tracks and began racing dogs to similarly enthusiastic crowds.

Early on, Ireland emerged as the powerhouse greyhound breeder and exporter in Europe. By the end of the 1940s, Irish dog breeders were selling about ten thousand dogs annually, valued at one million Irish pounds. It's hardly a surprise that the national government took notice. The economy was in terrible shape, and unemployment was so high that each month shiploads of young people fled the country to seek jobs overseas. Here was a promising new enterprise that not only generated jobs and track income but also a product for export. How could the government *not* support it? In 1958, the Irish Parliament got in on the action by passing the Greyhound Industries Act, which set up an agency to oversee the domestic operations at thirty or so tracks, and to promote the breeding and export of dogs. While England, the U.S., and Australia all had national racing boards, the Irish Greyhound Racing Board (also known by its Irish name, the Bord na gCon) was unique because of the government's extreme generosity. For decades millions of taxpayer pounds (and later euros) flowed into the sport and still do.

Raising greyhounds fit well with the Irish identity. It was a still rural nation, and Irish farmlands offered the wide-open spaces for raising and training dogs. But that was not all. Greyhound racing seemed to tap into a masculine aspect of the nation's "sporting" soul— one that was crazed for hurling, rugby, and Gaelic football, hunting, coursing, fishing, and horses, a soul that was connected to the land of which the Irish had been dispossessed for centuries. This love of sport was a common cultural thread that cut across all classes and included politicians and powerful men in the upper echelons of government who owned greyhounds or had family that did. With friends in high places, greyhound racing remained untouchable for decades.

In all four of the major racing countries—Australia, England, Ireland, and the U.S.—the industry killed excess dogs. Some dogs were just not interested in chasing; others got injured; all eventually got older and, somewhere between ages three and five, became too slow. During the first several decades of the business, euthanasia (as it was called) of young, healthy dogs became routine and unquestioned.

As racing became more popular, more greyhounds were born and bred to run. As early as the 1950s some industry observers complained that breeding was becoming too industrial, focused on quantity rather than quality—leaving a costly surplus of dogs. A 1952 article in the respected *Greyhound Racing Record* bemoaned the fact that fewer than 30 percent of all greyhounds were "usable" for the track, notes Thayer.

So, how could it be that human beings have used and killed hundreds of thousands of dogs for the purpose of entertainment and gambling?

For one thing, greyhounds were "the other." They were big, muscular animals, most often seen wearing Hannibal Lecter–style face masks as they sped around the track. Clearly they would kill and eat your children.

In fact, the reason they wore masks was simply that if you put six or eight animals of *any* kind in tight lanes, shoulder to shoulder, and set them all off to chase the same prey, there is bound to be infighting, or at least nipping. Still, the masks made the dogs look evil.

Even the Humane Society of the United States misunderstood these dogs and discouraged the keeping of greyhounds as pets. As late as 1975, a newsletter cautioned dog lovers that greyhounds didn't know how to relate to humans because they'd spent so much time in kennels, and as a result they were prone to biting.

It's important, also, to remember that before World War II, most of the world still saw animals as utilitarian because of their use in agriculture. Once an animal had outlived its purpose, you had to get rid of it because you'd go broke feeding it. Compassionate people had respectful relationships with their working animals and put them down humanely, but they put them down nonetheless.

The international greyhound adoption movement was, by and large, created and led by women. Yes, there were men in the industry who spoke out against the surplus, and a few even suggested early on that greyhounds could make good pets, but they were few and far between.

The movement started in England and the United States, where women, particularly middle- and upper-class white women, had been volunteering for animal charities for a long time. Though I have personally felt conflict at the idea of helping animals at the possible expense of impoverished and abused children (for example), it's fascinating to understand just how allied these and other social justice movements were.

During the nineteenth century, battles for animal welfare, child protection, women's rights, and the abolition of slavery frequently overlapped. Often the very same people fought for many of these issues. Child protection societies prosecuted animal cruelty. Animal defenders investigated and publicized child cruelty. Both borrowed language from and were inspired by the antislavery movement.

During the world wars and the Great Depression, these reform movements went quiet for a while, but after World War II they rose again. Civil rights, environmentalism, feminism, gay rights, and the American Indian movements of the Sixties and Seventies gathered force, emphasizing equality and justice. Animal rights rode that tide.

Despite the interrelatedness of these movements, justice for animals seemed the most radical proposition of all. The idea that animals had *rights* was a bit too much for most people. Fighting for animal *welfare,* on the other hand, was always far more palatable, because it did not challenge the bedrock social assumption that it was okay to use animals for food, clothing, medicine, or entertainment. Animal welfare merely sought fair and humane conditions and compassion for animals in the process of using them. It advertised itself under a banner of love. Who could argue with that?

But the greyhound movement was something unique.

⌒

ANN SHANNON was one of the very first. She was still a teenager in 1959 when she got a job as a kennel maid at Dumpton Park in southeast England. She handled the dogs at the track kennel, took them to their trial runs, and was at the track on duty for race nights.

Shannon fell in love with greyhounds from the start. It wasn't long before she became upset by what she witnessed. She saw dogs wearing muzzles 24/7 for months on end, dogs kept confined in their kennels for sixteen hours straight, dogs left without water, dogs with skin problems camouflaged with black boot polish on race nights. She heard owners calling out, "Have it put down or give it away," when a dog couldn't race anymore.

When she learned that many retired dogs were sold to laboratories to endure further confinement and painful medical experiments, she was devastated. She didn't ask permission, but simply took it upon herself to take out ads in newspapers seeking good homes for the "no-goers" and retired dogs. She raised funds to pay for their care. And she worked directly with owners who were keen to unload their dogs for "homing," as they called it, and relieve themselves of their obligations.

The National Greyhound Racing Club (NGRC)—the agency in charge of the business in England—was not happy when it got wind of Ann Shannon's homing plan. The racing manager came to see her and told her to stop immediately, because her ads were making the greyhound business look bad.

She was barely twenty years old but Shannon wouldn't let him intimidate her. She continued her adoption program, and eventually set up an old railway carriage as a temporary station for dogs needing homes. For support, she teamed up with the British Union for the Abolishment of Vivisection.

In 1965, a British teacher named Johanna Beumer got a greyhound for her twenty-first birthday. Her parents had wanted to give her a car, but she insisted that she'd prefer a dog. She'd been passionate about greyhound racing since age eleven and wanted to have her own dog on the track. However when she became an owner, she got a backstage view of the kennels, and it was a rude awakening. Beumer had always naively assumed that when a dog's racing days were over, he simply went home with his owner and lived happily ever after. She was deeply disturbed to find out that many were put down. And she was horrified to learn that many owners sold their used-up racers to laboratories, so as to wring out one last bit of profit.

She approached the family that owned Walthamstow Stadium in East London—her local track and one of the U.K.'s most famous. She asked them to give her two double kennels and funds so that she could start an adoption program at the track and save some dogs' lives. The track owners gave their full support, and Beumer began diverting four dogs at a time to adoptive homes. Years later, she expanded and got a kennel for forty-eight dogs. (Like Shannon, she is now in her seventies and still, more than fifty years later, finding homes for discarded greyhounds.)

Then came a third. Molly Redpath—a successful greyhound trainer at England's Portsmouth track—was upset by similar behind-the-scenes discoveries. She passionately believed that greyhounds deserved to have good lives and made wonderful pets. In 1970, she too started an adoption program, as did sportswriter Gee Lebon at the stadium in Southend.

As these women advertised retired greyhounds for rescue and rehoming, they made the dogs suddenly visible. The public had, conveniently, never really questioned what became of the dogs at the end of their careers. Discussion of euthanasia began to spread, and the British greyhound business had to do something or die. England was a dog-loving nation and had been a trailblazer in developing the modern idea that dogs could be beloved family members.

In 1974, the NGRC asked Ann Shannon, Johanna Beumer, and Molly Redpath to bring their groups together under one umbrella organization, called the Retired Greyhound Trust, which would be headquartered with the NGRC and funded in part by the industry. This was the first large-scale organization for greyhound adoption in the world. It was insufficient; it relied primarily on the unpaid labor of women and it provided only a fraction of the money that was needed, but it was a start.

During the 1980s and 1990s, similar movements followed in the U.S. and Australia. Animal lovers—usually women—protested the mass breeding and killing of greyhounds. They did this in a variety of ways. Most worked in peaceful collaboration with the industry, finding adoptive homes for greyhounds and working to change public perception of the breed so that people would understand that they made wonderful pets. Others had no interest in collaboration, but rather worked in opposition, exposing cases of cruelty, long hours in cages, broken legs on the track, fatal kennel fires, and the enduring issue of discarded dogs put to sleep by the thousands or sent to laboratories for medical experimentation.

At times, the issue came to seem like a gender war in which women defended the dogs, while men—the callous breeders, owners, and trainers—inflicted abuse. Of course, it was not so simplistic. Plenty of women bred and raced dogs, and plenty of industry men cared for their dogs and expended time and money to make sure they found adoptive homes.

In fact, according to greyhound adoption pioneer Joan Dillon, it was a man not a woman who started what was probably the first formal greyhound adoption agency in the U.S. After working at a Florida track, Ron Walsek was tired of seeing perfectly healthy greyhounds put down before they were five years old. He and his wife started REGAP (Retired Greyhounds as Pets) in 1982.

In 1986, the *New York Times* profiled REGAP's success in homing two thousand greyhounds in just a few years. The article also reported that around twenty thousand greyhounds were bred to run each year, but only half ever made it to the track. Of those that actually raced, "Only ten percent of the crop is saved for breeding purposes. Most of the others are either destroyed outright or shipped off for use in medical experiments."

The following year, the American industry established the American Greyhound Council, which provided grants to greyhound adoption groups. In order to qualify, applicants had to agree not to speak out against the industry.

By the early 1990s, Ireland remained the largest breeder and exporter in Europe, but the U.S. was the largest breeder in the world. In 1993, the U.S. produced thirty-nine thousand greyhounds for its fifty tracks, and bettors put $3.5 billion into the pot.

Around that time, a succession of media exposés dealt one blow after the next to the business. Perhaps the biggest was a National Geographic documentary that aired on American television in 1992. It portrayed the beauty and athleticism of the dogs, along with undercover footage of ex-racers being put to death not only in large numbers but with chilling efficiency. In one sequence, the film followed the last moments of a "retired" racing greyhound at a killing center, where, one after the next, young healthy greyhounds were put to death by injection, then thrown onto a dump truck with a heap of other greyhound carcasses. These were the lucky ones, put down humanely. The film also showed the less fortunate—skinny dogs crammed three to a cage and left to starve by owners who didn't want to spend the money on proper euthanasia.

The documentary brought a public outpouring of criticism, and tracks all over the country fielded calls from people who wanted to adopt racing dogs. Wherever there was racing, adoption groups sprang up in the United States.

Just as in England, it became increasingly common to see greyhounds as pets. There were not enough homes and many dogs were still put to death, but the stigma of owning greyhounds faded almost completely. In fact, if you walked down the street with a greyhound, it was a badge of honor for having saved a life.

No such thing had yet happened in Ireland. No greyhound adoption agencies had formed. In Ireland, the land of the Celtic hound, the stigma against greyhounds, and the perception that they were dangerous killers, remained strong.

PART II

Beverly at Fedamore. (Courtesy Beverly Wolf)

8

—

BEVERLY

1983–2001

"Marion and I were meant to be," Beverly would say years later. "We were a blood-brothership. We both thought the exact same thing. Nothing was going to deter us from taking care of the animals."

It was Dr. Carroll, the vet, who brought them together, though if it hadn't been him, it would have been someone else.

"There's an American woman you should meet," he told Marion one day. "She's picking up dogs off the street. She was in here today. She's just as mad as you are."

That night, Beverly's phone rang.

"Mrs. Wolf, my name is Marion Fitzgibbon, with the Limerick Animal Welfare Circle. I'm calling because I heard you picked up a sick dog today in downtown Limerick and took him to Dr. Carroll."

Beverly's first thought was, *Who the hell is this person and how did she get my phone number?* Instead, she replied politely, "That's right. I picked up a dog."

"Well, thank you for doing that. You may have noticed that we have a terrible animal welfare situation here. We've started a group because no one was doing anything. Would you be interested in helping?

"It's not a social group," Marion warned. "We're not interested in sitting around talking and having tea. It's hard work. We have no kennel. It's all foster homes. We have little money. But we want to do it right. We're having our next meeting at the Mechanics Institute Hall in downtown Limerick. I hope you will come."

Beverly didn't know what to make of this Fitzgibbon lady, but she'd been an animal lover all her life. In fact, in the earliest picture she had of herself, taken at two or three years old, she was holding a puppy in her arms and had a huge smile for the camera. Many times she'd held up that picture to her husband or children and said, See this? This is who I am. This is who I always was.

People were frustrating. So many were idiots. Beverly had a short fuse when it came to idiots. But animals were different. They were honest, and they were innocent because they were just what they were. Each one had a story to tell, each had something interesting it could do—bits of brilliance that she could often see, where usually others were blind. The thing that got her the most about animals was that they were voiceless; they literally could not speak to defend themselves when bad things happened, and this she could not bear. So if someone asked her to help with animals, she felt it was her responsibility to at least check it out. So she told Marion she would come.

The Mechanics Institute was in downtown Limerick, a grubby old place with no coffee and no heat, but they were allowed to use it for free. When a beautiful woman appeared in the doorway, fortyish and dressed to the nines, the other ladies must have assumed she was lost and would be asking for directions any minute. But Marion realized who it was and invited her in.

Before long, Beverly was asking questions. She had a commanding presence and a deep, resonant voice, the kind that filled up the space around her, as if she might have been an actress or a singer at one time.

"I don't understand how you do this," she said. "You don't have a van. You don't have an ambulance. How can you rescue anything? This is a mom-and-pop organization. You've got nothing."

She didn't win herself a lot of friends that day. The others hardly needed an American to come marching in and point out how poor they were. And that was even *before* they knew who Beverly and her husband were and what had brought them to Ireland.

Later, in private, Marion would try to explain. "Beverly, we're *used to* having nothing. You come from America, the land of plenty."

Until Beverly arrived in Limerick, there'd never been anyone who was willing to go as far as Marion. Yes, Marion had "the animal-welfare circle," her group of wonderful friends who gave years of volunteering to build something from absolutely nothing. All of them filled their homes with stray dogs and cats, all had made countless trips to the vet, all had stood on the streets in the rain begging for donations. But there was always a point when they shut it all out and went home like normal people for their tea. Marion did not. She was the one who would stay out in the cold late into the night trying to catch a sick cat, or spend a week chasing a dog that had a broken leg hanging off. Marion could call Beverly at 3 a.m. and say, "I just got a call about a horse in a ditch," and Beverly would say, "Okay, I'm coming," and arrive twenty minutes later with a horsebox on the back of her car. Not only that, Beverly was incredibly competent; she knew what to do in the worst of situations, perhaps because she'd lost a mother at age sixteen and, being the oldest, had stepped up to take care of her sisters and grieving father. She was the kind of person who grew stronger in an emergency, when others fell apart.

Beverly and Semon Wolf wound up in Ireland for one reason only: they were foxhunters. In 1976, Semon got an invitation to hunt at

Scarteen, in County Limerick. Anyone who knew anything about fox hunting understood the significance of this invitation. People came to Scarteen from all over the world to hunt.

At the time, they were living on the Upper East Side of New York City. Semon was a stockbroker; he and Beverly had been married only six months, but Beverly had fully embraced her life as a foxhunter's wife. She understood that hunting was Semon's passion, and if you believed people had souls—and she did—then it was part of his soul as well. She would embrace it.

Most people didn't understand the first thing about foxhunting. Beverly had to explain over and over that there were no guns involved. It was simply about the chase. The hounds chased the fox and the hunters chased the hounds.

From the very start of their marriage, the Wolfs spent their weekends in a rural corner of Westchester County, north of the city, riding with the Golden's Bridge Hounds club. Beverly knew how to ride well enough; in no time, she learned to jump. It came to her easily, probably in part due to her abilities with animals. She trusted her horse to do what he knew best, rather than trying to control him. She took care of him and protected him, and he never let her down.

There was something preternaturally adaptive about Beverly's nature, and this quality allowed her to embrace her new life and to do so very quickly. She'd learned this talent early. After her mother's death, Beverly saw what was needed and became caretaker of her younger sister. When she was twenty years old and needed to get a job, she walked herself into the showroom of a top clothing designer on Seventh Avenue and became one of three house models—just like that. If she were to go to France, after a week she'd be French. That was Beverly. Now the road led to a place named Scarteen in Ireland for a week of hunting with international people. She packed her bags.

Scarteen was the name of an estate, a large Tudor mansion that looked a bit like a Gothic castle. Scarteen was also the name of the hunt itself. The word had come to evoke tradition, a kind of life that no longer existed anywhere else—all owned and preserved by the Ryan family for more than three hundred years. Behind the big house was a major operation: stables and kennels, muddy lanes, hay being moved in and out for the horses and cattle, working men in wellies, and the hounds being turned out several times a day. Beyond were fields that the Ryans farmed because, although they'd inherited an amazing piece of real estate, the family needed to work for a living.

On that first trip to Scarteen, Semon and Beverly were in awe. It was a fairy tale, an epoch frozen in time. Thaddeus Ryan was Master of the Scarteen Hounds, a role he'd held for thirty years by then. Thady, as he was known, was the warmest and most welcoming Irish country gentleman you could ever want to meet. He treated a local farmer with the same respect with which he treated the wealthiest sportsman who'd traveled two thousand miles to be on his land. And while most fox hunting in Ireland was carried on by the Ascendancy—the descendants of British aristocrats who colonized the country—the Ryans were the rare Catholics who'd managed to hold onto their estate through centuries of British rule. The walls were covered with paintings of ancestors and hunting trophies from generations past. Beverly loved the large dining room table with two-foot-tall silver candelabras blazing with candles. The Ryans extended extraordinary hospitality, despite having little household help. More than once Beverly glimpsed Mrs. Ryan cleaning the guests' coats and boots by herself in preparation for the next day's hunting.

At Scarteen, the hunt was not a frivolous pastime for weekend fun. It was a serious year-round business that required constant work and sacrifice from the Ryan family. There were the horses to breed and manage and care for. There were relationships to cultivate and nurture with the farmers over whose land they passed. And, of course, there were the marvelous hounds, the famous Black and Tans of Scarteen. The Ryans had bred them over generations to be courageous and fast, but most of all to have great "nose and throat." Their job was to find and follow the fox, nose to the ground, guided by scent lines, then go into their deep-throated cry when they closed in. The first time Beverly heard their voices baying in the cold air, she was overcome by the haunting beauty of the sound.

Semon had hunted all over the U.S. and England, but nothing compared to fox hunting in Ireland. Nothing. The riding was rough and ready and wild. They didn't politely jump over post and rail. In Ireland, farmers dig gullies around their fields to help with drainage, a practice that creates mile after mile of ditches, which are filled with overgrown bramble and streams. Still, the Irish rode their horses at high speed across pastures of ever-wet earth and the checkerboards of small farms.

Once Semon had hunted in Ireland, he couldn't get it off his mind. As soon as he was back in New York, he was planning his next trip, and then the next. This traveling back and forth went on for two years. Then in 1982, Semon accepted the position of Joint Master of the Scarteen Hounds. It was a great honor, but Semon never kidded himself. Being the American Joint Master didn't reflect his bravery in going over fences, or great horsemanship (though he had both); it simply meant that he was able to contribute financial support to the enormous expenses of the hunt. He was grateful for the recognition and for the fact that the people of Scarteen had welcomed them.

One night, they were in Ireland at a pub celebrating a birthday with their hunting friends. A local lawyer joined them for drinks, and he and Semon hit it off beautifully. The lawyer asked Semon if he was thinking about buying a place in Ireland. If so, he knew about something very special that was coming up for sale. Would he like to see it the following morning? Semon turned to Beverly briefly, then looked back at the man.

"Yes," he said. "Why not?"

⁓

BEVERLY HAD met Semon when she was out riding with her daughter Briggie in Holmdel, New Jersey. She'd never been on a fox hunt before but had gone on a lark with her daughter, simply because someone had invited them, and she'd thought, why not? So there they were, she and Briggie, on rented horses, when he appeared out of nowhere, an impossibly handsome man wearing a red hunting coat and black hunting cap, britches tucked into knee-high leather boots. He sat astride the most beautiful brown horse. She realized he was staring at her. Was she enjoying the hunt? Yes, she was. They exchanged pleasantries—just a few words, that was all.

That night and the next day, the image of him came back to her. How ridiculous! She brushed it aside and laughed at herself, but he kept coming back into her head. Some days later, the phone rang, and she heard Semon's voice on the other end. She was not yet forty. She had a husband, and her three wonderful children were all teenagers. Could there be a worse time? No, she couldn't go through with it.

But then something changed. For a moment she glimpsed the future. There were many decades ahead. In only a few years the children would be grown up, living their lives. What then?

She went with Semon, and within a year filed for divorce. It was the 1970s, and Beverly's lawyer reminded her that as she was the one asking for the divorce, she would have to leave the marital home. She knew it would be an awful upset, but it was worse than that. Still, she believed that after the turbulence subsided her children would all be okay. And they were—but she had underestimated the toll it would take. Once it was done, she tried not to look back.

Of course, people talked. But she wasn't going to try to explain herself—who would understand, anyway? Did she even fully understand? She knew that she'd been struck by lightning and found the love of her life. But how could she fully explain that it was more than this. Her decision was not only about love; it was about life.

⌒

THE NEXT morning, the lawyer from the pub took Beverly and Semon to see Fedamore House, a Georgian manor that had come onto the market in County Limerick, right in the middle of hunt country. It had seven fireplaces, five rooms for gatherings, five bathrooms, a greenhouse, a jasmine conservatory, and espaliered roses in the courtyard.

Beverly walked through the rooms, taking in every arched doorway and window, all the moldings and coves. With American dollars and the exchange rate at the time, it was a great price. Fedamore was a perfect hunting location, close to Scarteen and at the center of Semon's dream. Beverly could envision them throwing parties for the hunters. When her children came to stay, there would be plenty of room. She said nothing but watched Semon.

He turned to her. "I guess this is it, isn't it?"

She nodded.

They sold their New York City apartment and Semon quit his high-paying stockbroker job. The house came with twenty-eight stables and multiple outbuildings, tack rooms, and barns. They decided to breed, show, and sell horses, which was Beverly's dream. They opened Fedamore House Stud. Beverly was the breeding end of the team. Semon took care of finances and money. As soon as they took possession of the house, they decided to throw a party. They didn't even have furniture yet, just the chandeliers and hunting paintings. Three hundred guests showed up.

Not long after that party, Beverly went into Limerick city center to do some shopping. She noticed a stray dog lying in front of a butcher shop, his ribcage thin, with open sores and elephant-like skin. She stepped up to him. He smelled disgusting. She'd been a dog breeder and an American Kennel Club judge in the Sates. She couldn't bear to walk by and leave him alone and suffering.

She asked around about a vet, and someone directed her to John Carroll. She didn't have a leash, so she had to carry the stinky dog. When she entered the examination room, Carroll immediately raised an eyebrow at the sight of her. She spoke, and he heard her American accent; he shook his head.

He sent Beverly home with bathing lotion, cream, and painkillers for the dog. And that was the night the phone rang, with its fateful call from someone named Marion Fitzgibbon.

The first time Marion went to Fedamore, she was stunned not so much by the house itself as by what lay behind the house: all those stables and rooms and outbuildings. By then Marion had spent nearly ten years begging and scrounging for donations and for space, imploring people to just give her a corner here or there for a couple more dogs or cats. She'd built a network of a few dozen foster homes and filled them all to the brim, including her own. She lived in continual fear of those awful moments when there would be a dog in desperate condition and she'd have no place to put him. For Marion, after all the years she'd been at it, here, finally, was a safety valve. Fedamore was so big that no matter what, there would always be a corner or a stall where she could put up a dog for a night or two. It put her mind to rest for the first time in ten years. Now they had a place.

Within a short time, Beverly had thirty dogs, and, soon after, forty. Fedamore, the hunt master's mansion, became the sanctuary for Limerick Animal Welfare. It was a shelter, an animal hospital, and 24/7 headquarters.

Marion and Beverly did everything they could, even crazy things that could have gotten them seriously hurt or killed.

Like the time she and Beverly were driving in downtown Limerick and noticed a terrier trotting along the sidewalk on Henry Street. She was in season, being chased by what looked to be a dozen dogs. Her scent had traveled for miles and driven them mad. They'd jumped over fences and raced into the street, nearly getting themselves hit by cars, in order to find her.

Now the terrier was surrounded. She tried to break free but she didn't have a chance. In each direction she hit a blockade of male dogs, one after the other trying to mount her.

By then the dogs were going berserk, barking and growling, fighting in their competition to get to the bitch. There was no underestimating the bloodbath it was about to become. A pack of stray dogs in heat could maul an animal or a child. Yet people kept walking by, ignoring the whole thing, or crossing the road to avoid it.

They parked the car. Beverly spotted a two-by-four piece of wood in the alley and picked it up.

"Marion, I'll get them off her. You get in there and grab the dog."

A moment later, Beverly ran into the mob, swinging the plank of wood at the snarling dogs, while Marion scooped up the terrier and ran full speed like she had a rugby ball under her arm and was crossing a goal line as she jumped into the car. Beverly kept swinging until the last moment, when she tossed the wood aside and jumped in behind the wheel. The dogs leapt and clawed at the hood, while the terrier shook in Marion's lap. As they pulled away down O'Connell Street, they could see the dogs in the rearview mirror, still chasing them.

Beverly and Marion brought out a fearlessness in each other. They were motivated by the cruelty they found: the puppies whose ears had been cut off with scissors, the pig that some children burned and watched die, the horse left to starve tied to a tree trunk with a foal at her side. They were adamant: they were not going to let these things happen.

They went anywhere—the deserted port at night and the worst council estates (as housing projects are called in Ireland), where they even once wandered into gunfire. They went into Travellers' camps, too, and some were rough. They did it to get sick animals out, buying them if need be.

If they saw a dog left unattended and in bad shape, they just took it. Same with dogs left to wander on the street by some irresponsible owner. If necessary they'd remove a dog from someone's home—like the time they got a tip about a Doberman being kept in a tea chest in a council house backyard. When they arrived, they found him emaciated and dying slowly of starvation. Marion and Beverly didn't need to exchange a single word because they both knew exactly what had to be done. They picked up the dog and took it to the car. What other choice could there be? They didn't just drive off, either, because it was Marion's habit that if ever they removed a dog, they always went to tell the owner. So Marion knocked on the front door and told the woman who answered that she was sorry, but the dog was in such bad condition that it needed medical care immediately. As Beverly sat in the car with the Doberman and the motor running, three young lads came up, looking like they had nothing to lose. What was she doing, they wanted to know.

"Picking up a dog," said Beverly. Her tone implied that it was the most natural thing in the world.

That's when they started to rock the car, side to side. They were strong and got it moving so hard she thought they would flip it over. She honked the horn to get Marion's attention. Marion turned from the front door and saw what was happening, then came rushing back to the car.

She said something like "Oh, come on, fellas. Can you let me get in the car, please? We've got to go home."

The lads backed away. She was firm—a bit like your mother.

"What the hell happened at the door?" Beverly asked as they drove away.

"You're not going to believe it. I was talking to that woman, and, behind her, water was pouring down the stairs."

"What?"

"It was just gushing down like a flood! And she kept talking to me!"

There was the time they untied a dog strapped to a railroad track and a five-year-old kid from the council estate came up to her and said, "My father knows where you live and he's going to come get the dog and fuck you in the arse." There was another time when Marion called her from Moyross, the most dangerous council estate, telling her she'd just saved a dog from getting firecrackers put up its rear end.

You had to be careful with Travellers; Beverly learned that the hard way when someone told her about a skinny Rottweiler who needed help. Marion was busy, so she went into Limerick by herself to look for the dog where he'd last been seen. Beverly found him sleeping on an old chair in a backyard. He was in terrible condition and stank to high heaven. "This dog is not staying here," she thought. She put the dog in the car and took him to the vet, got medicine, cleaned him up, and took him home.

A couple of days later, the doorbell rang. She opened the door to find two rough men.

"You have me brudder's dog, you know. We want it back."

Beverly didn't flinch.

"No," she said. "I have no dog. And I'm going to blow your fucking head off if you ever come here again." Then she closed the door.

That night the phone rang. Beverly could hear Semon pick it up and then his quiet tense voice saying, "Uh, yes, uh huh. I see." Then he hung up.

"Who was that?"

"Well, now you've really got us in trouble. They say they're going to burn the barn down."

Semon got on the phone and reached out to a connection who called in a favor. Luckily that was enough.

There was the time they found a bunch of starving goats, all tied together on a long rope, and realized that one was dead and was being dragged around in the dirt by the others. Another time they went to a house and picked up a litter of puppies that had distemper, an awful disease because it brings a miserable death and also because the virus is highly contagious, easily tracked about on shoes and clothes. As usual, they just charged right in, got the puppies, and took them straight to the vet.

Afterward, when they were driving back to Fedamore, Beverly said, "We're not going anywhere *near* my house with this distemper."

Inside the car, in the driveway, they stripped off their clothes and threw everything away. They would have to wash down the car with bleach. When they ran into the house in their underwear, that was the moment when Beverly said, "We've got to be crazy!"

They made it extra-hard for themselves by taking in all kinds of animals, even ones that most people would put down, such as the dog that had been run over by a car and left with a broken leg and pelvis. They took him to the vet, who reset his bones and gave him painkillers. Beverly put him in the jasmine conservatory, which was like a warm greenhouse, so he could be away from the other animals to heal in peace in a padded crate where he could feel safe. Each day, when she came in with his food and water, she found that he'd pulled off his bandages. She rewrapped all the wounds, and did it again the next day and then the next. He recovered. In fact, he turned into a devil of a little Jack Russell, bold and cheeky, chasing every horse in the yard.

In 1986, Ireland passed its first dog control law, which required that every county have a pound and a dog warden who would catch stray dogs, and then, if they weren't claimed, kill them. The purpose was to get dogs off the street and also to keep dogs from "worrying" livestock. Each county had to take action, and for many it was just eas-ier to subcontract the job to the ISPCA. Of course, this didn't happen only in Ireland; it happened everywhere. In an awful twist of fate, the organizations originally founded to protect animals from cruelty began to kill stray animals on a mass scale. There were just too many. It was a soul-destroying job that fell to an actual human being who would have to kill dogs week after week. The county councils tended to hire an ex-military person or, as in the case of Limerick, a former butcher— someone physically strong enough to handle the animals and desensi-tized enough to bear it.

County Limerick subcontracted the job to the ISPCA. The war-den's pound was a collection of hideous and filthy kennels, plus a trailer for an office. When it was time to put a dog down, the warden sat in a chair in the middle of a pit wearing a rubber apron and rubber boots. While the other dogs watched what awaited them, he held the animal between his knees and used a bolt gun, which was considered acceptable at the time but was hard to control. You had to pull back a tightly wound spring-loaded bolt, and then release the trigger so that the bolt surged forward with great force into the brain—no bullets needed. It was not an easy job. The blood ran down his apron and over his rubber boots, but he never missed.

This meant that Beverly and Marion had to move their battle to a new front: they had to stay ahead of the warden and prevent dogs from getting into his hands. As soon as they got a call that a dog was wander-ing or lost, they raced to the scene to make sure the warden didn't get there first. If they were too late, they'd have to go to his hellhole and beg him to give up the animal. The smell was so bad it made them retch. "Don't kill him. Give him to us, please. We'll find him a home."

Marion and Beverly shared a disapproval of the Limerick Society for the Prevention of Cruelty to Animals (LSPCA) for not doing enough and its monthly meetings where people socialized and discussed the sad situation of strays, while the dog warden was out picking up and shooting dog after dog. Still, they went to a meeting to voice their concern. Why wasn't the LSPCA doing more to find homes for the dogs? Marion and Beverly offered to work with them.

"You're not allowed to pick up dogs," said the head of the committee. "If you pick up a dog, you should bring it to the warden."

That's when Beverly lost it.

"Says *who* I can't pick up dogs? Did God come down and say I can't pick up hurt and sick animals and keep them alive?"

The other women from Limerick Animal Welfare—the ones who'd worked with Marion for years before Beverly arrived—didn't terribly appreciate that the hunt master's home had become the headquarters of their organization.

But what could Marion say? Of course it was a contradiction. But there was no one like Beverly—no one—when it came to hands-on care and dedication. She was a miracle worker with sick animals. She cleaned up shit and vomit and blood, cooked healing foods. She stayed up all night with the sickest ones, and solved canine disputes. The animals themselves seemed to think she was one of them. They gravitated to her and responded.

And there was so much room at Fedamore! Beverly played musical dogs, moving them among the different areas. She kept the puppies in the tack room, the sick dogs in the extra kitchen, and the large dogs out in the courtyard or in the barn. She had to constantly move them around as they came and went.

Beverly was a little older than Marion, but her energy was a force of nature. She arrived in Ireland in her early forties and for twenty years she built LAW with Marion. She and Semon ran Fedamore House Stud, breeding six mares a year, which added up to about a hundred foals over eighteen years. (That was enough—more than enough—for Beverly, who loved each one and suffered every time one was sold.) As well as all this, she rode in the Dublin Horse Show, trained horses for eventing, entertained guests who came to hunt, and managed an ever revolving circus of thirty to forty dogs at a time, of which about twenty a year were adopted.

When Marion heard negative remarks about Beverly, she put an end to it by simply saying that Beverly had been amazing for Limerick Animal Welfare.

It wasn't that Marion accepted foxhunting. To her, the whole idea of it was an abomination. How could you explain running horses into the ground just for the fun of watching one animal pull out another's guts? Rural Irish people called these types of pursuits "field sports." But what was sporting about setting one animal on another? As far as Marion was concerned, blood sports were 100 percent unacceptable. What bothered her most was the way people made a great, happy ritual of it. Fox hunting had the outfits, the horns, the rules and regulations of what to say and when, the smell of earth while they rode the horses hard, the heartbreaking cry of the hounds in the moments before they killed the fox. All of it bonded the hunters to one another and to what they believed "nature" meant. But this wasn't nature; it was the domination of nature. And on it went, year in year out, cementing the emotional connections with details as trivial as the buttons they wore on their jackets. Hare coursing was the same, just with a different class of people. It was an exercise in ritualized terror. Oh, it was a great festival of togetherness and celebration at coursing meets! Families, neighbors, friends gathering on the sidelines, imbibing warm drinks in the cold air, breath making steam, feet stamping on ground. They all said that they rooted for the hare. And, yes, sometimes it did escape. But when she (they always called the hare "she") didn't get away, that baby scream rang out followed by a gasp of horror from the crowd. It drove Marion mad. The moment of death would imprint in the children's minds as a jolt of thrill along with family togetherness and happy times and beautiful countryside. In the collective culture, that moment would be as firmly etched as the stars in the heavens that recur season after season and map out time. Tradition would repeat, and with repetition, tradition itself became the reason. Tradition causing pain. Tradition, the excuse for everything. That was Ireland. A sporting nation. A sporting culture full of sporting traditions. It was in their souls, people said.

Marion and Beverly were the same when it came to animals but different in their approach to people. Marion was the talker, the eloquent one, the political being. Beverly didn't want to go to meetings. First of all, it was difficult for her to leave all the horses and dogs, which seemed always to need something or other. Second, she found animal welfare meetings insufferable. "How do you bother?" she asked Marion. "They just talk and talk!" She preferred to be with the animals, hands-on—a paramedic, an EMT, a nurse, a mother to them all.

Marion's reply was always the same. "You have to go to the meetings if you want to change things."

That's how she talked Beverly into going with her to ISPCA meetings in Dublin to ask questions. The LSPCA was one of their member societies. Did they all know about what was going on with the dog warden in Limerick and his horrible bolt gun?

"We're a new group. We're Limerick Animal Welfare, and we've come to complain about the pound in Limerick." They described the hole in the ground where the warden killed the dogs while the others watched. "All he does is kill dogs! Did you know that? The warden seems to be positively *against* rehoming animals or even trying to adopt out dogs."

At the next annual meeting, the leadership of the ISPCA agreed that Limerick Animal Welfare would be invited to join. "Let's see what you can do," they said.

Marion and Beverly knew perfectly well that this was a good way to shut people up. Have complaints? Sure, you can join and help fix it.

9

—

A BURNING DONKEY

1987

The phone call came at night, as so many calls did, puncturing the dinner hour, the homework time, and the flicker of the television shows they liked to watch. Marion's children learned at the earliest ages that humans did bad things, especially at night. This was hardly a revelation, as all children know and fear this truth, but to grow up and personally witness the pain of burning skin, crushed bones, and starvation day after day—well, this was a deeper kind of knowing.

Marion answered the call as she always did, as though she'd been expecting it.

"Where exactly?"

It was always one of the first things she asked, because many people hung up too quickly.

"Childers Road?"

If the children had been listening, if John hadn't been watching television, they might have noticed that something in her tone was different from the usual.

"Burning? Did you say a donkey is burning?"

Keys, shoes, purse. John asking if she really had to. "Couldn't it wait until the morning?" But, of course she had to go now.

"Be careful, Marion."

"Yes, of course."

He didn't need to know where she was going. She just said good-bye as though it were one of the regular emergency calls.

The slam of the front door. The sound of her car starting and then heading off, engine fading into the distance. Quiet. More quiet.

The family had learned to tolerate it and tune it out as best as they could. She'd been like this for more than a dozen years. Perhaps it was temporary, and would end at some point. Perhaps someone else's mother or wife would take over.

On the ride there, Marion rehearsed her outrage.

How could you let this happen? A burning animal? There can be no excuse for this! None.

The site belonged to the Riley family, if "belonged" was what you'd call this collection of caravans and animals and cooking pots, clotheslines, and garbage sprawled out on a section of grass, which was mostly mud. "Belonged" in that the Rileys maintained a steady presence in these fields at the edge of a busy road. When they went off on their journeys, someone stayed behind to watch the site. They always returned to this spot. No one was bothering about the land yet; that wouldn't come until many years later, when the developers came to build. For now, the Rileys were, more or less, left alone.

When Marion was a girl, people called them tinkers or gypsies. They lived in wagons painted in bright colors and roamed the countryside. Their chief trade was tinsmithing. But they also bred and sold horses and dogs, and they picked crops and peddled goods. She could remember them at the door asking her mother if she needed her knives sharpened or had any odd jobs and whether they could fill their water jugs. Otherwise, they kept their distance from settled people. At night, they sat round their cooking fires, telling stories and drinking near their caravans. When it was time to sleep, the pregnant women took the wagons, while the rest slept under makeshift tents made of canvas thrown over the top of some sticks. They might stay at a particular camp for a month if the work were good. Then, all of a sudden, they'd be on the move, horses hitched and dogs running along. If you saw a wagon left behind and burnt to a skeleton, you'd know that a Traveller had died a tragic death and his possessions had been burned to send away bad luck.

Marion had been picking up animals for fifteen years, and so her work overlapped a great deal with the Travellers. She got calls about their horses. She wound up with their cast-off dogs, most of which had problems like mange, ticks, fleas, worms, and ear mites. They couldn't afford vets and were horrendous at animal care. When a dog was sick with a virus, they'd separate it from the others so as not to spread disease and bad luck, "staking" it in a field—which meant they'd tie the dog to a tree or a post and leave him behind to starve. Or they'd just dump the animal somewhere so as to lose it. This upset settled people greatly, and many saw it as evidence of their criminal natures.

Marion had made it a point to befriend the Travellers in her own neighborhood. They were the McCarthy clan, and when they came to her front door she gave them food and clothes and paid them to do small jobs. This encouraged them to come regularly.

"The itinerants" was how John referred to them. "Must you bring these itinerants here?"

But Marion saw these interactions as an opportunity.

"Can I give you some worm pills for your dogs? Do you have shoes on all your horses?"

"Here—take this or that to treat the parasites." They humored her, took the food or clothes. "Yes, Missus. Thank you, Missus. I'll say a prayer for ye."

Marion pulled off the highway toward the jumble of caravans and cars and horses and dogs, set up on a strip of grass at the side of the road. All was quiet, except for the sound of wind and the whiz of cars. An abandoned circle of coals glowed up ahead.

It was bone cold, the wind blowing hard. A few lurchers ran about, heads low, quietly whimpering from cold or hunger and scratching themselves, probably because of mange. She made a mental note to come back with medicine and show the Travellers how to treat it.

Like most Travellers, this clan had long ago given up horse-drawn wagons and now used recreational campers hitched to cars—vehicles invented for vacations when middle-class people wanted to leave civilization behind. For the Travellers, the caravans offered a huge step up, out of the elements.

A large silhouette came into view. It was a donkey in a heap beside the embers, its back to the remains of fire. She hesitated a moment, then collected herself and rushed in. The flesh on its back was charred and smoldering. The big, glassy eyes were frozen. She put a hand on its thick, bristly neck. He was gone. The smell of singed hair, meat, and death lingered about. Only the donkey's back was burned, but he was so emaciated and sickly that the fire had easily finished him off.

She bent down and peered under the vehicles. Sure enough, a couple of dogs had curled themselves into tight balls on scraps of carpet and cardboard. Another note to herself: all those rugs and paper had to be burned to get rid of the mange.

Oh, enough already.

She walked to the closest caravan and knocked.

After a few moments, the door opened a crack, and half a woman's face peered out with alarm.

"Sorry to bother you at night, but we got a call about this burning donkey. Do you know what happened?"

The woman could have been anywhere from twenty to forty years old. It was usually hard to tell a Traveller's age. The girls married as teenagers, then had so many children one after the next that they quickly aged way beyond their years.

The woman looked out at the corpse and shook her head.

"'Twas an accident. Such a cold night, the donkey got too close to the flames, trying to warm himself. Nobody saw it until it was too late. We'd all gone inside."

As the woman spoke, the door opened inch by inch to reveal numerous children huddled behind her, at least six or eight of them. (Marion was struggling to keep count.) They ranged in age from about two to twelve years old and looked to be of another world, because the public health nurse had evidently visited that day to treat scabies or some other parasites and shaved each child's head, then painted each scalp white with medicine. Marion had to steady herself as all those faces looked out at her, eyes enormous, to see what was going on. So as not to stare back, she glanced down and happened to see their bare feet on the dirty floor. How cold they must be! A two-burner cookstove glowed from the kitchen, red rings turned on for heat. It was all they had. Those many bodies must sleep on top of one another, in the two rooms of the caravan, to stay warm.

Oh, the bottom is very low, thought Marion. The bottom was here—right here.

Had the public health nurse told the mother that the scabies—or whatever it was—would only come back unless the dogs were treated and the sheets cleaned? How could the mother do it if she had no running water? And how could this mother even think about animals or scabies or running water when the children were so cold and clearly needed food?

Marion, who never lacked for words, now faltered. *Where would you begin?* Those were the only words that came to her. *Where would you begin?* She could manage merely to say goodnight, and then she went home.

For days after her visit to the camp on Childers Road, Marion was haunted by that mother and her children. Images of their bald heads and bare feet, their big eyes, kept coming back to her. No heat. No lights. No toilet. No water. Each time, it shook her, and she felt ashamed. Oh, how fucking sanctimonious she had been, how righteous with her little animal care lectures to the Travellers at her door. She had known nothing.

⁓

IRELAND HAD always been economically behind the rest of the Western world, largely because it had been oppressed for centuries by brutal English colonization, but also because of its isolated location—an island on the far western edge of Europe. After World War II, a better standard of living, from central heating to cars, finally arrived— slowly, but it did come. And when, eventually, it did, the Travellers' economy collapsed. Plastic replaced tin, machines replaced humans in the fields, and rural people got cars and went shopping rather than waiting for door-to-door peddlers. Modernity erased the Travellers' purpose.

Modernity also brought Travellers into closer contact with settled people. They moved their camps near to towns and cities so they could collect and trade scrap metal, beg, and search for new ways to survive. Suddenly their poverty, poor health, and lack of sanitation became visible and problematic to settled people. In the 1960s, the national government set out to solve the Traveller "problem." After a lengthy study, the commission concluded that the only way forward was for Travellers to come in from the road, settle in homes, and be "absorbed" into the mainstream culture. Social workers were dispatched to the camps, volunteers stepped forward to help, and the government offered apartments in public housing estates, health care, and the chance to sign up for the dole. Many in the Travelling communities gave up their caravans for permanent dwellings. But joining mainstream culture was another question. Once they were settled, Traveller children were more likely to go to school and become literate. Some went on to college and jobs, but the majority dropped out of high school by age sixteen. Many who moved into the housing estates would not give up their horses. They made makeshift stables in garages and tethered the horses in backyards, or simply left them to wander and graze anywhere. Then an odd thing happened: children—even the non-Traveller children, the ones who were simply poor—fell in love with horses and began owning them, much as children owned dogs, because their parents could get them ponies very cheaply. It was not an unusual sight in Moyross—the huge housing estate in northern Limerick—to see five- and six-year-old urban cowboy kids riding ponies bareback along expanses of grass, surrounded by graffiti-covered buildings.

With less to do, many young people had gotten involved in drugs and gangs. Horses were, at least, an alternative to crime. In the council estates, young unemployed men occupied themselves with horse dreams, of trading and riding and racing.

You'd see them swimming their horses in the Shannon to condition them. The men stood on the bank holding long ropes tied to horses standing in water up to their necks. The men guided the horses so they could strengthen their muscles against the current and the tide. Unfortunately, the young men lacked money for vets, shelter, horseshoeing, and hay. Limerick Animal Welfare received many calls about poorly kept horses, and Marion and Beverly were frequent visitors to Moyross.

⌒

MOST SETTLED people believed that Travellers were dangerous, and generally never set foot in a Traveller camp. Even those who sympathized and wished for Travellers to have better lives wouldn't have dreamed of crossing that line.

But after the night of the burning donkey, Marion decided that, rather than wait until animals were left by the roadside sick and injured, sometimes beyond healing, she should try to get to them sooner. Suddenly, it seemed obvious. She needed to go to the Travellers' camps and offer knowledge on animal care directly to them.

Of course, she'd have to find them first.

For a couple of weeks, while she was doing her errands, bringing kids or animals here and there, she scanned the sides of the roads, keeping a look out for the McCarthys. Finally, she spotted their caravans in Annacotty, a village right next to her own. The McCarthys were a small clan—only ten families, about fifty people in all, plus several horses and many dogs. Kathleen McCarthy was the matriarch, and her son John was the unofficial leader.

A handful of men hanging around in a clutch lifted their heads to watch her approach. A half dozen dogs trotted about, thin and filthy. Several horses stood, swishing their tails. Her method in these situations was to start talking and not stop. In the Irish way, she began with the weather, complaining about the rain. After that, it did not take long for her to spot a litter of puppies underneath a caravan, and then a horse showing signs of colic. This began the conversation.

"Oh, let me see that dog there. She has puppies. How do you treat mange now? And the horses. How are you doing with water for them?"

She walked over to a group of women and asked them questions about their history. They told her they'd been parking in the Castletroy and Annacotty area for as long as anyone could remember, and they considered the area their home. Each winter, they'd set up camp in these parts, then come spring they'd take to the road and begin their seasonal rounds. They visited relatives and shared news, made pilgrimages (they were very religious), and when summer came they might go to the seaside or perhaps a horse fair. In fall there would be harvest work, and then they'd come back here for the winter months.

In recent years, though, everything had changed. The area had become a sprawling suburb, with new buildings rising all the time. The Travellers' former camping areas had been paved over by development.

By far the greatest engine of this change was the University of Limerick, which was founded with seventy acres in the 1970s with a mission to be "the MIT of Ireland." It was the first purely Irish institute of higher learning. (All the others had been built under British rule.) Irish-American investment dollars flowed in, as did funds from the World Bank, so that by 1987 the university had steadily acquired more and more rolling meadows and woods along the banks of the Shannon, and one astonishing forward-thinking architectural design sprang up after the next.

Wherever the Travellers set up camp now, they were in the midst of things, and the settled people weren't happy. They called the police, who moved the Travellers on. Recently, tensions had been growing worse. The McCarthys had just left a site in Castleconnell, a few miles away, because they'd been refused water and badly harassed. There was nowhere for them to go anymore.

Marion returned a week or two later with more medicines and supplies for the animals, but when she turned her car down the road looking for the caravans, they were gone. The McCarthys had vanished, leaving only tracks in the mud and garbage. Chased away again. She drove around Castletroy looking for them, with no luck, scanning the edges of fields and roadsides. They had moved on, at least for now.

A few weeks later, they returned, and after that, it became a regular thing for Marion to keep close tabs on them, coming by every week or two to say hello and check on their animals, whether they liked it or not. It was a mystery to Marion why they accepted her. Maybe they were curious about her, or found her visits to be a welcome relief from boredom and struggle. Or maybe they could see that she genuinely wanted to help them, and they needed help.

"You solve their problems, Marion, that's why they let you in," said Beverly.

The first time she asked John McCarthy if she could take a mange-covered dog to the vet, he looked at her as though he hadn't heard her correctly. He was a man of few words, but eventually he nodded. Before he changed his mind, she put the dog in her car and zipped off to Dr. Carroll, who gave her the usual lotion and pain-killer. Mange was highly contagious: the parasites burrowed into the fur in search of skin, causing the dog to scratch so much that the fur came off and the skin opened up, bleeding, scabbing, and becoming infected. If untreated, it could be fatal. But the tragic thing was how treatable it was with the right drugs. She kept the dog at her house and bathed him in the family tub. When she returned him a week later, transformed—clean, his skin healing, and his eyes bright— the McCarthys were silent. She could tell they were impressed and appreciative.

Sometimes Marion bought the Travellers' dogs outright in order to save their lives. Beverly didn't hesitate to go with her to the Travellers' camps. They chose the dogs that were in bad condition, the ones most likely to be abandoned or tossed out or tied to a stake. They worked a lot with the other John in the McCarthy clan, Johnny Ryan—a tall, slim, dignified man. He always started off by asking for an outrageous sum.

"Fifty pounds for him, Mahry." (For some reason this was what they called her.) "He's worth every bit."

"Ten," Marion said without flinching.

"Forty. Can't go any lower."

And so they haggled and met in the middle and made a deal. Or, if the price was just too high, she'd have to walk away. But what upset her most, by far, was when a dog was sick and he insisted on leaving it to die somewhere and wouldn't let her have it.

"Can I give it water at least?"

"If you do, it will only take longer for him to die."

He drew this line firmly when it came to dogs that he believed were finished. Was this based on principle? Considering the Travellers' own dire situation, did he find it ludicrous that this woman wanted to spend good money on a vet for an animal that was so clearly done? Perhaps Johnny felt it was too out of balance. She could only guess. She never understood it.

At the camps, dogs had always been men's work. They didn't beat them, but they handled them roughly because they were a source of income, not companionship. Animals existed to be bred or sold at a fair, perhaps wagered upon in a coursing competition, or used for hunting when the men went out at night with lamps in the fields to catch foxes. Otherwise, they kept the dogs tied up much of the time. (Years later, when she and Johnny Ryan knew each other very well, Marion tied a Traveller child to a fence. "Does this look okay to you?" she asked him. But even Marion knew that this was going too far.)

The dogs slept outside, whatever the weather. If she came by early in the morning, Marion sometimes found them covered in grey ash, looking like they'd crawled out of a volcano. In fact, they'd slept in the warm embers of the fire, which explained what had happened to the donkey.

Dogs and horses—especially horses—had been central to the lives of Traveller men for centuries. Horses had pulled their wagons and made their way of life possible. But it wasn't so simple an equation, because Ireland as a whole was a horse-crazy nation. The annual Dublin Horse Show still drew crowds in the thousands. High society turned out for the jumping, dressage, hunting, and all manner of equestrian events. The Travellers had their own separate and oddly parallel universe on the margins of the mainstream horse culture. Instead of thoroughbreds and draught horses, they had the Irish cob, which they'd bred to be small and stocky, calm and strong, with long manes and feathery tassels of hair above their hooves. Travellers had many horse fairs of their own—such as the monthly Smithfield Fair on the cobblestones of Dublin or the annual Ballinasloe fair in County Galway, a tradition reaching back hundreds of years. They had their own horse racing events, too—mostly illegal sulky races, a kind of harness racing, held on hidden backstreets where the Garda couldn't find them.

Marion's regular visits to the camp were also noticed by the children there. One day she found a Traveller child standing at her door. He had a dog with him, baling twine around the neck for a collar and leash.

"Missus. Can you find my dog a good home?"

He was about ten or eleven years old. The dog was a shepherd mix, perhaps part collie, missing half an ear. He wagged and sniffed and wagged some more.

"His name is Lucky," the boy said, looking at Marion seriously. He was clearly upset but trying not to show it.

"Why are you giving him away?"

Marion knew the family. It was not a good situation. After the boy's father threw the mother through a window, she fled for the women's shelter and hadn't come back.

It took a little while for her to get the story. The boy's father wanted to lose Lucky. Twice he'd thrown the dog out of the back of the van and threw rocks at him, but both times, Lucky came back. The Traveller boy was worried about what steps might come next.

"Yes, I can find him a good place," Marion said. "I'll bring him to a home where he will be safe and happy."

The boy nodded, then bent down to say goodbye to his dog. Marion stepped aside to give them a moment. Then only Lucky remained.

Marion made good on her word and found Lucky a home at a healing center, of all places. It was a hippie kind of place, in County Roscommon, where the owner had faith in the therapeutic power of dogs. Food, open space to run, a soft bed, lots of attention—all the amenities a dog could want. In exchange, Lucky's job was to greet with openhearted acceptance and charm all the arriving guests, helping them forget their problems and their pain. He was well suited to the task, and lived up to his name.

Over the next two years, Marion continued to visit the McCarthys and observed firsthand how they were pushed out from one site to the next. At one point they were living on a traffic circle not far from her house, where their caravans flooded in the winter rains. When they parked on a quiet street in the nearby town of Monaleen, a mob showed up with a backhoe and dug a trench in front of their site, threatening to overturn their caravans if they didn't leave. Then there were the small indignities, such as the priest who let Traveller children make their first Holy Communion but didn't invite them to the celebration afterward. That was for the settled children only. Marion spoke to him, to ensure that the Traveller children could have cookies and milk with the rest.

Not long after the Communion, the local residents refused to give the Travellers water. The Travellers had to buy it, and because they had little money, it created hardship on top of hardship. People had no idea. But Marion did. She had walked into John McCarthy's caravan and found his wife, Bridget, washing six children's hair with a single bucket of water and two thin towels.

Marion told the McCarthys they could get water from the tap in her back garden. They came right away and parked on her street, then sent a couple of young girls with a large container. They made multiple trips back and forth from Marion's house to their caravan, which attracted a bit of attention.

It was one thing if that Fitzgibbon woman wanted to take in all of Limerick's dogs and cats, but now there would be Travellers as well? That was just too much. The neighbors stopped Marion on the street and told her not to allow it. She told them it wasn't that simple.

"Just shut off the tap!"

She did not reply. She was so shocked she could not speak.

That night, Marion was deeply upset. She looked at her family and said, "Deny people water? Whatever they would deny these people, how could they deny them water? I would never deny anybody or anything water."

At the McCarthys' camp, she saw things she could not have imagined. One Christmas Eve, she took them food. When she walked into one of the caravans, she spotted two shoeboxes on the counter and peeked inside. She could hardly keep herself from gasping. Twin babies, tiny and pink, not much more than newborns, lay in the boxes, each wrapped in a thin blanket. Freezing air blew on them through broken windows. And yet those babies were quiet in their little cardboard boxes, perhaps already accustomed to the life they'd been born to.

The more Marion thought about it, the more upset it made her. If the McCarthys were here first, how was it that settled people had moved in and built over everything but would not even give them water? How could the Traveller children go to school if they had to keep moving around? (She'd been talking to Travellers about school a great deal—they hadn't even known they had a right to public education.) How would the public health nurse find them? (The men had average mortality rates fifteen years lower than the rest of the population.) How could they make progress with their animals or anything else without some kind of home? Better lives for homeless people did not guarantee better lives for homeless animals, but it was a necessary first step.

At one point, the McCarthys parked at the Kilmurray Cemetery near the university. That changed everything. Local residents staged a major protest, throwing stones at the caravans and breaking their windows. In the early hours of the morning, they besieged the Travellers with car headlights and blasting horns.

The Travellers' camp at the Kilmurray Cemetery was not just a worry to local residents, but also a significant threat to some of the area's most powerful players. The university and Shannon Development Corporation were doing everything they could to establish the area as a major technology center in Europe, and trying to lure international companies to the adjacent corporate park. As they saw it, they were bringing desperately needed jobs. What kind of impression would it make on the wealthy corporate types if they saw the impoverished in full view? Shannon Development Corporation went to the circuit court to request that the city council evict the Travellers, but the judge refused to force the Travellers off on the grounds that they had nowhere to go.

Not long after the hearing, a truck arrived at the graveyard and dumped big mounds of dirt, sand, and rocks on the McCarthys' site, killing their dogs in the process. It was Good Friday, and the Travellers were, predictably, at church when it happened. It was one of the rare times they ever left their caravans unattended.

What would be next? The McCarthys left for safety's sake and found a place not far away, near a factory. The factory emitted particles of white dust that covered everything and made their children so sick that they had to go to the hospital.

In August, the children were expected at school in Castletroy. A few of the McCarthys returned and noticed that the barrier at the entrance to the University of Limerick was open. Soon all fifty or so arrived at the university gates with their banged-up caravans and cars. It was undeniably unsightly and a huge embarrassment for the university and the whole town. The Travellers used the university's railings as a clothesline; they cut the university's trees for kindling; and they used an adjoining plot on the university's grounds as a lavatory. The Travellers' (occasionally menacing) dogs roamed far too freely, and the Traveller children held out their hands to university personnel and visitors arriving on foot, asking for loose change.

Newspapers and television cameras arrived to report on the spectacle of the Travellers who were parked at the university gates and wouldn't leave until the council provided them with an authorized halting site. Marion couldn't believe her eyes one evening when she turned on the television and saw a newsman from the RTE six o'clock news interviewing Johnny Ryan outside his caravan, while he swept the area around his front door. He wanted to know how Johnny liked living at the university.

Johnny replied that he liked it fine, except sometimes when the college kids drank they got messy. He then returned to his sweeping.

Marion was fed up. It was the law, plain and clear, that the council had to make housing available to the homeless. Years had gone by and the McCarthys were still getting jostled wherever they parked, subject to fines of thirty-five pounds a day for trespassing. Meanwhile, the McCarthy children were growing up missing school and watching their families being intimidated, threatened, and harassed.

The university took action, filing a lawsuit against the Limerick County Council for not taking care of the Traveller problem. A judge allowed the Travellers to join the lawsuit as a third party. This meant they could also make a claim against the council for not meeting its obligations to them.

Marion turned to the Society of St. Vincent de Paul, whose mission was to help the poor. The society agreed to find and pay for a barrister who would represent the Travellers. In the meantime, Marion went through two-plus years of notes she'd kept on the McCarthys' situation, writing them up into a document that would later be used as an affidavit.

That was when the threats started. One day, she picked up the phone and heard a man's voice whisper, "You'd better watch where you're going."

She was confused at first. "Excuse me? Who is this?" He hung up.

The next time, there was no mistaking it. "Your husband will lose his job."

And the time after that, and after that.

"Your dogs will be poisoned."

"Your house will be burned down."

John called the Garda, who installed a tracer on their phone. The Garda would not tell them the caller's identity, except that it was someone near them. The hardest part was knowing that it was a neighbor who wished them harm, probably someone she even chatted with at the local shop or waved to on her own street. How violent would people be? How far would they go?

Marion knew from experience that people could go very far. A couple of summers earlier, one beautiful July evening at around eight o'clock, She'd been driving along the road to Fedamore House. Beverly was back in the States for a visit, and Marion was on her way to take care of the dogs. Her old Austin was being repaired, so she'd taken John's car instead. She could never have realized how much this simple decision would matter.

She spotted a Traveller boy, maybe fourteen or fifteen years old, walking down the road with a horse that had no shoes. She pulled over and got out, thinking she might know his family. She could see now that the horse had no proper bit or reins, but just a long piece of baling twine through its mouth. A lathery sweat was pouring down its legs.

"Excuse me. You can't walk that horse like this without shoes. It's very painful for him, you know. And can you see how badly he's sweating? He's very thirsty and needs water." She always asked children to imagine the animal's point of view.

She gently put a hand on the horse's neck, an unconscious move, perhaps to connect herself and the boy with the animal. Her other hand was on the makeshift reins. Maybe, from a distance, it looked like she was about to take the horse away from the boy.

A car sped toward her and screeched to a stop a couple of feet away. A couple of men jumped out and came at her. She recognized them as being from the Harty clan. When she realized what was about to happen, she began to shake.

"What are you fucking doing with that horse?"

Before she had a chance to answer, one of them hit her on the back of the head, and she went down. That first blow came with a shocking burst of stars, and confusion as her mind tried to catch up. They began kicking her ribs and legs and arms. Why was this happening? Pain replaced fear. Then she was looking up at the placid summer sky realizing there was nothing she could do but endure each punch and kick and wait until it was over.

It was difficult to breathe, and for the first time in her life, she was mute. So this is what it's like, she thought, to be beaten like an animal. Another car arrived and skidded to a stop. A carload of Harty women got out and started pulling her hair so that her scalp screamed in agony.

A man in the distance was yelling, "Stop it! Leave her alone!" But why wasn't he coming closer? She couldn't tell if the beating went on forever or only a few minutes. And then, finally, a kind of semi-darkness came over her, and she was out. How long went by?

When she came to, Marion pulled herself up to her hands and knees. From her concussed brain, she looked about and saw that she was not far from a pub. Had she known that all along? She began to crawl to the door, as there was no way she could stand up and walk. What amazing luck, she thought, that a pub was right there. On the heels of this thought, another shadow of a thought came: Why wasn't anyone coming out to help?

She finally arrived and reached up for the doorknob.

Was she so badly beaten that her hand wouldn't work? Was her wrist broken? She kept trying to turn it until she realized it was locked.

The window. The shutters had been drawn. Had they been drawn before? Then the sound of a siren coming. More car doors slamming. The Travellers screeched away as the Garda arrived.

It turned out that everyone in the pub had seen what was happening, but they'd all been too afraid to step out and help so they'd just called the police and locked the doors. The publican said he could identify one of the Travellers and would give a statement. But when the police returned to talk to him, he changed his mind. He was afraid that the Hartys would come and burn down his bar.

When John McCarthy and Johnny Ryan heard, they were upset and wished they could have helped. "If only you'd been in your own car instead of your husband's," they said. "Then they would have known it was you."

Just the same, the McCarthys asked Marion not to press charges because John's daughter was married to the toughest of the Hartys, the leader of the pack. And no, they weren't happy about that, but if Marion pressed charges he'd get sent back to jail and John's daughter would be on her own again. Plus, there could be serious trouble between the Hartys and the McCarthys. She agreed not to take it any further. A year later, the Harty leader was dead, killed in a street fight.

As for Marion, she saw double for a few days and the part of her scalp where they'd pulled her hair was still sore more than a year later. How could they do it? She didn't know what upset her more: to be beaten by a mob, or to know that the people inside the pub saw her and locked the door. She never could wrap her mind around that last one. From then on, she knew how bad it could get. She knew how far it could go.

⌒

FALL TURNED to winter, and the McCarthys continued to stay put at the gates of the university. When the court date arrived, Marion was there at 5 a.m., knocking on the caravan doors to make sure John McCarthy and Johnny Ryan were up. (They weren't.) It was a three-hour train ride to Dublin.

The trial would last two days, but Johnny Ryan's wife objected to them staying over. "You're not taking my man for a night. You have your own at home."

So, instead of staying in a hotel, they made the round trip two days in a row. She'd never spent so much time in close quarters with the Travellers, but she noticed immediately that confinement made the men uneasy. They couldn't read the signs on the station plat-forms, so they continually asked where they were.

"Gentlemen, we have a long ride on the train. How would you like to pass the time?"

She hoped to distract them. Maybe they'd play cards or some-thing.

After a brief silence, Johnny Ryan said, "I think I'd like to be able to write my name." Marion took out a piece of paper and a pen from her bag to show him how.

The High Court was a grand eighteenth-century building with a beautiful circular room where they waited to be called. People stared, wondering what a tidy middle-aged woman was doing with the likes of the Travellers. The barrister for the Travellers arrived and explained that the trial had been assigned to Judge Henry Barron, which was a good thing because he had a reputation for being fair and unafraid to go against the dominant powers.

In the courtroom, university representatives, the developer, and the county council all had their chance, represented by barristers who filled two rows. Marion, the two Johns, and their single barrister sat together on their own. Through questions and answers, the most difficult issue emerged early on: the Travellers readily admitted that they had no right to be on university land, and they would leave if they could, but they had nowhere to go.

Judge Barron, thin and bespectacled, held his head down much of the time. Mostly they could see only the top of his wig and his loose black gown. Marion wondered whether he was listening or sleeping. It was the former, evidently, because at one point, he rapped his knuckles on his desk to interrupt.

"Excuse me." Rap rap rap. "Excuse me. Would counsel for the County of Limerick please approach the bench?"

After a moment's hesitation, the barrister stepped forward.

"Refresh my memory, counsellor. What year did you say this is?"

"Your honor, it's 1991."

"Thank you, counsellor. For a moment, I thought we'd slipped back to the Middle Ages."

And then, with soft-spoken incredulity: "Are you telling me these people have no access to water? Are you telling me they have no access to lavatories?"

When Marion's affidavit was read and presented as evidence, Judge Barron looked up at her, noting that she was listed on the court paperwork as a member of the Travellers' Support Committee.

"Mrs. Fitzgibbon, who are you to these people and to this case?"

"I work with the Travellers to help them with animal care," she explained. He was waiting for more, so she added, "I'm just an ordinary housewife."

"You are no ordinary housewife," he replied.

Judge Barron called for the council to provide roadside toilets immediately. In his formal opinion, which came a couple of weeks later, in February, he wrote that the county council had shown genuine intentions to do well by the Travellers. Nonetheless, the council had neglected its duty by trying to please too many parties that had vested interests. His decision required the council to meet its legal obligations and provide a permanent site that the McCarthys could call home, within three months. That meant the council had until May. With such a short time frame, there weren't going to be a lot of options. Each time the council proposed a location, the local residents protested and created more fury.

Finally, the council zeroed in on an eight-acre parcel of land near the university. People were beside themselves that the Travellers would get this prime location, but time was running out and the court order had to be obeyed. They had little choice other than to shell out more than 350,000 pounds to secure the land. Between the time of the announcement and the move-in date, hundreds of people protested at the site. Some even brought their cows to graze on the land, and refused to move them. Ultimately there was nothing they could do. The council wouldn't back down: it had to fulfill the orders of the High Court. In May, the Travellers moved onto the land. The council had prepared it with a water hookup, electricity, and enough space for the caravans and dogs. To Marion, this was at least a step forward. Whether for animals or people, a home was a necessary thing.

Finally Marion could rest and tend to some other business. Except for one thing: there was a lump in her breast. For more than a year, her doctor had told her it was nothing. But it was getting bigger, and she didn't like the way it felt. She made another appointment.

10

—

A GRAND SCHEME

1994

Not long after Marion returned home after her cancer treatment, she found a phone message from a woman named Louise Coleman, who was from an organization called Greyhound Friends in Massachusetts. She wanted to talk to Marion about the Irish greyhound. Marion laughed: how could she possibly take on any new people or projects at that moment? A week later, she found a letter on her desk from the same woman. Coleman explained that she was coming to the World Greyhound Racing Federation conference in Dublin the following month, to put questions to the industry about how they were handling animal welfare. She wanted to meet with Marion to discuss the greyhound situation in Ireland. Marion put the letter aside, shaking her head.

The following month, Coleman phoned again. Now she was actually in Ireland, having just attended the conference, and she was staying with a friend in County Cork. Once again, she asked for a meeting. It was still a terrible time: Marion was in the midst of the initial court cases over custody of Stafford Taylor's tigers, baboons, and bear. But the woman was so persistent that Marion felt she should at least hear her out.

Beverly didn't like the sound of it at all. She could see this greyhound thing coming on, like a train barreling down the tracks straight at them. She'd been working side by side with Marion for more than a decade, and they knew each other so well that they could practically read each other's minds. Once Marion dug in on something, it was hard to stop her, but Beverly wanted to try nonetheless.

"Listen, Marion. This greyhound thing is just too big," she said. "Once you get in, it will never end. This is *Ireland,* Marion, not England. You're talking about a government-sponsored industry—thousands and thousands of dogs. You still have wild animals on Stafford Taylor's farm! Let's get finished with the goddamned tigers first. Not to mention that we can't even handle the dogs and cats we've got on the streets right here in Limerick. Plus, you're still recovering from cancer—you shouldn't take on another thing."

It had been less than a year since the cancer surgery, and Beverly worried about Marion. She was already doing far too much—traveling to Dublin for monthly ISPCA meetings and driving all over the country visiting every pound so she could see things firsthand. Not only that, but she was putting together a legal case for gaining custody of Stafford Taylor's baboons, tigers, and bear. The ISPCA was scheduled to take Taylor to court the following month.

"I'm not agreeing to anything," said Marion. "I'm just saying we can go and meet this woman and hear her out. We can give this just an hour, can't we?"

Beverly didn't like the sound of it, but she wasn't about to let Marion go by herself.

They drove east from Limerick to County Cork, following directions to an Anglo-Irish estate named Glenlohane. A drive led to the front door past a big pasture of grazing sheep. Horses meandered in the distance, their necks bent over the grass, and there were gardens all about. A stunning, ivy-clad Georgian country manor house stood in the center.

Though Marion and Beverly were soul mates when it came to animals, they diverged on other matters. Beverly respected Marion's guts in helping the McCarthys, but when she looked at Travellers, she saw animal-abusing criminals. She just didn't get what Marion saw in them. Similarly, when they pulled into a place like this, Beverly saw beauty and grace—her spirits brightened, lifted high—while Marion saw the Ascendancy class, and it gave her no particular joy. She might not have even been conscious of it, but somewhere in the back of her mind she checked off a box—another estate built on stolen land. Nearly every old manor house and estate in Ireland had been built for wealthy British landowners.

An American greeted them warmly at the door and introduced herself as Melanie Sharp Bolster. She was self-possessed, around fifty years old, as she led them through well-appointed rooms, she explained that her husband had inherited the place from his ancestors, who were British Quakers. He was the tenth generation of his family to live there. As for Melanie, she came from Greenwich, Connecticut, and had met Desmond in the States. She'd agreed to go with him to Ireland to claim his inheritance and turn Glenlohane into a guesthouse.

Beverly and Marion followed Melanie into an Irish country kitchen with a gigantic old cast-iron stove and a large wooden table in the center. A woman rose from the table and extended a hand. She was short, plainly dressed, and understated in every way—except for her extraordinary bright blue eyes. This was Louise Coleman, one of the pioneers of the greyhound adoption movement that was gaining steam in the United States.

They all sat down, and Coleman began by explaining that she'd been rescuing greyhounds for eleven years, mainly from the Wonderland track near Boston. She'd started in 1983, when she heard about a greyhound named Boston Boy who had been a champion and needed a home. His trainer didn't want to put him down but could find no one to take him. Coleman was a single mother of a young boy at the time. She and her son drove out to the track, and as soon as they met the dog, they knew they'd be taking him home.

Boston Boy turned out to be a wonderful guy—incredibly sweet and no trouble at all. They both fell hard for him, but he was also quite an oddity. In 1983, no one kept greyhounds as pets, and sometimes people weren't even quite sure what they were. When Louise and Nolan took Boston Boy out for a walk, heads turned and people stared.

"Hey, is that a dog or a greyhound?"—as though a greyhound were something other than a dog.

That would have been the end of the story, except the trainer was thrilled at the idea of "peting out" his finished racers, and he kept calling. He had this wonderful dog, and another wonderful dog, and they needed homes. Was she interested? Did she have friends who might want a greyhound?

It wasn't long before Coleman had ten ex-racers in her apartment, their long muscular bodies sprawled on her couch, chairs, and rugs, looking at her with ten bemused faces. She found good homes for each and every one.

The trainer—and then his trainer friends—kept calling.

In 1986, she rented kennels and started a nonprofit called Greyhound Friends. All these years later, she'd found homes for thousands of dogs. Early on, Coleman noticed that some dogs had Irish tattoos, and this captivated her. She had Irish-American roots, and, like many descendants of immigrants, took an interest in the country her family had left. She asked the trainers about the Irish dogs, and they told her that Ireland was a great breeder of greyhounds. Dogs were flown around the world for breeding and racing, and sure, lots of Irish dogs had passed through Wonderland. She knew then that she'd want to do something to help the Irish greyhounds.

That's why she'd come here for the meeting in Dublin. It was all industry people, and she'd sat through workshops and lectures about how to market greyhound racing and turn a better profit. But no one spoke about the welfare of the animals.

"When I raised my hand to ask about the dogs' welfare, they looked at me like I was crazy," she said. Then she asked the question she'd waited so long to ask Marion:

"And what about you? As the head of the ISPCA, what are *you* doing about the Irish greyhound situation?"

There was a pause.

"Absolutely nothing," said Marion.

Marion and Beverly knew perfectly well that the Irish industry killed thousands of greyhounds, and that the British, Americans, and Australians did the same. But on that day in 1994, when they first sat down in that kitchen with Louise Coleman, nobody was doing anything about it in Ireland. Occasionally, the newspapers ran a story about greyhound corpses found bludgeoned in a trench or washed ashore with a brick around the neck, ears cut off so as to prevent identification. But by and large, you only saw them at the track. Some wound up at the county pounds. But for the most part, when they were finished racing, greyhounds just quietly disappeared.

Some years earlier, one had come her way when a woman rang on the Limerick Animal Welfare hotline, frantic that a greyhound was on the loose in her neighborhood. He was limping, she said, and he was also hunting her cats! Could someone come right away?

Marion went to see about it, and not long after she parked her car, a big, beautiful ex-racer came trotting toward her and used his three uninjured legs to jump in. On the four- or five-mile drive to the vet, she felt him staring at her from the passenger seat. If she had to put a name to it, she would say he was looking at her with appreciation. She'd learned over the years that some dogs knew perfectly well that you were there to help them and therefore didn't put up any protest.

"He has a broken leg," said the vet.

"Oh, good," said Marion. That would be easy to fix.

"But then what?" the vet asked. "What are you going to do with a greyhound? Who do you think is going to take him?" His tone would have been equally suited to "What are you going to do with a llama?" Or, "What are you going to do with a wolf?"

"But he's a young, healthy dog!"

"Yes," said the vet. "And he has *probably* had a cat. He'll want more. I think you've got to put him down. You've really got no choice."

This was all true. Marion could think of absolutely no one who would be willing to take a greyhound for even five minutes. Her house was already filled to the brim with dogs and cats, and she'd pushed her family to the limit.

After an agonizing time of it, Marion agreed to put the dog down. She rubbed his head while the vet got the needle ready. As the toxic fluid drained from the syringe, the dog looked into Marion's eyes with trust and complete submission, and he kept on looking at her until his eyelids closed and he drifted away into death. It was so easy and quick. When his life was gone, she felt a thud inside. The impossibility of it all was overwhelming. Where would you find homes for all these greyhounds? Where would you get the money to fix all of these legs broken at the track? She made a decision that day: she pledged to herself that she wouldn't ever do that again. She just couldn't. If another greyhound came her way, she was going to keep him.

No greyhounds came her way for a long time, but then one day she got a call about an abandoned dog at the town dump. Marion and a longtime LAW colleague, Anne Kelley, went to investigate. They walked gently into Limerick's mountains of waste, looking about amid the stench until, finally, they found a small greyhound bitch. Rats had chewed her ears so badly that Marion couldn't see whether or not she had a racing tattoo.

After they'd taken the dog to the vet, Anne Dynan, their longtime treasurer, agreed to take her and slowly nursed her back to health. After a couple of months, she emerged as one of the loveliest dogs they'd ever known. Sweet and affectionate, with a light and pretty prance. When she walked, it seemed like her feet barely touched the ground, and that's why they named her Margot, after the famous ballerina Margot Fonteyn.

Marion and her partners put up posters all around town attesting to Margot's beauty and sweetness. What a wonderful pet she'd make, if someone would take her. And yet no calls came, not a single one. That's how they knew it was hopeless to rehome a greyhound in Ireland. Greyhounds were gentler, less demanding, and less likely to bite than terriers or Chihuahuas, but no matter how many times she explained that, no one believed her.

"I would never leave a greyhound alone with my child!"

"Are you crazy? A greyhound in the house?"

They worked with a British shelter, which found Margot a home in England. Before they shipped her off to her new life, they took her to the vet to be spayed and went to prepare her traveling papers.

It was an awful moment when the vet came out with the bad news: Margot was gone. She'd died under anesthesia. Back then, ordinary vets didn't know that greyhounds differed physiologically from other dogs, with their extra-large hearts and fast metabolism. They didn't have the fat to metabolize anesthesia and required smaller doses. Eventually vets would learn, but it was too late for Margot. Greyhounds were not only unappreciated, they were deeply misunderstood.

Beverly looked on cautiously, sizing up Louise Coleman, while Marion told her about Margot and how no one in Ireland wanted greyhounds.

"If you can't find homes for them here, why don't you send them to me? I have so many more people in the States who will open their homes to greyhounds, and you have no one here. Send me your hardest-to-place greyhounds. And I'll take lurchers too."

Marion and Beverly paused for a moment, imagining the logistics of crates and customs and costs and how the animals could safely travel on transatlantic flights in the cargo compartment of a plane.

Beverly thought it was absolutely crazy. "Are you suggesting that we start sending handfuls of greyhounds across the Atlantic Ocean, even though we have thousands of them over here and you have thousands of them over there? What difference would that make? People don't care about greyhounds. And anyway, where would we keep greyhounds once we collected them? I can't keep them in my yard. Not with all the other small dogs I've got. No way."

"Wait a minute," said Marion. "Doesn't Rosie have a greyhound?"

Limerick Animal Welfare (LAW) had formally become a charitable company in 1988, with directors and proper bookkeeping (in their first year they ran a deficit of 260 pounds). In addition to the space at Fedamore, they had about a dozen foster homes. One of these belonged to Rosemary Warren, a fellow hunter at Scarteen. Beverly thought the world of her and recruited her into LAW's network. Rosie was British and soft-spoken. She had an elegant manner and huge blue eyes. She'd come to Ireland in the 1980s for a wedding and fallen head over heels in love with Charlie Warren, one of the Scarteen fox hunters—technically Sir Charles Warren, baronet. As Rosie would later describe him, he was a true gentleman—honest, erudite, and a bit nutty. He had a sprawling farm in Limerick—a rambling twenty acres—which had once been part of a British castle. In addition to the main house, the property included a couple of cottages and several outbuildings, where Charlie tinkered and invented gadgets or built from scratch the odd windmill or dreadful old jeep. They married, and Rosie became Lady Warren. They had absolutely no money.

Or, as Rosie would later say, "Neither of us had a bean." And yet they were as happy as two people could be.

Together, Rosie and Charlie bred and sold draught horses for a while. Rosie grew vegetables and herbs and they also raised a special breed of pig, all of which she sold to restaurants. She raised angora rabbits, too. Beverly couldn't believe it one day when she found Rosie with a rabbit in her lap, cutting off the hair with tiny scissors. She spun the hair into yarn and knitted sweaters with it, which she sold. Everything brought in a little. Rosie had been fostering LAW dogs for a long time and she received a small stipend for the effort, and though it was not much, it helped.

A while back, Marion had seen a greyhound sitting on a big easy chair in Rosie's kitchen and expressed shock.

"My God, Rosie, is that a greyhound you have there?"

Rosie, being British, didn't think anything of it. She had no idea that Irish people didn't keep greyhounds in the house. The dog's name was Syd, because the racing tattoo on her ear included the letters CYD. She'd been abandoned and they'd found her hanging around their property, so they just took her in. She was a lovely pet, very sweet, said Rosie. "She doesn't even bother the hens!"

After their meeting with Louise Coleman at Glenlohane, Marion and Beverly went to talk to Rosie about fostering greyhounds that would eventually be sent abroad to adoptive homes. She said that sure, she'd give it a try. She and Charlie built a couple of new pens—nothing fancy, just wooden posts and chain-link fence—and set up sleeping quarters inside one of the outbuildings just for greyhounds.

Melanie Sharp Bolster agreed to take greyhounds, too. She had the space, though she stipulated that as she already had two dogs, horses, and hens to care for, and an inn to run, she would not permanently adopt any dogs. But she and her husband were both willing to foster dogs whenever they could.

"So next time we get a greyhound," said Marion, "we'll send it to

Rosie or Melanie, and if it's one that's in really bad shape, we'll get it well, and then send it on to Louise Coleman in the States."

At home, Marion hunted down the folder on greyhounds that Marion Webb had given her. It was time, finally, to have a look.

⁓

ABOUT SIX weeks later, their first opportunity arrived. The call came in at around 5 p.m. on a dank November evening. A man's voice said simply, "You should go to the graveyard. There's a greyhound there in bad condition." He hung up before Marion could ask him any questions.

Marion had nearly reached her limit. She still had Stafford Taylor's circus animals in custody with nowhere to send them, and the clock was ticking to their mandatory destruction date. She was still tired from her cancer; it was a tiredness that went beyond muscle and bone, deeper than sleep could reach. She considered ignoring the call, but instead she rang Beverly and told her she'd just got the strangest call.

"Maybe it's a hoax," Marion said

"It's never a hoax," replied Beverly. "You should know that by now. If we get a call, we have to check it out."

Marion couldn't go alone because her arm was still sore where the lymph nodes had been removed. If the dog was large, she wouldn't be able to pick it up.

Beverly arrived at her house in a few minutes, and soon they were headed into the city beneath the darkening autumn sky. They pulled up at the cemetery at Mount St. Lawrence in Limerick, where they found an attendant in the midst of locking up for the night. They convinced him to wait so they could go inside to find the dog.

They entered the cemetery and began walking. No one was there but the two of them, and the paths were thick with fallen leaves. A fog was rolling in, making it even harder to see. They went slowly past the rows of tombstones and monuments, not quite sure what they were looking or listening for. After fifteen minutes, they'd still found no sign of life.

They continued to the back of the graveyard, almost ready to give up, when they heard a rustling sound. Something was buried under the leaves, trying to hide and stay warm. They crept closer. Suddenly, a long, pointed snout peeked out, then big, ghostly eyes. It was a greyhound. A piece of wire had been strung through its collar and double-wrapped around the tombstone. The dog was emaciated and probably dehydrated; she'd clearly been there a long time, and from what they could tell, the only water she'd had was whatever rain she could lick off wet leaves. She looked to be on the verge of death, so weak that she couldn't stand.

"Oh my God," said Beverly, bending down to untie the dog. "What jerks. Oh, this poor creature." Then she lifted the animal in her arms, and she and Marion rushed her to the vet. When the cemetery caretaker saw them leaving, he shook his head and pointed to the direction of the Limerick greyhound track, which was just a couple of blocks away.

"That one got punished," he said. "A slow one has to starve and die slow. A winner gets a bullet."

11

—

RISING TIDE

1994–96

Only much later, when Marion looked back, would she understand that energy was gathering force—fragments, small bits of luck, garbled messages coming through, not just from her immediate vicinity, but from far beyond. Louise Coleman's visit had marked the beginning. Then came BBC journalist Donal Macintyre, an investigative reporter with a reputation for infiltrating gangs, drug rings, and corporate crime scams, shining a light on the worst of human nature. When he turned his attention to the greyhound business, he found plenty. In October 1994, his exposé "Not All Dogs Go to Heaven" landed like a bomb on the pages of the *Irish Times*.

> *Everyone knows that greyhound racing has financial problems—few enough know about its accounting problem—it has failed to account for the thousands of greyhounds that have retired from the sport. . . . Discounting for natural wastage and some stud dogs there should be about 100,000*

dogs enjoying comfortable retirement after hectic competitive careers—but where are they?

Are they looked after by caring and loving owners after their three or four-year racing careers and allowed to live out their natural lives of about 15 years? Or are they variously abandoned, put down, bludgeoned to death, sent for vivisection or exported to race in appalling conditions in Spain when they have served their useful purpose?

For years, the greyhound industry had been getting negative press. But this article went beyond anything previously published. Macintyre's sources told of greyhounds tossed from moving cars on the way back from a bad race, greyhounds drowned, greyhounds buried in mass graves with their ears cut off to prevent prosecution of the owner. Greyhounds pumped up with drugs to subdue pain so they would push on around the track despite injuries. Greyhounds sold to university research laboratories. Greyhounds sold to lower-grade tracks in England, Scotland, and Spain.

Macintyre quoted Marion in his story:

"It's nearly impossible to get a home for a greyhound in Ireland. We have had to get homes in Boston and in England because we have had no luck here. People just don't see them as pets . . . I am ashamed by how we treat our greyhounds—I despair. These dogs have raced their hearts out and are then often left to fend for themselves—it is a disgrace and worse it is subsidized by the Government."

People all over Ireland were shocked. They asked themselves, how could they not have known? How could this have been going on right in their midst?

After the article ran, a small trickle of greyhounds began to appear at Rosie's door.

~

BASED ON her condition, the vet estimated that the graveyard dog had been tied to the tombstone for at least a week. She would need very special care. Marion picked up the phone and called Melanie Sharp Bolster. She had not forgotten the peaceful beauty and order of Glen-lohane, the location where they'd met with Louise Coleman. It would be the perfect place.

Later, Melanie would admit that when she heard the story, she was sickened and hesitated to say yes. This was not a case of neglect or abuse stemming from the usual ignorance, anger, or despair. What had happened to the graveyard dog reached a far deeper level—a type of cruelty that stole life away for the pleasure of it. Melanie was not the theological type, but the only word she could think of to describe it was evil. It was beyond repentance or explanation or hope. Did she want to take that on? Did she want a dog who would remind her every day that a sadist was out there who would likely do the same again—to animals, humans, or both? Once you saw certain things, you could never unsee them—never unknow.

She pondered. Then she called Marion back about the graveyard dog.

"Yes. We will foster her until you can find the right home. She can stay as long as she needs to."

As soon as Melanie saw the animal, her fears melted away. She was a filthy and cowering mess with red, open sores running down her legs, so weak she could still barely stand. She and Desmond had arrived with a leash and a blanket, but no matter how gently they approached, no matter how softly they spoke, the dog's body rattled in terror. When the dog saw she could not escape, she curved herself into the wall, trying to hide, and twisting her head so as not to see them. Finally, Desmond just swooped her up in his arms and carried her to the car. On the way back to Glenlohane, Melanie came up with the name Demi, because the dog was half white and half auburn. Later it occurred to her that the name fit because Demi was half alive and half dead.

For the first two days, they left Demi alone to eat and drink and sleep as she wished. On the third day Melanie allowed her own dogs, a greyhound and a Welsh corgi, to come and meet their visitor. The duo became Demi's companions and mentors.

A couple of weeks more, and Melanie looked out of the window to see Demi spring into a play bow toward the other two, as though a great wind had come down from the sky and breathed the animal spirit back into her body. She emerged as a gorgeous animal, her soft white fur and big auburn patches shining, her expression sweet and gentle. In a short time, Demi's physical health and beauty returned completely. But psychologically speaking, she was still not at all well.

Humans were her biggest problem. She could not bear them. She would not take food from a human hand, would not allow herself to be touched or petted, and would not look a human in the eye. If a human approached, she tried to run, and if she could not get away, she twisted her head as far as possible in the other direction, to keep said human out of her vision. She was utterly unadoptable. Who would want a dog as damaged as this?

Louise Coleman asked Jill Hopfenbeck, a young vet who volunteered at Coleman's shelter, spaying and neutering greyhounds, as payback on a debt. A decade earlier, when she'd been a student at Tufts Veterinary School, she walked into the lab one morning and found more than a dozen greyhound corpses laid out on tables awaiting dissection. Most were only about three years old, and each had a number tattooed onto their thin pink ears. Their owners had sold them to Tufts after their racing lives were finished. The only way Hopfenbeck could move ahead and pick up her scalpel was to silently vow that someday, when she was an established vet, she would do something for the breed. That's why, even though she already had two greyhounds, she agreed to foster Demi. The plan was that Hopfenbeck would help the dog recover so that she could be adopted. If that was not possible, she'd keep Demi herself.

One morning in January 1995, when it was still dark, Marion and Melanie met at Shannon airport to see Demi off on her trip to Boston. Most dogs could travel as baggage along with a passenger, but not greyhounds. Aer Lingus required them to travel as cargo. This method was more expensive, and also meant they had to arrive extra early at a special building, where they would be muzzled and packed into a small box, its dimensions specified by the Irish Greyhound Board. In short, Demi would be a commercial shipment.

Demi tried to run. They had to force her inside against her will, as gently as they could, quickly shutting the door and saying over and over again words that Demi couldn't possibly understand, "You are going to a better life. You will be okay." Demi crept to the far corner and shut herself down, going inward to the place dogs go to hide or to die.

About ten hours later, Marion got a phone call that Demi had arrived safely in Boston. But after that, it was rough going. Demi quickly claimed refuge on a cushion in Hopfenbeck's bedroom and emerged only to eat or go outside, after which she zoomed right back. No one could get near her. If Hopfenbeck approached, Demi leapt away so fast and hard that she slammed into the wall. When Hopfenbeck got home at the end of the day, her other two greyhounds came running to the door for a celebratory welcome, carrying on and leaping, while Demi was nowhere to be seen.

After a few weeks, Hopfenbeck came home one night and spotted Demi in the background, standing at a safe distance just outside the bedroom door, wagging her tail. A couple of weeks after that, Hopfenbeck was sitting on the floor watching television when Demi poked her nose out of the bedroom and finally, of her own sweet will, crept, one tentative step after the next, to Hopfenbeck's side, where she simply stood very still. That was when Hopfenbeck knew that

Demi was going to be okay. She also knew that she wasn't going to let Demi go to any other home.

~

ROSIE MET a couple of trainers who hated to put down a healthy dog and were happy to learn that they could bring a greyhound, who had raced with heart and given so much, here for a second chance. That's how Louise Coleman and Marion got a brilliant idea: they could work with the good guys in the business.

They called upon the most famous dogman in Ireland. He bred and raced dogs on both sides of the Atlantic, and at the peak of his business he might have six hundred dogs at a time. His dogs' bloodlines were legendary. He regularly flew them around the world to compete in the biggest derbies, where he won the biggest purses. He'd been in the business full-time since age eighteen and was now in his fifties. Everyone admired, or at least envied him.

When Marion and Louise arrived at his place in Tipperary, he greeted them cordially and took them outside for a tour of the kennels. The dogs had large pens with access to a huge green paddock, a perfect diet, lots of socialization, and exercise six times a day. They looked fabulous, alert, and interested in everything.

Afterward, in the living room, the man's wife served tea and biscuits. Marion took a sip, to be polite, and returned her cup to its saucer.

"We are here because we know that there are many high-quality people in the industry, such as you, who really look after their dogs. But too many dogs go unaccounted for each year. That's why we'd like to form a group of Concerned Greyhound Breeders and Owners who can work with us and the Bord na gCon to improve conditions for all greyhounds across the industry. We are hoping you will be part of it with us. If you lead, they will all follow."

After a respectful silence, he said, "Ladies, I appreciate what you're doing, but I just can't help you. I'm sorry."

Then he and his wife changed the subject. Soon they were discussing the horrors of abortion. Louise and Marion left, with the sound of the heavy door closing shut behind them.

Once Marion got started on the greyhound cause, it was as though she had a fever inside her brain. There was no way to cool it off.

She forced herself to go to the grimy Limerick track so she could witness the industry in action. She learned that for the dogs, the most dangerous places on the track were the turns, which placed pressure on their inner legs and caused the most injuries. The first time she saw a dog go down with a broken leg, there was no vet on site; handlers ran onto the track and dragged the dog off to the side, where he lay yelping in agony for thirty minutes until the vet arrived and administered the shot that would kill him and stop the noise.

"Give me the dog," Marion cried out from trackside. "I'll take him and fix his leg. It won't cost you anything. Give him to me!"

But they didn't listen. Some people even laughed at her. If a dog broke a leg, that was the end of the dog. Period. Who would fix the leg of an animal that wouldn't be able to work anymore? It made no sense unless the animal had champion bloodlines, in which case they would fix the leg and use the dog for breeding. After a while, Marion stopped going to the track because it was too awful. She hated the way the handlers walked the dogs in a proud single-file ritual toward six dark boxes. Hated the way each runner went compliantly inside, with a quick push in the rump from the handler—door shut. Then they barked and moaned and scrabbled to be set free to chase after the whizzing piece of fabric that fooled them every time.

She forced herself to attend the monthly auctions where greyhounds were sold, bought, traded in, and traded down. First, the dogs ran timed trials to provide current numbers. Then they were paraded onto the auction block, where a small crowd, mostly men but some women too, looked on with skepticism at the elegant animals, while their own clumsy human bodies—wearing ridiculous shoes, cloth caps, cigarettes in mouths, pencil stubs in hand—hunched over columns of numbers, comparing past and present performances. Time broken down to imperceptible fragments of speed and distance—and these fractions of seconds were plugged into formulas that created a monetary value.

Sold, to the highest bidder!

Next, the foreign agents swooped in to scoop up the unsold dogs. They'd been hired to make purchases for Scotland, England, Pakistan, Spain, sometimes Morocco, looking for bargains. They paid, received official papers, and in no time walked their new purchases out to the parking lot. Marion made it a point to follow them and let them know she was the chairperson of the ISPCA, there to observe them.

"Did you give the dog water? How often will you stop to give them exercise? You can't pack them this way! Do you have papers? Have these dogs been vaccinated?" (So *this* was what Marion Webb had been talking about.) Once, she made a big scene, holding back a truckload of thirty-six dogs for two weeks and demanding proof of vaccinations.

Not that it did any good. The dogs were eventually allowed to leave.

Generally, the men paid no mind to her as they loaded the greyhounds into lorries, pulling them by the neck as they shoved them into crates because most of the dogs were terrified and resisted. Crates, doubled up and stacked, or just tossed into the back of the lorry with nothing to stop them sliding around. The worst was when the dogs were all packed up, their eyes looking out, hopeful of release. The gate slammed down and they disappeared.

The most unlucky dogs wound up in a truck to Spain. Over the years, thousands of greyhounds had made the four-day trip—six hours on land, then at least eighteen hours at sea, then another twelve hours on the road from Brittany down across the Pyrenees and on to Barcelona, all the while rocking and slamming about in their own shit and puke, sometimes in hundred-degree heat, sometimes in an open truck under a canvas tarp.

For years, they'd heard rumors, complaints, and firsthand accounts that the dogs at Spanish tracks looked sick and abused. Back in the 1980s, Ann Shannon (who had helped start the greyhound adoption movement in England) had been obsessed with the situation, which she publicly described as "appalling cruelty." For nine years, she'd written letter after letter, trying to pressure the Bord na gCon to stop selling dogs to Spain. She spoke out to the Irish press about "appalling conditions" and misery. The Bord insisted that conditions in Spain were fine.

But by far the most influential person on this matter was Anne Finch, a British woman who, with the support of her husband Arthur, more or less went off the deep end.

It began innocently enough (as animal welfare efforts usually did). Anne was a nurse who had a soft spot for Labradors, especially those who had been seeing-eye dogs. She felt a kinship with these dogs, who had spent their lives being of service to others, and she enjoyed adopting the ones who couldn't work anymore, giving them a nice retirement. She took it a step further and decided to help out by walking dogs at a local shelter. How surprising to find that the place was teeming with greyhounds! She took an interest in a particularly depressed and unresponsive greyhound who had lived there for years. No one knew anything about the dog. Finch wanted to help, but despite the walks and toys and attention, the dog never warmed up or showed any affect. When the greyhound died, Finch took it hard. She decided she wanted to learn about the breed. She went to the track kennels to find out something of what their lives were like. When she learned how many were put down, abandoned, and killed, she was horrified. First, she adopted a greyhound named Emma. Then she began working with Ann Shannon and the British Retired Greyhound Trust to find homes for dogs who would otherwise be killed. Over the years, she personally ferried hundreds of dogs to adoptive families all over England.

It might have rested at that, but in 1991, Finch opened a newspaper and saw a photo of a greyhound behind rusty bars, looking starved and sick, clearly in misery. The accompanying story told of greyhounds exported from Ireland to Spain, where they were raced to death in the sweltering heat.

That's when everything began to unravel. She couldn't get the photo out of her head. Two months later, she and a friend set off on a secret mission to Mallorca. They haggled with trainers and managed to come home with three greyhounds, plus a fourth left behind in safekeeping with a friend, to be retrieved later. The media in Ireland and England loved the story. "Mercy Mission Rescues Irish Greyhounds," the *Irish Independent* reported, calling it a "dramatic undercover rescue mission." Photographs showed Finch smiling beatifically next to one of the saved dogs.

The Bord na gCon immediately denied knowledge of any abuses and asked the World Greyhound Racing Federation to send an investigative team to the Spanish tracks. The WGRF investigators cited crowded kennels, untrained handlers, dogs sleeping on concrete floors with no bedding (disastrous for greyhounds), extraordinary temperatures and no air conditioning despite the Mediterranean summer heat, and far too many races per week, which left dogs no time to recover from injuries.

In response, the Bord announced that it would suspend all trade with Spain. Technically, this occurred, but in reality, nothing changed. Though the Bord no longer dealt directly with the Spanish industry, middlemen saw an opportunity and stepped in to make a profit. They simply attended the Irish auctions, purchased dogs, and sold them in Spain. Time and again, the Bord told the media that under free trade agreements, it was powerless to stop independent agents from coming to the Irish sales and buying dogs.

Finch continued making trips to Spain. She worked directly with the trainers, most of whom were uneducated and impoverished. She wrote and produced a video in Spanish on the proper care of greyhounds and gave away a thousand free copies. She brought medications to the tracks, and the trainers readily gave her their most hopeless dogs instead of putting them down or selling them to hunters in the rural north, where their fate would be even worse. Everybody knew that in Spain hunters killed their hounds when the three-month season was done. It was easier to get fresh dogs at the start of the next season than to pay for their food and care for the other nine months of the year.

Finch built networks—first in Switzerland and Germany, later in France, northern Italy, Belgium, Slovenia, and Austria—with welfare agencies who would take greyhounds and find them good homes. She and her husband were not wealthy, but for years she did all of this at her own expense, taking from savings and using credit cards. At night, she wrote reports and letters recounting what she described as atrocities. She sent these firsthand accounts to the Bord na gCon, the Queen of Spain, news outlets, the appropriate government ministers, and the shipping companies that transported the dogs.

But nothing changed. Foreign agents kept coming to the Irish sales, and the dogs kept getting trucked to Spain. And the Bord na gCon did nothing to stop them.

Clearly, eyewitness reports from an empathic British nurse were not going to be enough. Something more serious was needed. During the circus rescue, Marion had learned that to really have impact you needed the voices of qualified people. Having an independent vet involved added an instant boost to credibility (as did several male team members, if possible). She went to Ciaran O'Donovan, the chief executive officer at the ISPCA. He agreed to support an investigation.

Then came reality.

Marion asked and asked again, but she could not find a vet who would go with her on a fact-finding expedition to Spain. Every single one made excuses, begged off, or said quite directly that they were doctors—not animal rights activists.

Her sense of powerlessness became unbearable. She had to *do* something. That was when she started going to the auctions and buying a couple of slow, leftover greyhounds at a time. At least save a few lives, she rationalized. She brought them to Rosie or Melanie—at least now she had two people who would foster them. If she could not find Irish people to adopt them as pets (they almost never could), then the dog was sent on to England, where they had good contacts, or to Boston, where Coleman would find it a home.

Shipping dogs across the Atlantic was expensive and ridiculous. It was an ordeal for the animals—Marion would be the first to admit it. She much preferred for them to find homes with Irish families, but that was not possible yet. She used this to her advantage, letting the Irish newspapers know that she was flying greyhounds out of the country to save their lives because no one in Ireland wanted them. She appealed to Aer Lingus to let greyhounds fly like other dogs, as baggage instead of manifest cargo. In the meantime, Rosie had an idea.

"Oh, let's just disguise them. You know, send them as something else."

"What do you mean? Put them in a collie suit?"

They laughed—but the joke inspired a grand scheme.

Rosie found a vet who was so absurdly "incompetent" that each time he prepared traveling papers for their flying greyhounds, he somehow put down the wrong breed. The check-in clerk studied the papers but never looked inside the crate. In this way, dozens of greyhounds traveled from Shannon to Logan under false identities, passing for Labradors or sheepdogs or collies for the price of eighty or ninety pounds. Melanie, Rosie, Marion, and Beverly cornered unsuspecting souls traveling to the States to ask if they wouldn't mind taking a dog with them. My friend Elizabeth was one such recruit. A dozen years later, this was the route Lily would take from Rosie's shelter to New Jersey. But at this point, no one could foresee how big the circles would become.

⁓

ABOUT SIX months after the Macintyre article, Marion received a letter addressed to "The Chairperson of the ISPCA." It came from Germany and read like this:

I am trying you again in the hopes this letter will reach you. It is my second attempt. I read the article about greyhounds by Donal Macintyre. If the situation is so bad as this man says, I must do something to help. I have raised funds to help dogs in hopeless situations. I believe the Irish greyhound may qualify.

It was signed Johanna Wothke, founder of a nonprofit organization called Pro Animale für Tiere in Not e.V. (which translates to Pro Animale for Animals in Need). Marion read and reread the letter. Could it be real?

A few weeks later, she was in the restaurant of a Limerick hotel, shaking hands with a soft-spoken German woman who had an overwhelming aura of seriousness. On the table next to her lay the Macintyre article.

"You're late."

Marion looked at her watch, confused. "Yes, so sorry. Ten minutes." (For her, that was more or less on time.)

Johanna waved off her apologies and offered a few pleasantries, then began the interrogation.

"Are you honorable?"

Honorable? Marion stumbled. "Well . . . yes. I try to be."

Johanna corrected herself. "My English is not good. I mean . . . how do you say . . . Do you get money from this work?"

"Oh, you mean voluntary. Charitable. Yes, we are a charitable organization. I make no salary. No one does."

Johanna smiled then, and the fierceness in her eyes softened. Marion relaxed a bit too, and soon they hit it off. Johanna was a retired schoolteacher who had built many animal sanctuaries in Germany and was now branching out to other countries, such as Poland, Turkey, and Russia. When the conversation turned to greyhounds, Marion stopped her.

"Why don't we just go and have a look?"

Rosie received them wearing her jeans, wellies, and her usual British elegance. She led them through her house, past Syd the greyhound asleep in her easy chair, out back to the kennels that she and Charlie had recently built. These "greyhound facilities" were admittedly modest. But at least they proved to Johanna that efforts were underway.

The dogs came forward, sleek and big-eyed, and leaned their long backs against the fence asking to be petted. They poked their snouts through the links and licked hands.

"They're lovely really," said Rosie softly.

Silence.

Johanna walked about taking photographs but saying nothing. Her demeanor and head-shaking made it clear that the facilities were not up to her standards. She nodded when she was done, and they led her back to the kitchen. Would she give them a grade, maybe a B or a C? A promise of help? Why was she here?

She sat down at the table, pulled her huge leather satchel onto her lap, and reached inside. Marion would never forget it. She took out a large stack of bills, which she placed on the table. When she finished there were a couple of thousand pounds, at least.

"You will make proper kennel for greyhounds, and I will pay. The old house out there—make tile floors. Make heat. Make bathroom to wash the dogs, and I will pay for all of it. Every greyhound that needs a vet, I will pay. If you cannot find homes, I will send my transporter and he will bring them to Germany and we will find homes. Give me receipts for everything. We will take this little step forward. We are going to build some kind of proper space for ten or fifteen greyhounds right here. It is just a start."

Marion and Rosie looked at each other in shock at the sight of all that cash. In fact, Marion felt a bit woozy and unsteady. Was this really happening?

"Now," continued Wothke, who seemed absolutely buoyant after getting all this business out of the way, "let's have a drink of wine to celebrate." She reached into her magical sack and produced a bottle. Rosie got glasses so that they could all toast their new greyhound mission.

⌒

MARION AND Beverly agreed on most things, but had always diverged on one basic aspect of strategy: stay small and focused, helping as many animals as possible locally, versus getting involved in politics and risk accomplishing nothing at all.

Marion insisted on doing national work with the ISPCA. During all those prior years of picking up dogs and cats, and going out in the middle of the night to investigate horrors, she'd never had any clout. Zero. She was not a vet, not a lawmaker, not a minister. Now, she had this one small thing—a title. She intended to use it while she could. "A rising tide lifts all boats," she told Beverly. This became a mantra.

After she finished out Marion Webb's term, the ISPCA reelected Marion for another two years as chairperson. The job involved lobbying for better animal welfare legislation nationally and sometimes even internationally, in the EU. On occasion, she and O'Donovan went to Brussels for meetings at Eurogroup for Animals, where they voted for an extra couple of inches on veal crates and lobbied for stricter regulation on animal transport. Many millions of farm animals went through grueling journeys across the continent only to be slaughtered at the end so they could be sold as fresh meat rather than frozen. And of course, she continually tried to get greyhounds on the European agenda.

More than anything, she wanted to use her leadership of the ISPCA to build a truly national organization that would raise standards for all Irish animals. This had been the original idea back in the 1940s, when the ISPCA was founded to unite all the smaller societies around the country. To date, there had been only minimal success. Each of the more than two dozen affiliates was autonomous and pursued its own standards. One local SPCA still electrocuted dogs as a means of euthanasia. Some openly supported hunting and blood sports such as coursing.

As chairperson, Marion reached out to every local society, and especially those that had allowed their memberships to lapse. She invited representatives from all member groups to attend the ISPCA's monthly meetings in Dublin, and attend they did. They came from north, south, east, and west, across the rural–urban divide, and represented every corner of the animal kingdom. They were cat and dog people, horse lovers, pig and cow protectors, advocates for wildlife, and spokespeople for the elephants and bears that were being held like museum objects at the Dublin Zoo. She was especially glad to bring in the small, impoverished societies that had little support.

With fifteen or sixteen organizations represented at the table every month, the meetings were more than interesting and at times rather noisy. (Some might say emotional.) But Marion's goal was to create an environment that welcomed new ideas and debate. She believed this coming together was necessary and good. For decades, they'd all been isolated, uncoordinated. Now at least everything was transparent and they all sat at the same table and discussed national legislation and court cases. The dog people had no choice but to know that the marine people existed. The rural people *had* to hear about the urban horses. The urban people had to witness how little they knew about cows and pigs and sheep compared to farmers who had for generations believed that if you looked after animals they would look after you.

She wanted to start with the awful condition of the local animal pounds, because they took in thousands of cats and dogs each year. Coming from Limerick Animal Welfare, with its no-kill policy, Marion could hardly bear the mass euthanasia of unclaimed animals. The least they could do was make it as painless as possible. Early in her tenure, she got hold of a bolt gun and brought it to a meeting. At a well-chosen moment, she pulled it out of a bag and held it up for all to see. Everyone stared dumbfounded, as though she'd just produced a grenade. The room went silent.

"Ladies and gentlemen. *This* is how most of dogs are put down at the pounds managed by the ISPCA."

She handed the bolt gun to the person next to her so it could be passed around the room, allowing each person to feel the cold weight of it. Then she reached down again into her bag and pulled out a photo she'd had blown up to a large size. In it, a dog lay on asphalt, with a huge red mess pooled under his broken head.

"As you all can see, the bolt gun penetrates the skull with great force. But you have to aim it just right, and that's not easy to do when an animal is squirming around and terrified. This dog was lucky," she said. "He got shot once. But unqualified people are using this tool. If they miss, the dog must wait in agony for a second shot while it lies there with half its brains blown out."

She put the photo down.

"Of course, the heads of puppies and kittens are too small," she continued. "You could blow your hand off. So our societies put them in a box and gas them."

Discomfort. Sighs. Bodies shifting in seats.

"You can't really call this putting them to sleep, can you now?"

Then she reached inside for her tone of utmost authority and confidence. "If there is no choice and we must put an animal down, the most humane method is intravenous injection performed by a qualified vet. I propose that we make this policy at all our pounds."

A respectful pause followed—then the naysaying began.

"Where will we get the money to pay a vet to do this? The counties will never pay!"

"We can keep the bolt gun if we make sure it's used correctly. Then it is perfectly humane and quick!"

"The dog wardens will fight this. They have a union, you know. It's their livelihood to put down the dogs."

Marion agreed that there were challenges, but she would not relent.

"If you had to put down your own pet, you wouldn't use a bolt gun, would you?"

Silence.

"Well, then, we should treat the animals in our shelters the same way as we treat our own."

The goal was to get everyone on the same page, with a clear definition of what the society did and stood for, and what "prevention of cruelty" meant. If an organization wanted to be part of the national group, they would have to agree to those terms. She and the board prepared a national policy statement and sent it out for ratification to all the member organizations. She expected some resistance, but she never could have foreseen what would come thanks to a single sentence that made up Article 7: "The ISPCA is in principle opposed to the taking or the killing of wild animals, or the infliction of any suffering on them."

Had she been naive?

The Irish Master of Foxhounds Association declared a small war and urged its members to join their local societies—as many as possible and as quickly as possible, to make themselves heard. Soon, they were marching en masse into small society meetings in the countryside—meetings that usually drew a handful of dog and cat lovers. Bewildered members looked up and saw dozens of hunters walking in the door. It was a brilliant tactic. Paying a membership fee of as little as five pounds gained these new members the right to vote. Then, with their instant majorities, they struck down the constitution.

"Hunters Infiltrate ISPCAs!" went the headlines.

The battle raged on, and after a while, some of the most passionate animal welfare advocates got nervous.

"We have many good hunting people in our local SPCAs," went the chorus.

As much as it annoyed Marion, she knew it was true. Well-to-do British people had founded many of the SPCAs in Ireland. They had the means and desire to look out for dogs and cats and horses, which they especially loved, but saw no conflict in killing wild animals. In fact many of the founding members had been hunting people.

"This is ridiculous!" insisted Marion. "We are the ISPCA, as in *prevention – of – cruelty – to – animals*. Our local societies cannot be speaking out in favor of hunting!" Her message became a chorus of its own.

"Sign or resign."

No doubt, Marion's confrontation with the hunters revived the old question of how on earth she could keep LAW's animals on property owned by a Joint Master of the Scarteen Hunt. She had no trouble explaining it. What would they do without Fedamore? The Wolfs had taken in hundreds of dogs over the years. Surely Semon would have been happier if she had just disappeared. But he tolerated her, and she owed him the same. The standoff with the hunters dragged on for months. One, two, and then three local societies had to leave the ISPCA because they would not oppose hunting. The tension was becoming unbearable. Something had to be done.

To resolve the matter, the governing council of the ISPCA decided that at the next annual general meeting, it would put forth a motion and let the membership decide whether to uphold or strike down Article 7. Each member society could contribute a single vote. It would be the moment of truth.

The day began with anti-hunt protestors picketing in the street outside in support of Article 7. Up in the conference room, introductory speeches came and went, and the air was electric as everyone waited to hear which side would win. Finally, Ciaran O'Donovan rose from his chair to speak and the room fell silent. Everyone seemed to lean forward.

"Ladies and gentlemen, the votes have been received and counted. The results are: Article 7—that the ISPCA is in principle opposed to the taking or killing of wild animals—has been upheld and remains in force."

Booing and cheers burst out simultaneously.

Marion was gobsmacked. She'd never imagined it would hold. Later, the hunters tried to overturn the decision, saying it wasn't valid. But she had all the paperwork in order, and there was nothing they could do about it. Article 7 became a permanent part of the ISPCA constitution. From then on, it would be known as Marion's article.

⌒

MARION KNEW the greyhound movement was gaining momentum when she learned that Clarissa Baldwin had gotten involved. Baldwin was in charge of the much-venerated National Canine Defence League (later renamed Dogs Trust), which was the UK's largest dog welfare charity. It was an old and wealthy organization that had the support of the Queen.

Too many greyhounds were turning up at the League's rehoming centers with special needs—from teeth problems to old racing injuries—and because they were not as popular as terriers and Labs, many simply stayed on forever. Baldwin wanted to know why the industry was dumping its dogs and leaving her charity to pick up the bill. To address the issue, she formed the UK Greyhound Forum and gathered members of Parliament, animal welfare groups, and greyhound industry people around the same table. Now she wanted to do the same thing on an international level. Since 90 percent of British greyhounds were imported from Ireland, she wanted to replicate her efforts in Dublin. Marion was there at the start, of course, as were animal welfare people from Britain, Ireland, Northern Ireland, Scotland, Wales, Sweden, the European Union, and the United States.

Baldwin called it the International Greyhound Forum, and they met every six months. At first, the Bord na gCon was patronizing at best, sending a different representative each time.

Oh, well, Mr. Such and Such, he's gone. We're sending a new man today.

The new man would show up and say, "Now, what seems to be the issue here?" And they had to start from the beginning. But eventually, the Bord realized that it had to meet with the welfare people— because they weren't going to go away.

Clarissa Baldwin's vision was to change the laws so that greyhounds were better protected. She knew the process would be arduous and slow, but she was in it for the long haul. That meant working cooperatively with the greyhound industry, treading a line between making them comfortable enough to stay in the room yet keeping the pressure on.

Marion was far less polite, and struggled to restrain herself at each Greyhound Forum meeting. She frequently returned to the same questions. When would the Irish Bord establish a sanctuary for finished racers? When would the Bord have a vet on site at every race? When would the Bord require accountability, so that if a greyhound was tossed onto the street it could be traced to its owners and prosecution could follow? She seldom failed to mention the "wastage" issue. It didn't help matters that she criticized the greyhound business in the media time and again.

In 1997, according to the *Limerick Leader,* Marion claimed that fourteen thousand greyhounds—including five thousand puppies— were disposed of in Ireland each year. The Bord's Sean Collins vigorously denied this, calling her accusations "preposterous" and "outlandish."

After some years, Baldwin told Marion that the industry men were suggesting that a smaller working group would be more productive. They thought they could get more done without her.

~

ROSIE'S GREYHOUND facility had been quickly overwhelmed by greyhounds.

"Now it's time for you to go and find land," Johanna told Marion.
She'd raised the equivalent of 200,000 euro from Pro Animale's supporters for the purpose of building a proper sanctuary for the Irish
greyhound.

Johanna had many requirements. She wanted a place that was
far away from people, yet accessible. They needed good drainage
and grazing land in case other kinds of animals arrived. And beauty:
beauty was important to Johanna. All of her sites were in peaceful
natural settings.

Everything took so long back then. Marion and Beverly drove to look
at properties, and each time they had to photograph it, develop the film,
mail the photos to Germany, and then wait. A few weeks later Marion
would receive Johanna's response, which was usually a rejection.

"What is it with her?" asked Beverly.

Land was hard to come by in Ireland. The Irish people had been
deprived of it for so many centuries that now, when they had it, they
tended not to let go of it.

Finally, Marion and Beverly found thirty-eight acres with a farmhouse in Woodford, amid beautiful countryside in County Galway.
As soon as the deal was done, Johanna sent her architect to draw up
plans, and then the builders arrived to get started. She asked Marion
to think of a name—something that would convey what her organization, Pro Animale, stood for, which was to bring shelter, happiness,
and peace to neglected animals in dire need.

Marion gave it a lot of thought. Then it hit her.

Avalon.

It was a name for the islands off the western coast. In ancient
times, the Irish people believed they were blessed, a kind of paradise

where the land was so fertile that fruit trees sprang spontaneously from the soil. After their battles were finished, wounded kings and heroes were put on a boat and sent across the water to Avalon, where they remained forever. King Arthur made this journey after he received his mortal wounds. When he arrived, nine priestesses awaited him; they had powers to heal the incurable and to shift between the animal and human worlds

Nearly three years after Marion had her first meeting with Johanna, Pro Animale opened Avalon, its new sanctuary in County Galway. It could accommodate about ninety greyhounds at one time, as they waited for their new homes: some in England, a few in Ireland, but mostly in Germany. Avalon also offered room for some goats, horses, and other animals in need. Instead of cages or little pens with wire doors, the dogs lived in groups of six to eight individuals, like small families. This was an essential feature of every Pro Animale station, as Johanna abhorred cages of any kind. Each group of greyhounds had a bright airy room; the rooms were named Patience, Tolerance, Faithfulness, Honesty, and Strength. Each animal had a soft bed and blanket,

At Avalon, there are no cages. (Courtesy Pro Animale für Tiere in Not e.V.)

and there were huge paddocks for running. It was a vision from another world—microscopic in the big picture, but it was real.

Marion was one of the directors of Pro Animale's Avalon. Of course, a part of her felt sad that it had taken expatriates and foreigners from America, England, and Germany to care about Irish greyhounds. Why did it have to be Pro Animale that built the first greyhound sanctuary in Ireland? It should have been the Bord na gCon. Oh, she knew the reasons why: the poverty of Ireland, its isolation, and its history. Everything came later here. She had to believe that things would change. For now, she pushed those thoughts aside and celebrated, because for the most part, Marion had never felt so hopeful.

~

THE LIMERICK Animal Welfare hotline continued to ring.

"I'm worried about my dog."

"What is the problem, ma'am?"

"He isn't eating. Can you come over right away?"

"Maybe you should take him to a vet?"

"I can't carry him to the car." The woman's voice was shaky and faint. She sounded a hundred years old. Marion was going in that direction anyway, so she agreed to stop by.

A frail, ancient woman met her at the door and led her into the house, where Marion found the dog curled up on a rug. She reached down and tried to lift him. He was stiff and cold. Then came a tinkling sound: his nails had fallen off and scattered about the floor.

You have got to be kidding, Marion said to herself. And then, "Ma'am, I'm afraid I have to tell you the sad news that your dog is dead."

It was not an easy moment.

The woman started to cry, and Marion heard herself promising that she'd get him buried. Somehow she carried the dog out and put him in the boot of the car, which was absurd. *Absurd!* As she drove away, she realized that the ground was too cold and hard for shoveling. She called Beverly and told her what had happened.

"Now what would I do with the body? I promised a burial! Can you believe this?"

They burst out laughing at the same moment, because they both knew that Marion was going to find space in someone's freezer to hold the dog until the thaw.

At least they laughed.

The worst times of all were the calls to Moyross, the public housing estate on the far edge of town, brilliantly placed out of sight. A writer in the *Limerick Leader* observed that as Ireland's economy was getting better, conditions in Moyross—particularly the violence—seemed to grow worse. Was it because of frustration among the poor, who felt themselves being left behind? The women of LAW had developed informants there who would call the hotline if they saw an animal being abused or neglected. Marion regularly went with Beverly or Anne Kelley, and sometimes with the Garda.

In the space of a few months, LAW got calls for dogs tied to the train tracks, mutilated horses, and a strangled goat—all carried out by children. Once she found a group of young boys, ten or eleven years old, about to light a calf on fire. She had been watching this particular group of boys and suspected they were responsible for the death of a pig—stabbed twenty-seven times—the previous week. She looked each child in the eye and asked if he'd done it.

The confessions came forth readily. Nobody in the gang seemed to feel ashamed of his actions, as though the torture had not mattered. Marion later recounted the conversation to the *Limerick Leader*:

"One of them said to me, 'Well, I was there, missus, and I only stabbed the pig twice.' Some of them had stabbed the pig five times."

She didn't feel the need to mention to her family when she was going to Moyross. They'd had some close calls, finding themselves at least twice amid gunfire and another time far too close to a knife fight. When she went in after dark, Marion and the LAW women wore green vests with the words "Limerick Animal Welfare" in big letters so that people would know why they were there and hopefully wouldn't shoot them.

As though eccentric cat ladies might actually do this work! The stereotypes of animal welfare were so condescending. Most people had no idea of the cruelty that went on in their very midst at any given moment. But people like Marion knew. On a regular basis, she and her partners saw the strong crush the weak: humans on animals, adults on children, and all kinds of people on one another. She constructed theories to make some sense of things, but none of them were satisfactory. So they lived with an intimate knowledge of a kind of violence that was inexplicable and would never end. It just was. They existed with it, lived under it, and, in their tiny pathetic way, fought back as best as they could.

She never could have done it without John. When she had to go to Dublin for the national meetings, he made sure she was up on time and had the car ready to drive her to the early train. "Do you have your watch? Do you have your glasses? Do you have your papers?" He took care of things at home. Though he asked her to slow down, he never asked her to stop.

That man has a halo around his head.

At the end of 1996, her final term as chairperson ended. She was elected president, an honorary title, which meant she no longer managed the organization's day-to-day affairs. In some ways, it was better.

"You're always going to Dublin," said Beverly. "I need you here."

And Marion repeated it: "A rising tide lifts all boats."

12
—
UNDERCOVER

1997–2001

It might have been easy to underestimate Finbarr Heslin back then. With his fresh young face and fresh new degree from the University College Dublin School of Veterinary Medicine, he had only a few years of practice under his belt, along with a youthful determination to keep his integrity. (He had been the kind of kid who at six or seven years old knew he wanted to be a vet.) He had quite recently joined the ISPCA as an advisor and inspector, agreeing to do so under the strict condition that he be kept as far away as possible from the crazy, emotional animal people. As an animal health practitioner, he believed in reason and scientific objectivity, not ideology. He told Ciaran O'Donovan that he would give his professional opinion and if anyone tried to get him to alter a report or testimony, he'd be on his way. O'Donovan was fine with that. Heslin's first gig was to inspect the dog pounds run by the local authorities.

Marion met him at an ISPCA meeting in Dublin. When she realized who he was—the new independent vet hired by O'Donovan—she chatted him up at the hotel bar. It didn't take long for her to steer the conversation toward her two-year search for a veterinarian willing to do a greyhound investigation.

"Dr. Heslin, are you aware of the situation in Spain?"

"I've read a little. But not terribly much."

It was as though he'd pushed the Play button. Marion began on the overbreeding and the missing dogs and then moved on to auctions and the lorries and the government funding of the . . .

"Sure, I'll go with you."

"Excuse me?" Was he serious? Or just trying to get her to stop?

"I'll go with you."

Yes, he seemed to be quite serious.

For added professionalism, Marion also wanted someone from the Royal Society in England, which is why she reached out to Mike Butcher, an ex-cop and chief inspector with the Special Operations Unit of the RSPCA. He'd built a legendary career infiltrating gangster organizations that ran dogfighting rings (and usually drugs and guns as well). A while back, Butcher had had a case in Ireland. A member of the IRA was running a huge dogfight in Dublin, involving as many as a hundred people, which brought together IRA men and their sworn enemies, unionists loyal to Britain. They put their dogs to fight each other in the ring. The police refused to raid and catch them in the act because there would be an instant gunfight. Instead, Butcher had to build a case based on photographs and other evidence. The ISPCA had lent a hand, and a successful prosecution followed. That's why, when Marion Fitzgibbon called him for help, he saw it as a chance to return the favor. He said he'd be happy to go to Spain.

O'Donovan agreed to go too, so as to contribute the added credibility of the ISPCA CEO's office. Louise Coleman connected Marion with her best greyhound people in Spain—a Spanish vet named Alberto Sorde and his wife, Anna Clements. Sorde and Clements had been working on the issue with Spanish animal welfare groups. (Later they would found their own organization, SOS Galgos—Spanish for "greyhound.") They were eager to help, and Clements said she'd be the interpreter. Now they were ready, a team of five.

They met at a hotel in Barcelona. It was October 1999, a lovely bright autumnal day. They wasted no time in getting started, and set off in a rental car for Canódromo Meridiana, the biggest greyhound racetrack in Spain. It was a seedy place, only half filled with sorry-looking gamblers and retired men. They waited in the lobby for the track manager, who had been told of Marion's visit. Finally a tanned, middle-aged man appeared, his face visibly shifting from friendly to uncomfortable as he took in the sight of the whole team.

Marion introduced them all, but when she was done, he made no attempt to hide what had quickly become outright hostility.

"Ms. Fitzgibbon, this is *not* what we discussed. The invitation was for the president of the ISPCA only, not a delegation of people. I'm sorry, but your tour is canceled. I cannot allow you to go to the kennels or behind the scenes. If you want to go to the track along with the public, we won't stop you." Then he turned on his heel and left.

They were stunned and stood for a moment looking at one another. As it became clear that they would have to find another, perhaps not so aboveboard approach, the other four turned to Mike Butcher, who appeared utterly unfazed.

"Now what?" Marion asked him.

"Plan B."

"What's that?"

"Don't worry. It's better than Plan A. You never want them to know you're coming." Then he gave them each an assignment, and they prepared to go forth and conquer.

Clements and Heslin were about the same age, and made a convincing couple as they walked up to the door at Santa Coloma kennels, a set of huge grey barracks in an industrial suburb outside Barcelona.

The kennels were built of corrugated metal, with a row of tiny windows near the ceiling. It was hard not to see the similarity to a prison camp.

They'd practiced their cover story on the way over. They were a boyfriend and girlfriend team, there on behalf of some Irish breeders who wanted to sell their dogs directly to Spanish owners, without the middlemen. They'd come on an exploratory business mission.

Anna Clements smiled when a man opened the door. "You are expecting us, yes?" she asked in Spanish.

The trainer nodded with mild interest.

"May we come in and have a look at your facilities so we know where our dogs would be headed?"

They followed him into a main corridor with rows of rusty cages on either side. Some of the cages looked to be only about eighteen inches wide, yet held two dogs. Others, only about three feet wide, held three dogs. Paws and noses poked out between the bars—if they were lucky enough to have bars. Some were shut behind wooden doors and could see nothing. Heslin observed their dark noses sniffing underneath the door, seeking any information they could find.

"If we sell dogs to you, must we provide vaccination records?" asked Clements.

No, he didn't think so.

Heslin wandered down a row and peered inside the cages, making a mental catalog: eye infections, overgrown nails, rotting teeth, ankles wrapped in bandages, bald itchy skin, pink broken skin from lying on concrete, possibly urine scalding, infected pressure sores. Many of the dogs had knobby pelvic bones poking out because they were so thin. Some looked fine and alert. Others trembled with fear at the sight of him. The intense heat amplified the stench of diarrhea, while an industrial fan ran its motorized hum over the dogs' yips and cries.

"Tell him his dogs look good," said Heslin.

Clements turned to the trainer and translated, then she went in for the kill. "Do you mind if I take some photos so that we can bring these back to our people to show them how good everything looks?"

She shot pictures while interpreting for Heslin and the trainer, who were now hitting it off like colleagues swapping notes. The trainer seemed genuinely interested in improving care. He told Heslin about the drugs he used—caffeine, amphetamines, and sometimes cocaine—to mask the dogs' pain so they could run. He explained that when dogs got too injured or old to run anymore, they were sold for next to nothing to the gypsy track on Mallorca, which would take practically any dog that could stand, or he put them down with an injection of Anectine. He clearly didn't understand that the drug only appeared to produce a peaceful death. In fact, Anectine works by paralyzing the animal piece by piece, but offers no sedation. Death came as the dogs observed their own bodies stop working, including the moment when their lungs froze and suffocation came. Finally, without oxygen, their brain function ceased.

The trainer took them to another barrack, and when Heslin remarked that it was noticeably better equipped (including air conditioning), he said, "This is where we bring inspectors."

"But still no bedding?"

"We only put that out for visits. After they leave, we take it away."

Back at the Meridiana track, Butcher disappeared among the spectators with a tiny video camera concealed in his lapel—taking photos or video was absolutely prohibited—while O'Donovan and Marion wandered about, observing.

Marion had expected the scene to be difficult, but nothing could have prepared her for what she saw. She'd taken in plenty of animal suffering in her life, but she'd never witnessed so many animals in such poor condition at once. Trucks filled with dogs came and went, making the trip from kennels to track and back again, packed with fifty to sixty greyhounds at a time, doubled up and squashed into cages. When a fresh shipment of dogs arrived, the trainers rushed out to retrieve them from the truck and pull them into a trackside holding kennel, where they were shut into boxes behind windowless doors to wait before their races, alongside other dogs waiting to leave. Their noses poked under the doors in a desperate attempt to find out what was going on. Out on the track, the traps flew open and at least two of the six limped so badly that they could barely walk, let alone run. And yet they tried. Later, Marion asked why the trainers had so many dogs, and why they ran them so much, and so hard, not giving them a chance to rest and recover from the inevitable injuries. That's when she learned that in Spain, a dog's condition had little to do with winning. In fact, every dog that participated in a race got an appearance fee. The only requirement was that they ran out of the traps—that was all. Whether they came in first or sixth barely made a difference financially. Winners only got a fraction more, so there was little incentive to keep the dogs in decent condition. To the contrary, the system made for investing as little as possible in the animals.

At the end of the day, Marion's team met back at the track and followed in their rental car behind the transport truck, watching as dogs were tossed into the back of the vehicle, and then tossed out again on the road. The scale was shocking.

In all her years, even in the worst situations, Marion usually found something she could do to help. But now, for the first time, the scale was too enormous. If she could airlift five hundred dogs out of there right at that moment, two weeks later five hundred more Irish greyhounds would come over the Pyrenees to take their places. The government would just keep on funding the Bord na gCon to breed more dogs, with no concern for where they wound up. No sanctuary could be big enough.

After they finished at Meridiana, the investigative team reprised their roles at the other Barcelona dog track, a place called Pabellon, and then they flew to the island of Mallorca, where the track was run by gypsy families, with grandparents and children helping to manage the dogs. In Mallorca, the greyhounds looked the worst of all. These were the cast-offs of the cast-offs—greyhounds traded down from Ireland to Barcelona, and then here, which was the end of the line. They would run until they died. Some collapsed on the track.

At one point, a group of ill-looking greyhounds mustered up the strength to wag their tails and put their noses through the fence, hoping someone might come over and pet them. That killed Marion. For six months, she would have trouble sleeping, unable to get their faces out of her mind. She'd close her eyes and see truckloads and truckloads of greyhounds.

On their last night, Butcher, Clements, Heslin, O'Donovan, and Marion sat at a near-empty bar, still open in the off-season, celebrating. They'd gotten all the access they'd hoped for, and done what they'd come to do. They shared a lighthearted moment and toasted O'Donovan and Marion, who had tried for two years to make this investigation happen. It was a merry night, with much drinking.

But at a certain moment, the conversation got serious. Someone asked how people could use animals and not see their suffering. They all agreed that the trainers and the gypsies had no intention of cruelty; they were part of a system. Heslin told the team that when he and Clements were in the Santa Coloma kennels, he noticed small bunk beds in the corner, a gas camping stove, and a few belongings. Some of the trainers lived there. They needed to earn money.

But still—why couldn't they see the sickness and suffering of the dogs? Was it because of ignorance? Poverty? Or were human beings just so messed up that they only saw what they wanted to see?

That was when Mike Butcher told them about gangsters and their pit bulls.

"They love their dogs," he said. "When we raid them, we take away their drugs, their weapons, their money—and they say okay, because they expect that, and they don't fight us. But when we say, 'We're going to take away your dog,' they say, 'No you're not,' and throw themselves at the police and fight. It's a bloke thing. A man thing. They have this real connection. They love the dogs. They have a genuine respect for a dog that will fight for them. I've seen videos where they stand up and cheer when their dog has two front legs broken. That's because what's important isn't which dog is strongest. In the dogfighting world, it's about heart and gameness. They love the dogs, even if they're hurt. They call it respect, and loving the sport. And that's not made up. Whether we like it or not, there is a genuine bond between the dogs and the men. The dogs get hurt and go back and do it again. If a dog runs away from the ring out of fear, it's called a cur and gets killed. But when a dog has game and heart, the owner will do all he can to keep it alive, stay up with it all night, and fight the police to keep it. When we finally take them away, they accuse us of cruelty. They call us animal killers and murderers because they know we're going to kill the dogs. We have to put the dogs down because they've been trained to kill."

When they returned to Ireland, Heslin quickly submitted a twelve-page report to the ISPCA. The entire document was written from the veterinarian's objective perspective, and it went over the conditions point by point. He described a litany of neglect, abuse, sickness, and cruelty, noting that, based on positive prior reports from Irish and other officials, he was amazed to find conditions as bad as they were. Because his team arrived unannounced and undercover, "we were able to view for ourselves the unsanitized version of the industry." He called for a review and overhaul of the entire system. For assurance, Heslin noted, "The people we were in contact with have a deep feeling about this problem and are not radical extremists with other hidden agendas."

Butcher made Marion a DVD of the video footage he'd captured.

She couldn't believe the power of a tiny camera to dispel the lies and cover-ups. It was all there, brought into the light of day.

The ISPCA called a press conference in Dublin and the media took serious interest. Irish television dedicated a program to the abuses of the greyhound industry and filmed scenes at the Limerick racetrack. Many newspapers ran stories, and the video and report were circulated throughout Europe and America. Even *Der Spiegel*—one of the biggest news magazines in Germany—sent a team to do a major story on the "Slave Market of the Sprinters."

Finally, the Bord na gCon announced that it was going to set up funds for a retired greyhound trust, just as other countries had done long before. It offered a 50,000-pound trust for retired racers.

"It's a pittance," said Marion in the *Irish Times*, "compared to what the Bord na gCon is spending on tracks and facilities." She pointed out that the Bord had earned 10.6 million pounds alone for the sale of a property that year.

Word was that many Irish dogmen were sickened by the whole thing. They'd had no idea that the Spanish system used the dogs as slot machines, and that performance was so unimportant that the dogs needed only to be healthy enough to get out of the traps. Of course, some brushed it off and continued business as usual, but many vowed never to send a dog abroad again.

Marion had postcards made with a photo of a wretched greyhound in a rusty cage, and the caption "Could this be your greyhound?" On the back was a list of conditions they'd seen and a warning: "Don't sell your greyhound to Spanish agents." She put the postcards on the windshield of every car in the parking lot on auction days. She put them on the seats where the auctions took place.

It came as a shock when they got word eighteen months later that the Pabellon and Mallorca tracks were shutting down. Marion wanted

Greyhounds in Spain. (Courtesy John Mottern)

to rejoice, but she couldn't. What would happen to those dogs? Sure enough, they got word that some had been turned loose on the streets, others sold off to hunters.

In the spring of 1999, Louise Coleman, Anne Finch, Marion Fitzgibbon, Marion Webb, and Finbarr Heslin met up in Mallorca, where they worked alongside Anna Clements, her husband, Alberto Sorde, and representatives of other Spanish animal charities to gather all the released greyhounds into a holding area. Then they went to the Pabellon in Barcelona. They managed to get hold of four hundred greyhounds in total, almost all with Irish tattoos. Sorde and Heslin checked and vaccinated each one. They recorded tattoos and health conditions, then signed off on each dog's medical papers after blood tests ensured they were free of parasites.

Managing four hundred dogs was a nightmare. They had a temporary site on a farm next to a motorway, and the day before Marion arrived from Ireland, one of the greyhounds had run out and been killed by a car. They still hadn't had time to dispose of him. Marion kneeled beside his broken body and cried, apologizing for not having been able to save him.

They needed a place safer for the dogs in which to work. That's when Johanna Wothke showed up with her satchel of cash. From Marion's point of view, she was a miracle worker. Johanna arranged for a temporary kennel north of Barcelona to process the dogs. It was amazing how quickly they pulled the site together. ("Money walks, bullshit talks," Marion muttered to herself.) Then they began the outreach. The international animal welfare networks lit up and buzzed. Greyhounds were sent to welfare agencies—in Germany, England, France, Italy, Belgium, and the United States. The groups vowed to find each and every dog a good home. Greyhound Friends of North Carolina brought in ten dogs. When they arrived, a small group gave them a heroes' welcome at the airport, and national media came to cover it. The story of rescued greyhounds went out on national televisions shows and was printed in East Coast newspapers. It was a defining moment: an international movement was firmly grounded. All of the greyhound welfare people were connected from this moment forward and would work together again in the future. Suddenly, they seemed strong, and Marion felt more hopeful than she had in years.

If only it weren't for one thing . . .

⁓

SOMETHING HAD gone wrong with Beverly. She seemed distant and especially weary.

True, she was over sixty now, but a sixty-year-old Beverly had more energy than most forty-year-olds. In addition to caring for thirty-five dogs herself, Beverly and Semon still ran Fedamore House Stud. She could barely leave home because of all the animal care. Guests stayed at Fedamore House, and they needed meals and towels in the warming drawer, and much else too. She had one household helper, which wasn't enough. She also had to attend the hunt balls at Semon's side (where she could imagine people wondered at his crazy wife who kept stray dogs in her stable—but she just paid no attention).

Yes, weary perhaps, but Marion knew there was something more. They still worked together, and called each other about the dogs. But Beverly was suddenly cool, all business. She got off the phone quickly.

Meanwhile, Ireland was transforming around them. The new millennium had arrived, and their little island was the fastest-growing economy in Europe. The Irish miracle had taken place. Multinational tech companies were booming in Ireland and, for the first time in history, workers were migrating to the country in search of work instead of away from it. Dublin was suddenly filled with international people. The real estate market had gone wild. Everywhere you looked, new housing developments and shopping malls were going up. For a fleeting moment, it seemed the Irish were no longer poor. With all the free-flowing cash, Marion was able to get a great lease on a storefront in downtown Limerick. LAW established a thrift shop, from which all proceeds went to animal care. Almost immediately they started to make a small profit.

The economic boom meant that donations to LAW were up, and Marion, who was always looking for more space to keep more animals, started talking about using LAW funds to build kennels at the homes of some willing supporters and volunteers.

It took a long time for Marion to realize that this might be rubbing Beverly the wrong way. Evidently, the strengthening Irish pound had caused some financial stress to Beverly and Semon. When they first arrived, in the Eighties, the weak Irish pound had given them a competitive advantage in everything, including exporting horses back to the American market. But now everything had changed, and Beverly was complaining about the exchange rates and the skyrocketing costs of living in Ireland. Marion always assumed they were fine. Everything had always looked so idyllic at Fedamore House. Perhaps she hadn't been paying enough attention.

Over nearly two decades, Beverly had sunk thousands of dollars into the animals, and she'd never taken a cent from the LAW coffers. She'd never wanted to. But now, she and Semon were getting older. Their money was going half as far. Beverly just kept giving and giving to the dogs: money, energy, and time.

It's hard to imagine that a friendship like theirs could break apart so suddenly and completely. But that's what happened. Beverly stopped taking Marion's calls. No matter how hard Marion tried to speak with her, Beverly refused.

During their eighteen years of working shoulder to shoulder, talking multiple times a day, and moving from one animal emergency to the next, Marion had witnessed Beverly's ability to shut people out forever. It was all part of the same fierce personality: this was a woman who would go up to strangers and yell at them if they were pushing their animal too hard, who got out of bed at 3 a.m. to get a horse from a ditch, who refused ever to speak to the chief veterinary surgeon of Ireland again because he hadn't the balls to take a stand against the slaughter of dogs with a bolt gun at the pounds. This was Beverly. And Marion had never expected to be on the receiving end. She didn't know what to do. Months went by with silence.

It was Rosie who called to tell her the news.

Beverly and Semon were leaving Ireland and going back to the States. They'd sold Fedamore House. The stables and house were all empty. Beverly had been in a frenzy for a month, packing up the rooms and finding homes for all the animals.

"Semon has already gone ahead to the States," Rosie said. "Beverly's alone at the airport now."

Marion paused for only a moment, then got into her car.

In the main waiting area at Shannon International, Marion spotted Beverly sitting alone, quietly, with two dog crates at her feet. When she saw Marion, they looked at each other and it all melted away. Whatever problem had been between them was suddenly gone. It was just Beverly and Marion, two warriors and friends.

They acted like they'd just seen each other yesterday and simply began talking about the animals, of course. Beverly told Marion where the last dogs and horses at Fedamore had gone.

"I killed myself to find them all homes," she said.

Marion believed her and said she understood.

Beverly's gate was called then. Her baggage was already checked, and Marion picked up one of the dog crates and carried it to the gate. They hugged and said goodbye. There was no need to say they would stay in touch. No need to say that they didn't know if or when they'd see each other again.

And then Beverly was gone.

PART III

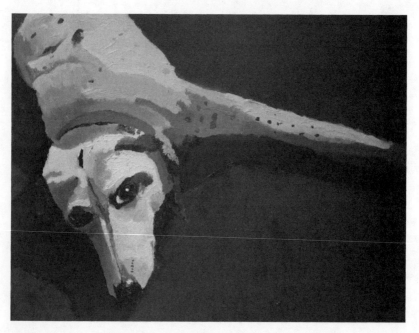

The Lily Series, No. 2, by Simon Schaffner, oil on canvas. (Author's collection)

13
—
DOMINION

"Lily, tell me," I said one morning when we were walking to the park, "what do I owe you?"

She declined to answer, which was typical. The information from her nose was far more fascinating, as she worked over every blade of grass, leaf, and bit of dirt.

Since meeting Marion, questions like these were increasingly on my mind. What was fair to the animal?

Years ago, before we got Lily, I took my sons to Florida to visit my sister. She designed a busy itinerary of Florida adventures with her nephews in mind. One afternoon, on the way back from St. Augustine, she surprised us by pulling into a place called Marineland, just off the highway by the ocean.

It was some kind of aquarium amusement park, but it gave off an odd feeling. It was too easy to get a parking spot. The line to get in was short. We followed my sister through the entry gates toward a large blue pool, center stage, surrounded by bleachers. A sparse crowd of vacationing families sat patiently waiting, squinting in the Florida glare, ready for the show.

Along the way, we learned that we'd entered a landmark in the history of animal entertainment. The place had first opened in 1938 as Marine Studios. It was originally designed as an outpost of Hollywood, where underwater scenes could be shot in a pool filled with amazing sea creatures. Four men with ties to Hollywood had come up with the idea. Three of them—W. Douglas Burden, C. V. Vanderbilt Whitney, and Sherman Pratt—were scions of wealthy Gilded Age families, while the fourth was a cameraman, Ilya Tolstoy, grandson of the Russian novelist Leo Tolstoy.

What they shared was an old style of conservationism, reminiscent of Teddy Roosevelt. They loved nature passionately and wanted to protect it from the encroachments of capital and markets and civilization. But they also felt a deep need to conquer and possess it. One of them (Vanderbilt Whitney) was a celebrated master of all things equine and owned an extensive stable of horses. The other three were adventurers who went on African safaris to hunt elephants and tigers, or to the Indonesian islands to shoot Komodo dragons, or to the northern reaches of Canada to film caribou. They brought back specimens and treasures to the American Museum of Natural History in New York and decorated their homes with trophies.

On what were then the remote sand dunes of northern Florida, these four men built two large aquarium tanks at the edge of the ocean and, in a feat of engineering, devised a system that pumped millions of gallons of fresh ocean water into these tanks each day. Nothing like Marineland had ever been built before. Cetaceans, such as dolphins and whales, were particularly mysterious, and, up until that point, most attempts to capture and hold them up wound up killing them.

When everything was ready, Tolstoy set out on a boat with tranquilizers and nets. He captured porpoises, manta rays, sea turtles, sharks, coral reef, and other specimens to create the world's first "oceanarium," a simulation of the real undersea world.

Two hundred observatory portholes built along the perimeter gave extraordinary views into the underwater world. It was fascinating just to watch, which is why someone thought of selling tickets to the public. On the first day, thousands of people arrived to look into the portholes and see the porpoises and sharks and iridescent fish up close, as they'd never been seen before. They watched as keepers wearing diving helmets fed the fish. For a small fee, an ordinary person could glimpse the mysterious and unknown.

Ten years later, the founders went to the next level. What if they could take the on-site entertainment idea further and train the porpoises to perform tricks? After all, the circus had trained seals. The problem was that no one knew whether porpoises were smart enough. They called in a legendary wildlife trainer from Ringling Brothers circus to try his hand at training Flippy, a bottlenose dolphin, the friendliest one they had.

Flippy quickly figured out what his trainer wanted him to do. Knowing that a bucket of fish awaited, he eagerly leapt through hoops, pulled a surfboard with a woman and a dog on it, jumped hurdles, played fetch, shot hoops, and rang bells. (Since then, study after study has revealed the high intelligence of dolphins, who have large brains, ingenious problem-solving abilities, self-awareness, and a range of basic emotions including something that appears to be empathy.) On the first day, between twenty and thirty thousand people came to see "the world's first educated porpoise" perform in the world's first ever dolphin show. Flippy became a national celebrity and inspired the long-running television series about a boy and his dolphin named Flipper.

Huge crowds kept coming for two decades, until the early 1970s, when Disney World and Sea World opened their doors, offering even bigger and more dramatic spectacles. Marineland began its long downward slide.

Now, here we were in the early 2000s, my sister and her husband leading my younger son up into the stands, while Gabriel and I lagged behind. I looked down to see what the trouble was and discovered that Gabriel had come to a complete halt and was emphatically shaking his head no.

Confused, I looked up ahead and saw what he saw.

In the big blue pool, several dolphins were racing madly from one side to the other. The trainers stood on the sidelines getting ready. Through the glass walls, we could see the dolphins missiling toward us in the blurry water, larger than life. When they reached the wall, they curved their sleek grey bodies and, in a single smooth burst of force, shot off in the other direction. Then they turned again. For a fleeting moment, a wave of childlike awe rose in my chest. They seemed magical.

"I'm not going in there," he said.

"Why not?" My tone was matter-of-fact, as I tried to casually move him forward. No luck. His legs were tree trunks, tap-rooted into the ground, and his big dark eyes became red-rimmed, welling up with not-quite tears mixed with fury.

"I'm not going!"

A prickle of annoyance went down my back. *Really?* said my inner voice. *Really??* Why couldn't he just go along?

Deep down, I knew that dolphins were magnificent wild creatures who swam forty miles a day, possessed high intelligence and had language, complex relationships, and inner lives. I had temporarily shut off that switch in my brain so that I could go along with a fun family day. Gabriel could not. Why is it so easy for most of us to be in the presence of animals and not to see them? Why was it not possible for him?

"It's a prison! It's a prison!"

A tantrum was coming, so we reversed and went outside the Marineland gates, where we waited quietly for the show to end.

WHERE DID we in the Western world get the idea that human beings are superior to all other creatures? Certainly the ancient Greeks get a great deal of credit, and in particular Aristotle, the giant of Western philosophy, who believed that logic and reason ruled the universe. Only man possessed a rational mind, and this made him supreme. Animals lacked reason and therefore were inferior.

> *Plants exist for the sake of animals, and brute beasts for the sake of man—domestic animals for his use and food, wild ones for food and other accessories of life, such as clothing and various tools. Since nature makes nothing purposeless or in vain, it is undeniably true that she has made all the animals for the sake of man.*

Aristotle envisioned the universe as a Great Chain of Being, built on a vertical hierarchy of power. Humans were in the top slot, followed by land mammals, then dolphins, reptiles, birds, amphibians, and fish. At the bottom were rock and earth.

Within this hierarchy, other hierarchies existed. In the human category, women ranked below men because, although they possessed the ability to reason, they lacked authority. Slaves may have had certain faculties and abilities, but by nature they were inferior to women. Aristotle had no problem with slavery, which he saw as the natural order of things. Some people were simply born with inferior minds, so it made logical sense that they would be the property of more rational men who would tell them what to do.

In sum, men ruled women, slaves, animals, land, and sea. A rational mind could see these immutable truths of nature. And yet, why couldn't Aristotle's brilliant mind see his own inherent self-interest in proclaiming the perfection of man?

The Dominican monk St. Thomas Aquinas (1225–74) was a great admirer of Aristotle. In his 3,500-page *Summa Theologica*, he drew heavily on Aristotle's ideas and laid the foundation of Catholicism for centuries to come. Because the Greeks had been pagans, some revision was necessary. In Aquinas's version, the Great Chain of Being was revised as *Scala Naturae*, which was more or less the same except for the addition of a couple of layers at the top: God and the angels at the apex, reigning over man. God was rational and the author of everything. He had made man rational, giving him free will to choose sin or obedience to faith.

Aquinas kept the part about men ruling over women, slaves, animals, mammals, fish, earth, and sea. And he explicitly explained that men should not worry about killing or causing suffering to animals because they had no souls and were as dumb as trees. We wouldn't feel bad about cutting down trees, would we?

In sum, it was St. Thomas Aquinas who allowed the guilt-free usage of animals. "Charity" does not extend to "irrational creatures," he wrote. And "humans have no fellowship with animals."

This was why Sister Theresa Concepta wouldn't let my sister take her two dogs on the last spaceship away from earth. It was because of Aquinas and Aristotle that we were not allowed to be friends with animals, and we certainly were not supposed to love them.

⁓

AT THE park, the Golden Age of Dogdom was on full display. Lily and I joined the usual group of people and dogs who regularly walked together on a loop around the green. One, two, three times made a mile. I took my role with the other dog parents. I did it for Lily because I believed she needed to be with other dogs.

A play bow here, a play bow there. Over time, she became comfortable enough with a core group: Boomer (a shepherd mutt) and Charlie (a little white fluff who was really a ferocious giant), Delilah (a majestic Rhodesian ridgeback), Bella (a retriever mix puppy), and Pooch (a dachshund mutt), who had come up from the South on a rescue truck. ("Down there, shelters still gas stray dogs"—grave nods, because in Dogdom we've all heard of these atrocities.)

"Darius! Come here this instant," called one of the dog moms. "Darius! You cannot go to the pond and eat bird poop. You'll get a sick stomach. Just like the last time! Remember?"

The large black dog ignored her and barreled ahead, tongue to the ground, slurping up green goose shit. The woman threw up her arms and performed a comic gesture of exasperation. What could she do with the wild-child dog?

I struggled not to roll my eyes.

In Dogdom, I was sometimes judgmental, which I knew was wrong. And, really, I was worried. Was I becoming one of them?

For a long time, I worked for a children's mental health center in New York City, where I wrote about children who were in serious trouble. These were kids who were unlucky to have been born poor or to have had horrible things happen to them. They'd been abandoned or abused, poorly educated by crummy schools. Some were in foster care. Many had loving families who were overwhelmed and alone, barely hanging on by a thread.

During those years, I went to remote parts of the city to interview the children, teens, parents, and therapists. It was like going to another country, especially in the neighborhoods where poverty had beaten down generations. As I absorbed stories and struggled to retell them, I often reused a particular sentence that I hoped would galvanize donations. "All children have the right to safe and loving homes." Who wouldn't agree with that? And yet each time I wrote it I wondered if it was bullshit. If, in reality, neither the cosmos nor the law delivered any such thing, how could a safe and loving home be a right?

When we speak of rights—animal or human—are we really just expressing a wish?

∿

"WHAT A good girl. What a good girl!"

If I say it too much and, God forbid, use an overly sweet mama-type voice, my younger son will get on me.

"She is a *dog*, Mom. A *dog*."

He hates when I make a fuss over Lily and tells me that by treating her as a child, I am denying her true nature. That nature is animal. To take it away is an insult to her dignity.

Animals seem to be embedded in the human imagination at birth. Children respect them and crave a connection to them, but as life goes on, we see them less and less as real beings. They become things we must use.

Even at age ten going on eleven—well beyond the magical fantasies of early childhood—my soon-to-be-an-adolescent son number two lamented, "Of all the things I could have been, I was born the most boring thing."

"What do you mean?"

"Human! I was born human! Humans are boring!"

When I asked him to explain, he became impatient.

"Come on! Birds can fly. *They can get up off the ground*."

Then, thinking it through, he added, "Okay, so if you're an animal, you give up some years. But who cares? You really don't need eighty or seventy-five years, do you? I'd exchange all those years for a pair of wings and a chance to live in the wilderness. We are chained to the ground. It's so boring. We walk. We eat. We sleep. We think. Sure we can run. But not in the same way a wolf can. Wolves have incredible speed. They're interesting. They work together to take down their prey. Five wolves could take down a moose because they work together.

"They can't speak. So they can't argue. They don't argue!"

Naturally, I did not dare to disagree.

~

WHEN I couldn't make it to the park in the morning, I went in the evening and walked Lily over to the little island on the pond, pulling the gate shut. A cluster of geese sensed our presence and nervously waddled en masse toward the water's edge. But not fast enough. Lily sprang, ears perked, muscles flexed, and gave her most growling kind of low bark. Lily the beast. Lily the killer. A flapping clatter of wings. Squawks of alarm. Sudden emergency liftoff. The birds landed on the water just out of her reach. Lily gave a couple of extra barks and leaps for good measure. The encounter clearly gave her an energy boost. She ran a few sprints, sniffed some more, and then let me know she was done.

One evening during this routine, I spotted two black-and-white streaks at the periphery of my vision. Energy in motion, circling around the park. Could it be a double suspension gallop? Yes, it was. They looked about Lily's size and shape and color, except with long feathery hair. Lily saw them too and leapt toward the gate. When the hounds came round the circle in our direction, one of them caught sight of Lily on the island and ran toward her. Soon they were nose to nose through the iron bars, ears relaxed, tails wagging. Lily acted as though she already knew the other dog, and the other dog did the same. Windhounds, the owner explained, a mix of greyhound and border collie. The second arrived, and all three dogs enthusiastically wagged with recognition as if to say, "Yes, we're all sight hounds."

I broke my vow of safety that day and let her loose. Within a moment, all three were gone. Lily galloped in perfect sync with the windhounds, making a high-speed blur of flexing spines and pumping legs and lots of air above the ground. After about ten minutes, the other owner called his dogs and they came running. Soon they got in the car and were gone. Lily trotted to my side panting with tongue and teeth showing, blinking, her face looking relaxed.

"Lily, tell me. What do I owe you?"

That time, I heard her answer. She said, "To run with the windhounds."

Marion at Greyhounds Reach the Beach, an annual event at Dewey Beach, Delaware. (Courtesy Marion Fitzgibbon)

14

—

AND THE SHEEP CAME TOO

2008

Marion picked me up at Shannon Airport, wearing an "Adopt a Greyhound" sweatshirt and track pants. A cellphone hung around her neck on a long rope, something like a necklace. Despite the outfit, she still somehow looked prim and neat, with her short blond hair in place and little pearl earrings. She gave me a hug for having just crossed an ocean and led me to the parking lot. Her car was filled to the brim with a jumble of lamps and chairs and other household goods headed for the Limerick Animal Welfare charity shop. A King Charles spaniel jumped onto my lap.

"Oh, that's Harley. Unfortunately, he's not much for brains, you know. He came from a puppy mill. They overbreed them to get this brown and black color."

I'd come to Ireland because my friend Elizabeth was here and had invited me to stay at her cottage. I took her up on it because I'd never been, but also because I was curious about Lily's gypsy greyhound lineage, and I was curious about Marion and her band of animal rescuers—though probably more for their bad-ass rule-breaking than their good deeds. As a writer, I suspected there might be a story.

We passed the Shannon River, rushing its way toward the Atlantic. Above, the clouds churned grey and white. On that car ride, Marion and I picked up the conversation we'd begun in her son's New Jersey kitchen eighteen months earlier. We would continue speaking, on and off, for many years to come.

I enjoyed listening to her brogue sing its way down one forest path after the next, though she could go quite far afield. I quickly learned that if I waited long enough, she would loop back to the main road—eventually—at which point she might take a breath, but not always. After fifteen minutes of light conversation, she got to talking to me about an abandoned sheep that had come into the care of LAW, which they'd named Shirley.

"Oh, I was so upset about this sheep. It's been driving me crazy."

She explained that Shirley was in such terrible condition that when they cleaned up her filthy, matted wool, they found many open wounds. Her skin was crawling with maggots. All they could do was feed her and treat her kindly and then call the vet to put her down.

"No creature should have to die that way. I've been asking the Department of Agriculture about her. And people are saying, 'Oh no. Now she's going to get started on sheep, is she?'"

～

WHEN BEVERLY went back to the States in 2001, Marion took it very hard. Not only had she lost a friend, she'd also lost Fedamore House. She couldn't drive by there. Couldn't look. She decided that she couldn't let that happen to her again.

Fedamore was gone. Avalon belonged to Pro Animale. Suddenly it all became clear: Limerick Animal Welfare needed a place of its own.

The idea took root, and nothing was going to stop her. Not the cancer (which returned after ten years) and the mastectomy that followed. Not the national work, where she'd already given so much.

In fact, she made a decision about the ISPCA. The tide had changed there, along with a series of chairpeople who followed after Marion. They had little interest in continuing her battles with the Bord na gCon, the hunters, or the veterinarians' union. Nor were they inclined to bring together the member societies in a great national force. One of the subsequent chairpersons restructured the ISPCA as a more professional nonprofit corporation, with a board of directors that held meetings behind closed doors, as was usual for professional nonprofits. From that point forward, the local SPCAs from all around Ireland only came once a year for the annual general meeting. In this new structure, the honorary president's position ceased to exist. And though Marion probably could have served as a board member, she wished them well and retired from national leadership. It was time to focus her energy back home with Limerick Animal Welfare.

Luckily, there was a little money stashed away.

Back in the early 1990s a friend handed Marion an envelope, saying that it was a gift and she wished to remain anonymous. Later, when she opened the envelope, she nearly fainted. It was a check for 20,000 pounds. The women of LAW were thrilled. Imagine all the food and vet bills it would pay for!

But after the initial thrill settled, they all agreed that since they'd never in a million years expected to receive this 20,000 pounds, they should put it aside and forget about it. Save it for the future, add what they could, and maybe it would really add up someday.

Bit by bit they put in small amounts, mostly from their street and church gate collections. Ten years later, the sum had grown to 95,000 pounds (soon to be converted to about 120,000 euro).

In 2003, Marion heard about a big piece of land going up for sale at the edge of County Limerick. She went to have a look and found the setting to be beautiful and more perfect for their needs than they could have hoped—twenty-five acres and far enough from people so the animals wouldn't bother anyone. The only problem was that they were almost 100,000 euro short.

They put out a call to their most loyal supporters. A longtime friend of LAW stepped forward and offered Marion an interest-free loan to close the gap. This brought the twenty-five acres within reach. The night before the auction, Marion picked up Anne Dynan and the two of them drove out to the land with a small shovel and two statues of St. Joseph. It was an old superstition that St. Joseph brought luck when it came to real estate matters. They buried the statues on the land and said a prayer.

The next day, they bid and won the property for 212,000 euro.

The women were amazed with themselves, and amazed by Marion's boldness in doing such a thing. To take on so much debt, even without interest, required courage. They worked with an architect to design a grand vision: one large central building that would be the gold standard of animal welfare in Ireland, plus several auxiliary buildings to serve as isolation units for sick animals.

After the purchase they were broke again. Five years of uphill struggle followed. They had no choice but to build the project in phases. The most important thing was to start construction. This would be Phase I.

They built the small auxiliary buildings, which had a lower price tag. After three decades of jostling animals among dozens of foster homes and rented kennels, Marion and the women of Limerick Animal Welfare opened an animal sanctuary. They called it the Field of Dreams. In May 2008 they had an official ribbon-cutting. Hundreds of people came for the festivities. There was a craft show, food, games, tours, and dog agility events. A priest arrived wearing white robes to bless the animals and the facility, and Marion gave a joyful speech in which she recalled how a handful of women had started the whole thing on the streets of Limerick, how they'd started with practically nothing. She thanked dozens of people, while the dogs barked over her voice. She reminded the crowd that this was just Phase I. It had cost 500,000 euro, which had been donated by the generous people of Limerick. How they would ever raise more money to go on to the much bigger Phase II was a mystery. But at that moment, anything seemed possible. For once, they had a day of pure and unfettered jubilation.

⌒

THE FIELD of Dreams was about an hour away from the airport. It was late 2008, a few months after the grand opening, and Marion was taking me there to see it now.

The town of Kilfinane looked like it could have come from a picture book of charming Irish villages. Rows of buildings lined the Main Street, each tinted a different pastel hue of blue, orange, green, or yellow, stark against the treeless sky. Pubs, butchers, betting shops, and restaurants, one after the next, in an unbroken façade. Beyond the town lay the forested Ballyhoura Hills.

Marion turned her car up a slight hill onto a country road. We drove past woods and fields until we came to a clearing and turned into a gravel parking lot. A bright sign greeted us with the words "Limerick Animal Welfare Sanctuary."

I followed Marion toward the sound of barking and yipping. Up ahead was a cluster of animal enclosures. The biggest was a new-looking rectangular building, about a hundred feet long, with at least a dozen doors on each side—clearly the dog kennels, which let out to a series of separate grassy paddocks accommodating small groups. My heart sank as I took in the sight of eight-foot-tall fencing enclosing the whole thing, but as I got closer to the raucous barking and leaping, I began to grasp the practicalities of containing so many dogs.

Inside, the dog kennels were immaculate and bright. Volunteers were taking dogs on leads for walks about the countryside. People seemed happy around the dogs, smiling and saying hello.

"The main building isn't even started yet," said Marion. When I asked how much more she needed, she said, "1.5 million euro."

And the total cost?

"When we're all done, this will have been a little over 2 million euro for the whole project."

I was silent while I took this in, then followed her along. We passed paddocks one, two, three, and four. Then we came to a paddock where lurchers and greyhounds mixed with other dogs.

"When we bring people here, it's a chance to educate them. Most people still think that greyhounds are killers, you know. You're far more likely to get bit by a Jack Russell. But when they can come and see for themselves that a greyhound is just fine in the pen with other dogs, and that children are there petting them, they start to understand."

Anne Kelley walked by with a brindle greyhound. I bent down and petted her. She had Lily's face.

"The Irish government just keeps on investing in the dogs and breeding more and more. We're producing more than twenty-five thousand pups per year. The government props up the industry. The business could never stand on its own."

I checked that later, and she was right. At the turn of the new millennium, the Irish government radically stepped up the money it invested in the Bord na gCon, by establishing a Horse and Greyhound Racing Fund that guaranteed a growing subsidy to the business. With the influx of government cash, the Bord refurbished many of the stadiums with shiny bars and restaurants that would bring out a new generation for a night at the races.

Most distressing of all to Marion was that they'd gotten approval and loans and subsidies for a brand new stadium in Limerick, to be built from the ground up. A Taj Mahal of the sport. "It's a twenty-million new facility," she said with horror, guiding me along, beyond the dog paddocks, where several enclosures marked different pastures.

We stopped in front of two black potbellied pigs, named Wayne and Colleen. They were busy, noses to the ground, their bodies short and dense. They were not terribly big, but my fear of animals kicked in and a wave of nervousness put me on edge. I could see Marion smiling with affection.

"They were some of the first animals here," she said. "A man brought them to us when they were only a couple of months old. He'd found them in a ditch. They were very small—the size of small terriers."

We came to the cattery, which held forty cats. Did I know about feline AIDS? Marion asked. Oh, it was a terrible problem. Cats were the hardest because they got terrible diseases.

Next was the rabbit field, an enclosure set up with tunnels and structures so the rabbits could retreat or hide. "You can't believe how many people will bring them to the vet and just never come back to pick them up," she said.

Across a small road, three goats, with horns and bulging eyes, were bent over, grazing. Then we met a very small pony, followed by an ancient donkey who had been locked in a farm shed for years.

"When we came here to the countryside, we were really surprised at the kinds of animals that came our way. We never had these animals in Limerick. But ever since we got here, people call us about sheep and pigs and goats and any animal you can think of. Sometimes we find them at our door. Our policy is, we take whatever comes in."

Marion's vision for the sanctuary was ambitious and clear. She talked about it the way any executive would discuss a large construction project. She spoke with confidence and showed me the plans.

The main building, to be built at the center of the property, would hold two hundred animals. It would include a large dog rehoming unit, a cat rehoming unit, meeting rooms, a classroom, and a reception area. There would be places for people to sit and pet an old dog or cat who might not be up for going on a walk. There would be an on-site veterinary clinic—that was very important to her—and they would finally hire a vet and save so much money. They would have accommodations for overnight staff. Outside, Marion wanted to build a Garden of Remembrance for the pets who had passed on. People could come and bury the ashes of departed animals and know they would always be here.

She told me that it was hard to get people—particularly older people—to even comprehend what she was trying to do. "Spending money on dogs? People think we're mad!

"When they see the bacteria-resistant floors, they say, 'Well, what do you know! It's a hotel for dogs! You making any money, missus?' They still can't believe that there's no money in the animal sanctuary business. Why else would I do it? They think like, maybe we're selling the dogs. 'You wouldn't be into the bodhrans, would you, missus?'" She pronounced it "bough-rawns."

"Bodhrans?" I asked.

She explained that Irish hand drums, or bodhrans, were made with dog skins. Then she paused, and added that the younger people were appreciative.

Marion's project with LAW had come far. They'd begun with bake sales and were now looking at a 2-million-euro project—and they owned this amazing piece of land. But it was also clear that what she'd accomplished was, at the same time, insufficient. I saw that she was obsessed and wouldn't stop until it was done. All she needed was money. Just money.

Neither of us said the obvious, which was that an economic crisis had just arrived. It was the last week of September 2008, and a sense of economic doom had crept over the country. In a few days, Ireland would officially be declared in recession—a mere formality, because everyone already knew it was. Billions would be needed to keep the banks from collapsing, and few people knew yet that the country was bankrupt, that the banks had borrowed a terrifying amount of money they could never repay, that the real estate and construction boom— which had employed a fifth of all workers—was built on debt and lies. All of that would come out in time.

Once people started losing their jobs and homes, a dog sanctuary would be a mighty tough sell—if not impossible.

We finished up at the end of the road, where Marion took me to look out at the pastures and fields beneath the hills. Somehow she got to talking about the Irish language, which the English had forbidden shortly after colonization took hold. She wanted me to know that Irish was a superior language, very lyrical, and expressive of the Celts' deep love of nature. There were poems that simply couldn't be translated; English didn't have the words. We paused, looking out at the valley. There was something about the place that was not just beautiful but also deeply peaceful.

"A lyrical place makes lyrical people," said Marion. "You know, I was thinking the other day of the Bible, and of the people who say animals have no value. But aren't I supposed to be a good shepherd?"

As we walked back, Marion said, "That sheep really drove me crazy. The cost of a sheep is thirty euro. A vet visit is eighty! Animals used to be valuable to people in Ireland. But now sheep have no value!"

She said this last sentence with a certain outrage, then paused. "That's why I got so upset about Shirley the sheep."

*In the U.S., around ten thousand greyhounds were bred in 2015, down from nearly four times as many in 1993. Source: National Greyhound Association. (Photo: Steve Herbert, courtesy New York Times/*Redux*)*

15

—

LAST RACE AT WONDERLAND

2009–10

I t was hard to find, but then I realized that the obscure address was probably intentional.

I drove past the auto body shop and lobster fishing company, over a rickety bridge above the Saugus River, with its brackish smell. I was looking for the North Shore Dog Kennels. It was supposed to be about six miles up the road from the Wonderland track, just outside Boston, but the address brought me to a boat dealer. It made no sense.

"Excuse me. I'm looking for kennels?"

Blank face.

"You know, the place where they keep the greyhounds."

Oh. He nodded with recognition. "Back there," he pointed.

Behind him was a long road and a fleet of yellow school buses parked in a lot. There were kennels back there?

As I got closer, a chain-link fence came into view, with a security guard sitting beside a locked gate. I told the man I had an appointment with Bill O'Donnell. He shook his head resolutely. "Not here."

"I'll wait, then."

"Suit yourself."

I pulled over to the side of the road. In the distance, barking rose into a chorus and then fell silent.

Finally O'Donnell's car arrived, and the security guard opened the gate and gave me a nod that I could follow.

It used to be that anyone could raise dogs in his backyard and bring them to the track to race. Then the rules changed. In the United States' greyhound system, you have to keep your dog at the central kenneling compound where you are racing. Every track has one. This kennel held dogs that raced at Wonderland. Bill O'Donnell owned it. On the phone earlier that week, he had vacillated about whether to talk to me. I told him I wasn't an advocate or an activist, just writing a book. First he said yes, which quickly turned to no. An hour later, my phone rang and he said, "Okay, come on."

I followed his car past the school buses toward a collection of low, grey, barrack-type buildings. For the trainers and handlers who worked here each day, these were simply the kennels where their dogs lived when racing at Wonderland. But to me, it wasn't a stretch to see it as a concentration camp.

In 1993, the U.S. greyhound business had reached its peak.

Over the next ten years, television, magazines, and newspapers produced one exposé after the next of dogs being used and hurt. They ran the gamut from an incident when seventy dogs were burned alive in a kennel fire to profiles of vets whose job was to put down healthy young racers, to 2,600 ex-racing dogs donated to Colorado State University for experimental research. One of the worst revelations featured the excavation of a mass grave in Alabama filled with a thousand greyhound skeletons, evidently shot in the head for ten bucks apiece by a security worker at the Florida tracks. (He died before going to trial.) The National Greyhound Association condemned abuse and violence, regretted errors, and tried to crack down on the few "bad apples," but couldn't get ahead of the negative publicity.

Meanwhile, new kinds of gambling and entertainment posed a growing threat. Before the 1980s, Las Vegas and Atlantic City offered the only major casinos in the U.S. By the end of the decade Indians were opening casinos on reservations all over the country, and by the mid-1990s many state legislatures had approved new lotteries and gaming licenses, realizing that gambling revenue brought in easy money for closing budget gaps. Gambling became a part of American life.

Several states granted gaming licenses to greyhound tracks on the condition that they continued the dog racing, so that track employees kept their jobs. The problem was that dog racing had come to seem old-fashioned. Dogs sprinted in thirty-second heats, followed by boring intervals when the racers slowly paraded off and onto the track, and serious gamblers studied the stats. The dogs couldn't compete with the allure of instant-win slot machines and poker. When I went to the Daytona racetrack in Florida, it took only a moment to see the problem. Dogs ran before empty bleachers while, down the hall, the poker rooms were packed, humming with the sounds of chips being tossed and antes being called. Big money was there. You could feel the heat of it. But in order to have the casino, the track owner had to keep the dogs running.

Still, I'd say that the greyhound women delivered the biggest blow. By the early 2000s, there were about three hundred greyhound adoption groups in the United States, mostly small, female-led organizations. As more greyhounds appeared on leashes at the park or downtown, they transformed in the public imagination from racing machine to real dog. The word "rescue" became associated with the word "greyhound." ("Is she a rescue? Did she run at a track?" People asked me this all the time when they saw Lily, and they seemed disappointed when I had to tell them that no, she'd never raced, and wasn't even a full greyhound.) In the bizarre world of greyhound racing, each side loved the dogs and each side had its heroes.

A significant contingent of women wouldn't go along and work nicely with the industry. These were the unapologetic activists who set out to break it. One of them was the Arizona-based Joan Eidinger, who, in 1992, founded the anti-racing newsletter *Greyhound Network News* when the bodies of more than 140 greyhounds were found in an orchard in Chandler Heights, Arizona. For the next sixteen years she, along with contributor Susan Netboy of the Greyhound Protection League, embarrassed the industry time and again, reporting on deaths, abuses, injuries, and mistakes made at every track in the country.

Nationwide, greyhound track attendance continued to drop, which lowered the betting pool, which lowered profits and accelerated the downward trend. By 2000, racetracks in nine states had shut down for good. And that was just the start.

Nothing could have prepared the dog industry for Christine Dorchak, who was a force of nature like they'd never seen before. In 1992, only a couple of years out of Boston University, she and her dog Kelsey were out walking when they were hit by a train. Dorchak was severely injured and lost her memory. It took her two years to recover. She believed that she and Kelsey had been spared for a reason.

> When I awoke from one of my early comas, the first thing I said was "How's Kelsey?" She was the only thing I could remember and my only anchor in a new and mysterious world of disability and fear . . . It was through my experience with her, and our recovery together, that I found the courage to learn to take care of myself again, and to realize a new focus for my life. Shortly after regaining consciousness, I said if I ever got up from my hospital bed, I would work to help dogs.

In 1995 she went to Wonderland track, took her place outside with other anti-racing warriors, and held up a protest sign. She had found her life's work, based on her near-mystical conviction that she was destined to fight for greyhounds. Along with her partner, Carey Theil, she joined the GREY2K Committee of Massachusetts. Jill Hopfenbeck—the veterinarian who had adopted Demi from Ireland five years earlier—was a leading member. The group collected thousands of signatures to get an "end greyhound racing" motion on the ballot in the 2000 election.

After a bitter fight, the dogmen and track owners won, by a 51 to 49 percent vote. Dorchak, Theil, and Hopfenbeck vowed to rise again. They formed GREY2K USA, a successor organization, dedicated to ending racing not only in Massachusetts but nationwide. For added firepower, Dorchak got a law degree. She also married Theil, a sophisticated communicator and strategist who shared her dedication.

In 2008, GREY2K got a greyhound racing ban on the ballot in Massachusetts once again. This time, they were better prepared and had help from the state's SPCA and the Humane Society. Whereas the prior campaign had painted a national picture and used graphic images, this time they focused almost entirely on data from the state of Massachusetts regarding deaths and injuries. In a major upset, 56 percent of voters called for the business to end. After January 1, 2010, greyhounds would never run in Massachusetts again. And GREY2K turned its attention to a national fight.

⁓

"YOU'VE COME to my funeral," said Bill O'Donnell, shaking my hand. He was a slim, older man, at least seventy, wearing a baseball cap, chinos, and work boots.

"You're the first one who came. None of them would come and look at my kennel. I asked them to come." He paused. "Are you sure you're not an activist?"

I followed O'Donnell into kennel building number seven, which was freshly painted with immaculate floors, everything organized and neat. The walls were lined with two rows of greyhounds lying on shredded newspaper inside metal cages. There were about a hundred of them—females in the top row, males on bottom. When I entered, ears pricked up and dozens of heads turned my way. At least half got up and stood in their crates to watch my entrance. Then they began barking. It was not aggressive in tone, but rather a curious and excited kind of barking to mark the arrival of someone new.

"Do you see dirty conditions?" he asked. "Do you?"

I'd never been around so many animals in a single space. And, of course, these weren't just any animals; they were dogs—the most spectacular dogs I'd ever seen, bright-eyed and alert, sleek-coated, buzzing with energy. I was aghast at the sight of them in cages, yet I was also overwhelmed by their beauty and exhilarated to be near so many of them. In an instant I understood why people on either side would want this life—whether racing the dogs or saving them. O'Donnell led me into the kitchen and proudly showed me the meat, ready and portioned into dozens of bowls. He took a handful of the raw meat in his hand and lifted it to my nose.

"Come on. Smell that. Not rotten at all. They say it's bad meat, but would we feed our animals bad food if they had to run?"

He repeated again that it drove him crazy that he was attacked and never had a chance to show the world how clean his kennel was, how hard he worked to take care of the dogs, and how beautifully conditioned and happy these dogs were.

O'Donnell introduced his trainer, Casey O'Neil, a fit and youthful guy in his late forties with close-cropped hair and a friendly face. "Twenty-eight years," he said when I asked how long he'd worked there. "Since 1981, when I got out of University of New Hampshire with an animal science degree."

They both told me how they'd fallen in love with dogs as children.

O'Donnell's parents were vegetable farmers, not far from there, and his uncle was a dogman. O'Neil told me that he knew he wanted to work with dogs when he was four years old.

There was a time when Wonderland was a prestigious venue and people used to fight to get their dogs to race there. The famous Irish dogman Pat Dalton won huge money back in the 1980s, but then the money got so low that it wasn't worth his while.

"I remember back in 1944 or 1945, when my uncle raised dogs, they used to have a purse of $800 to $850. Can you imagine that much money back then?" In the last year of Wonderland, he tells me, the purse only reached about $300.

It was turnout time, and O'Neil began opening the cages, one at a time, attaching a plastic muzzle to each dog's face as he went. Each muzzle had a name written in marker: Apple, Andicot, Dybala, Skul—whom O'Donnell said was his favorite dog. They ran toward the door with tails wagging and I followed, marveling at the muscles of their haunches: females into one pen, males in another. There was no room to run, but it was large enough for them to pee and roughhouse with one another. They drank from a huge water bucket. It was September, a beautiful fall day, mellow and sunny. Some dogs lounged in the sun.

A few came up and nosed the men's hands, asking to be petted. The men obliged.

"I think of them as athletes, and I'm the coach," said O'Neil. "I try to get the best out of them."

"What are you gonna do?" I asked, acknowledging that he was out of a job.

He shrugged. The O'Donnells had a big, multigenerational business, with kennels in Florida and a breeding farm in Kansas. They would reshuffle dogs about, but O'Neil was the employee.

"I don't want to move. I've got kids."

While he spoke, he had a hand on Dybala's head, as she leaned against his leg.

O'Donnell pointed to various dogs, naming them and telling me about their personalities.

"Those two there are sisters. Always together." And then, "You've got to see how this one smiles. See?" I knew he was shamelessly pouring it on. Then he went for the coup de grace. "Dogs give you unconditional love," he said, petting one. "Dogs are better than people."

Of course, I knew that, seeing as he'd been in the business since 1958, he'd surely destroyed his share of dogs. How could it have been otherwise? There was nothing else to do with them back then. How many had been injured? And yet, I was sure he believed what he said.

There were ten kennels. O'Donnell had one and his two sons each kept another. The site had capacity for eight hundred to a thousand dogs, though this was highly unlikely now.

When O'Donnell's son Johnny arrived, he looked at me with suspicion. When his father told Johnny that I wanted to write about the last race at Wonderland, he immediately vented his feelings.

"We're labeled as killers. When I drive my dog truck down the street, people call out that I'm a killer. They say we use crates that are too small. But the adoption people use the same size."

His was a different kind of bitterness than his father's, perhaps because O'Donnell senior had already had his career. Johnny was in his forties, I'd guess, and still had many years to go. Would this business still exist?

"They live on donations," he said with disgust about the adoption people. "And the ballot questions are a huge industry for the Humane Society. Did you know that they never had a shelter until last year?" Actually I did, because I understood that they were an advocacy group. "They only built their first shelter last year. People don't know that." Clearly he hated the Humane Society.

The men told me that they worked fourteen to sixteen hours a day, including weekends. That's what the dogs required. It was a hard-working life. When I suggested that they reminded me of farmers who worked day and night to take care of livestock, O'Donnell and O'Neil both stopped me in my tracks, vigorously shaking their heads.

"These dogs all have personalities. We know them each. It's different." They said it almost in unison. "These are *dogs*."

Soon, it was time to go to Wonderland. Johnny and his father went to the board and looked at the list of names—the twelve they'd be taking that night. They gathered leashes.

The dogs obviously knew what was happening. They began barking. As O'Neil went to get the special twelve, opening and shutting the cages one by one, they barked louder and louder. It was all so clear: they wanted to be chosen to go to the track and race. Their barking, a hundred dogs at once, was so loud that it shook the building. I felt the vibration in my bones.

O'Donnell leaned in toward me and said, "They're talking. Do you hear it? They're saying, 'Pick me! Pick me!'"

Only a couple of hundred spectators came for the last night of live racing at Wonderland. Management, which was fighting the result of the Massachusetts ballot, would not acknowledge that it was the last race that people were arriving to see. When the artificial lure, named Swifty, was set in motion, the announcer called out, "There goes Swifty!" for the last time. Then there was nothing more to say.

The dogs were loaded into trucks. Some would go to Florida. Others, back to the farm in Kansas. Officials say that about a thousand Massachusetts dogs were adopted into homes after the ban took effect.

～

AFTER THE closing of Wonderland, Dorchak and Theil honed their messaging and never veered from it.

Greyhounds endure lives of confinement.
Greyhounds suffer serious injuries.
Greyhounds are killed.
The greyhound business is not economically viable.
The business is inherently cruel, outdated, and has to end.

They replicated the Massachusetts strategy and buried the enemy in a barrage of state-specific data and statistics, much of it gathered from public records: the numbers of injuries, deaths, abuse reports, positive drug tests, and track violations. The group had enormous success in getting their stories into the news outlets. GREY2K's list of supporters and followers grew to over one hundred thousand.

By 2015, more than forty tracks had closed since the early 1990s, and breeding declined from about thirty-five thousand dogs per year to ten thousand. Betting was down by 79 percent. Greyhound racing remained in only a handful of states. Florida—which has by far most of the remaining tracks—was in GREY2K's crosshairs. They began lobbying the state legislature to end the requirement that gambling subsidize racing. As of this writing, they have not succeeded, but they have adopted a message that they repeat time and again: "The question now is not if dog racing will end, but how soon?"

In the meantime, GREY2K USA renamed itself GREY2K Worldwide, and began working with other activists to end greyhound racing wherever it exists on the planet.

Sometimes, when I think about all the violence in the world, from humans toward other humans, and humans toward animals, I wonder why some people organized themselves with such fervor against this single animal issue. What about factory farming, in which billions of animals each year are slaughtered? What about horse racing? Horses get injured in races, traded down to worse conditions, and eventually slaughtered and turned into meat. Why not help them? But if the greyhound activists had challenged the horse racing industry instead, they would have been taking on some of the wealthiest and most powerful people in the country, and they would have been far more likely to fail. If they fought factory farming, they'd be going up against the biggest corporations in the world. Greyhound racing was always a marginal sport that suffered from a lack of respect. It was easier to target. And after all, greyhounds are *dogs*. Most people cannot adopt a horse, but millions are willing to take in a dog.

Compared with thirty years ago (and certainly compared with the Irish system), the progress of animal welfare in U.S. dog racing is considerable. When I walked into a track in Daytona, I was nearly knocked over by two friendly ambassador greyhounds on leashes. There was an information booth filled with adoption literature at the entrance.

When I spoke with Gary Guccione, the director of the National Greyhound Association, in 2015, he told me that it was incredible how much the attitudes and culture had changed from the 1950s, when it was automatic that losing dogs were killed. Guccione grew up near the Butte dog track in Montana. His father raced dogs and ran a kennel. He remembers being nine years old, knocking the ice out of the dogs' water buckets in wintertime, and helping his dad build pens. "I fell in love with the sport and the dogs and couldn't imagine doing anything else with my life other than being involved with them," he told me. He went on to a career as a journalist writing about greyhound racing, and eventually became the executive director of the industry's governing body.

"I never asked my dad, how do you feel about having them euthanized? The men back then kept that personal. I don't know how they felt. Knowing people as I do now, I imagine that there were some who were callused, and there those who never got used to it. The people I know took their dogs to the vet to be euthanized. There wasn't any talk about what were the different options for the dogs. I was a product of our culture. It was just reality.

"I've celebrated seeing how much the old attitudes toward the dogs have faded away," he continued. "Greyhound adoption is great. The idea of euthanasia has become abhorrent. It didn't happen overnight. There were old-timers who clung to their ways. But they have changed. People's attitudes are changing as we speak. Now, 90 to 95 percent of dogs either go back to the farm to breed or get adopted. It's been an incredible change."

But when I asked for specifics on how the NGA keeps track of adoptions and returns to farm, or how much the industry donates to adoption efforts, he couldn't verify any of it.

"We don't keep tabs," he said. "The tracks donate money; the trainers and owners give voluntarily to adoption agencies and participate in fundraisers. But there are no mandatory contributions."

16

—

AVALON

Two and a half years had passed since my visit to Kilfinane. It was
2011, and I found the Field of Dreams transformed. More of
the land had been committed to pastures, and there were now many
horses and many more goats, birds, and bunnies. The dog kennel and
cattery were filled to the rafters.

There seemed to be many more volunteers, as well. They bus-
tled about, moving dogs from inside to out and outside to in, taking
them for walks, folding laundry, managing food, cleaning kennels,
and sweeping. The tone was unmistakably cheerful. It was June, and
wildflowers dotted the fields.

But the biggest change, by far, was the new building—an enormous facility, still under construction. This was the centerpiece of the
sanctuary. Marion had been trying to build it for a decade.

"It's just a shell," she said. "When I go in it I have to cry. But at
least the base is set down."

When she took me on a walk-through, it looked to me like much more than a shell. Inside, many walls had been built and doors framed. There was electricity and lighting and kennels with mesh doors. You could see exactly what it was to become: the veterinary clinic, the reception area, the rehoming sections.

Marion and her team had thought through countless details. The building was M-shaped, creating two different wings, one side for incoming cats and the other for incoming dogs. The space was set up for seamless processing. When the animals arrived, they would be checked by a vet and their blood was tested. Their medical record would be entered into the computer system. Then they would go into isolation until they were vaccinated and healthy, at which point they would be placed in the main rehoming center with the other animals waiting for adoption. Little dogs went quickly, usually in less than three months. In contrast, a big black dog could be there for a year.

The entrance points were all about preventing the spread of disease, especially in the cat wing. Marion pointed to a big ventilation system in the ceiling. "Cats carry so many diseases and viruses— much more than dogs. This air exchange will turn over the air every ten minutes. It cost 45,000 euro." She explained that the doors, at 5,200 euro, were coming in the next week. The antibacterial floors would cost 35,000 euro.

I asked her how she'd funded the project.

"I took out a loan."

No doubt she took some criticism for doing this, if not directly to her face then behind her back. She knew people thought it was hubris, or simply biting off more than she could chew. She paid no attention.

LAW had a 500,000 euro annual budget by then. The two thrift shops cleared 100,000 euro a year, and she had just opened a third shop to try to get that up to 150,000 euro. The rest came from donations and adoption fees. Somehow they were making their bills each month—or coming close. It was nerve-racking.

Despite her progress, Marion seemed deeply stressed by her sanctuary project and upset at the suffering she was witnessing in post-recession Ireland. Earlier that year, she'd written to me, "The depression is seeping into every crevice of society. We meet it every day in the most unexpected places. It is palpable in a strange way now and we have to struggle just to remain upright. . . . I am getting older and slower as time passes."

The recession had crushed the U.S. and Europe, but Ireland was an extreme among extremes. When it was all done, Ireland had the most debt per capita in Europe. To help and to punish, the European Union swooped in with a 90-billion-euro bailout, in exchange for a promise that the Irish would inflict harsh spending cuts on the national budget. The E.U. was now in charge, and that was not a good feeling. Money for children's programs, education, and health care was slashed. People lost jobs and homes.

"In Greece the people got a similar deal," said Marion. "But they went into the streets and protested. In Ireland, we just take it and go along."

During hard times, welfare agencies for humans and animals always receive more cases of desperate need and fewer funds. This is exactly what happened at LAW. People surrendered or abandoned the dogs and cats they couldn't feed anymore. But the pet situation paled in comparison to the horse crisis. After the 2008 crash, animal welfare agencies all over Ireland, Britain, and the U.S. were inundated with unwanted horses. During the boom, horses had been a bit like real estate. Lavish lifestyles and easy credit brought them within reach. Now there were thoroughbreds and sport horses dying in ditches, left wandering in fields to fend for themselves, and brought into abattoirs to be turned into meat.

Earlier that year, Marion and her team had taken it hard when they'd picked up two horses that had been severely beaten and abused, and could not save them. Both had to be put down. At one point, Marion got a phone call about forty horses at the horse pound in Mallow, about to be put down. They'd been picked up in terrible condition—bones sticking out, matted fur, open wounds, torn-up hooves. She could see it in their eyes that they'd given up and didn't want to live anymore. She was so upset that she called Johanna Wothke in Germany and asked her for help.

Johanna came and they took all forty horses, most of which went to Germany, while Marion, who only had so much room at Kilfinane, took just a few. Then Johanna did an amazing thing: once again she turned to her donors, and Pro Animale came up with the funds to start a horse sanctuary at Avalon, right next to the greyhound sanctuary. They bought one hundred adjoining acres and built stables. In 2010, Avalon Horse Sanctuary had had its grand opening with one hundred horses in residence, on the fields across from the greyhounds.

"Johanna is the fixer. She was the only one I could think of to turn to," Marion said.

We exited the big building, and Marion walked me around the Field of Dreams to take a look at the animals. She kept up a constant stream of stories: who they were, how they'd gotten here, and any escapades they'd been involved in. "See Mabel? She's our oldest goat. We didn't know she was even pregnant, and look at her baby!" she said, pointing to a very large white goat. Next she wanted to talk about the grass and hay the horses needed, and a possible grant they might get from a local tourist agency if they were willing to put walking trails on the sanctuary. She pointed out the foals who had no mothers and a rooster who had been left on the steps of the Garda. She suspected he'd been involved in cockfighting: "Maybe he wasn't any good at it," she said.

We turned the corner and headed toward the dogs. The funny thing was how it felt like coming home to family. The goats and pigs and horses and birds had been going about their business. They really didn't care about us. But here were the dogs, jumping and happy, as if our arrival were a long-awaited reunion.

I went to the greyhounds and lurchers in paddocks five and six. One of them came up and sniffed my hand through the chain-link, a black female they'd named Toots, with amber eyes and a sad face. A LAW worker pulled back her ears to show me what a mess they were inside, full of scar tissue because someone had poured acid on them to remove the identifying tattoo before dumping her on the road.

I asked Marion about a new greyhound welfare bill that was about to be passed in Ireland, establishing much higher standards in greyhound care. It would drastically improve things, wouldn't it? She waved her hand. "It's a self-regulated industry. They pour millions into it and provide a pittance to welfare," she said. Later, I looked up the numbers. The Bord received 11 million euro in government funding in 2013 and contributed a little under 52,000 euro.

⁓

AN ENORMOUS man with a big white head of hair and Santa Claus beard came walking toward me at the train station in Howth, an old fishing village near Dublin. When he extended his massive hand and smiled, I had the distinct feeling that I was meeting a supernatural character, a friendly giant who'd just stepped out of a tale, perhaps related to Hagrid the gamekeeper at Harry Potter's Hogwarts.

It had been more than fifteen years since Brendan Price took Molly the bear across the English Channel, and since then, he had devoted his life to the Irish Seal Sanctuary. As we walked to the water's edge near the tied-up boats huddled at the dock, Price pointed at the water, and sure enough three sleek heads rose to the surface in succession. The seals rolled onto their backs, then dove back down into darkness. When I asked Brendan about Marion, he said, "She is a direct successor to Humanity Dick Martin." It was obvious that I hadn't a clue as to what he meant, so he told me about Richard Martin, an Irish member of the British Parliament who passed the world's first animal welfare law.

It seemed incredible to me that all animal welfare law traced its way back to an Irish man, but it was true.

Martin, who was also known as the King of Connemara, descended from one of the original "tribes" of Galway. His family had come to Ireland from Normandy in the thirteenth century. Over generations, the Martins acquired some 200,000 acres, nearly a kingdom itself, filled with bogs, lakes, forests, and the breathtaking mountains and coast of Connemara. Born in 1754 at Ballynahinch Castle, young Richard Martin inherited all of this land. He grew up in the wilderness, riding horses, fishing, shooting, and hunting.

For hundreds of years, the British had forbidden Catholics to own land. Somehow, the Catholic Martins had evaded persecution—perhaps due to friends in high places, or simply because their land was too remote for the British to bother with. By 1745, this was no longer possible, so Richard Martin's father renounced the Pope and converted to the Church of England in order to keep his estate. Almost certainly he didn't mean a word of it, but these were years when Catholics were not allowed to vote, hold office, go into the major professions, or send their children to university. They were not allowed to serve in government, own a firearm, or possess a good-quality horse. By giving up Catholicism, Robert Martin paved the way for his son to be born into the Anglican Church and have every opportunity for success.

Legend has it that when Richard Martin was seven years old, his father took him sailing on Lough Corrib, where he informed the boy that he'd soon be off to boarding school in London, and after that, university. Robert Martin also made his wishes clear: he wanted Richard to become a member of Parliament and fight for Catholic emancipation.

Richard grew up to be a colorful figure. He was a famous duelist, an actor, and a benevolent landlord in Galway. He fulfilled his father's wishes and dedicated forty years of his life to the cause, first in the Irish Parliament, and later in the Parliament of the United Kingdom, where he continually spoke and voted for Catholic relief and ultimately emancipation. Martin also voted against slavery, fought to repeal the death penalty for minor crimes such as forgery, and stood up for other laws that would protect the weak from the powerful. But he is best remembered for what he did for animals.

Martin was a gifted speaker, who often entertained Parliament with his wit. (When asked why he cared so much about animals, he said, "Sir, an ox cannot hold a pistol.") His friend King George IV nicknamed him Humanity Dick. In 1822, he presented his animal welfare bill to Parliament.

Two major failures had gone before him. More than twenty years earlier William Pulteney, an evangelical Christian, had put forth a bill to end bull-baiting, a brutal practice in which a bull (or bear if available) was tied to a post in the center of a pit and a pack of dogs (as many as six) was sent in to attack it. The larger animal defended itself as best as it could, as one dog after the next clawed and bit it to shreds. Spectators of the high-stakes drama were notoriously rowdy. Some bet on the dogs, others bet on the bull. Either way, the fun was in seeing how well they would fight.

The bill's primary opponent, the great orator William Wendham, pummeled it with some of the arguments still used today against animal protection laws: 1) Bull-baiting was an old tradition that went back a thousand years with no proven harm. Why change it now? 2) It was not government's role to legislate morality, which was a private matter. 3) Why take away the pleasures of the lower classes, who had so little? (Though it surely wasn't lost on the members of Parliament that if bull-baiting was banned, their beloved upper-class blood sports, fox hunting and coursing, might be next.) Pulteney's bill lost by a narrow margin.

Nine years later, Lord Erskine introduced a bill for Preventing Malicious and Wanton Cruelty to Animals. It passed in the House of Lords but lost in the Commons.

Martin—with the help of Erskine, the famous abolitionist William Wilberforce, and others—adopted an intentionally narrow strategy. Martin's Act to Prevent the Cruel and Improper Treatment of Cattle was modest in ambition. The bill made it a crime to cruelly beat or abuse livestock, including horses, sheep, and donkeys, with fines up to five pounds. If unable to pay, the offender would get up to three months in jail. Members of Parliament ridiculed and jeered it, but ultimately passed the law in a landslide. It was called Martin's Act.

Martin personally enforced the law. Woe to the man who was caught whipping his horse in the streets. Martin might punch him, or at a minimum drag him to court. Within just a few years, dozens of prosecutions had resulted in convictions. In 1824, when Arthur Broome led the founding meeting for the Society to Prevent Cruelty to Animals, Richard Martin was present.

For years after his initial success, Martin continually tried to expand his law so as to outlaw bull-baiting and give protection to more animals, but Parliament tired of his efforts and would have none of it. In 1826, he lost his bid for reelection and no longer had parliamentary immunity for his debts, of which he had many. On the brink of being arrested, he fled to France, where he died in 1834. The following year, Parliament finally prohibited bull-baiting, dogfighting, and cockfighting with passage of the Cruelty to Animals Act.

⌒

THE NEXT day, Marion picked me up in the rain. On the way out of town, as we sat at a traffic light, I saw a monstrosity by the side of the road, an ugly conglomeration of cement and steel which was evidently a huge construction project abandoned before it was even halfway built. I asked Marion about it.

"Isn't it terrible? It was going to be a shopping mall, but they ran out of money."

It felt unnerving to look in and see the unfinished floors and concrete walls, steel beams reaching up to nowhere, as though the workers had dropped their tools and fled due to some catastrophe. In fact, this is exactly what happened, though instead of the volcanic ash of Pompeii or the huge waves of a typhoon, it was an economic disaster. This was just one of many incomplete real estate projects left behind from the boom years of the Celtic Tiger.

It receded behind us as Marion continued north. In Ireland, it never takes long to get from city to countryside, and soon we were surrounded by green, leafy trees on a road that ran alongside the River Shannon.

After more than an hour, we turned west and crossed into County Galway. That's when the terrain changed, as though we'd entered another dimension. The bright green landscape was gone, and suddenly the car was climbing a rugged small hill that led to an open plain of brown untilled fields on one side and a bog on the other. The sky hung low and grey, and the vista was gloomy yet beautiful, with brown moor grass and rushes dotted with yellow wildflowers and heather.

In the distance, the hills rose up into the Slieve Aughty Mountains. Patches of dark earth lay in small heaps of broken rectangles left behind by local turf cutters. I remarked on the untillable soil and Marion said, "To hell or Connacht," with an ironic laugh. We were in the rocky, harsh part of Ireland's west, the place to which Cromwell banished the Catholics after he stole the fertile land in the1600s and gave it to English Protestants.

"I remember when Beverly and I first came here and found this land," Marion said, changing the subject. "It really shook my foundations when she left. I thought we'd be saving dogs together until we dropped."

We turned down a dirt road that led to a large wrought-iron gate flanked by a wall of round, smooth stones, beautifully placed by hand.

A sign hung in front, bearing the word "Avalon" inscribed in Celtic-style letters.

"Whenever I come here, I feel happy because I know Avalon will be here after I am gone. The sanctuary in Kilfinane, I cannot be sure. But Avalon will always be here."

Marion had been one of Avalon's directors from the start. And though she felt responsible for helping bring Avalon into existence, Avalon was Johanna's project. It was part of Pro Animale. Marion didn't have to tell me what she was thinking: How could it be that now Johanna had more than thirty sanctuaries while Marion couldn't even complete one?

We drove up the road, passing through a stand of trees, and then beyond to open meadows and rolling fields for grazing and running. We had arrived at an animal heaven. The long necks of horses came into view, bent over to graze. Sheep stood in distant, misty fields. The most dominant presence was of greyhounds, dozens of them, barking aggressively. In their paddocks, they came leaping toward us and jumped up, forepaws to the fences, pink bellies and fangs showing, ears up, barking so forcefully that I felt afraid and checked the height of the fence.

The entry road led to the main building, covered in climbing roses and vines. Inside, every wall was hung with art—paintings, woodcuts, and sketches of animals. The floors gleamed with stone tile.

There were a few humans here, mostly Polish men, walking horses between fields. An Irishwoman named Noreen was in charge. She'd studied animal science and spent her life on farms before coming here. She sat us down at the kitchen table and made tea. She and Marion began to talk about Johanna's high standards, how everything had to be just so.

Marion recounted how in 1996 Johanna invited her to Germany to see some of her sanctuaries. Marion and Johanna were similar in age and had started their animal work at around the same time, by bringing dogs into their homes. On that trip, Marion learned that Johanna had started with no great financial means—she'd been a schoolteacher. Early on, she'd had the idea to write a newsletter— first, for her friends and acquaintances—to let people know about her work, and also to appeal for donations. She continued to write these newsletters a few times a year, and her subscribers and sup- porters grew. In time, some donors left bequests to Pro Animale, which allowed her to build several sanctuaries in Germany. When the Soviet bloc fell, she bought cheap land in Poland and, later, in Russia, Austria, and Turkey. She kept a notebook for each sanctuary and spoke several languages, which helped. She ran these sanctuar- ies down to the last Deutschmark. Each one was designed the same way, with art on the walls, gardens, and tiled floors. Johanna had not involved herself in advocacy as Marion had. She was not a social being, but focused every hour that she could on creating sanctuar- ies. She was a workaholic. From what Marion observed, she slept only four hours a night.

They drove across Austria and down into Italy. Johanna had just acquired about ten acres of prime land in Assisi. At sunset, they reached a secluded valley with a broken-down mill and an orchard. A stream ran through the middle of the property, and at the center stood a farmhouse with thick walls and Gothic windows with deep ledges where you could sit and look out at the green valley. To Marion it was all incredible.

Johanna was about to open yet another sanctuary right there in the shadow of St. Francis, on this spectacular piece of land. She had raised her money by writing stories about the suffering of animals. People had responded. Germany was a wealthy country. Marion pushed away any feelings of envy.

The Assisi property came with a flock of sheep, which were still in their winter coats. While she was there, neighbors arrived with shears and got to work. They also brought a big feast and set out tables. Everyone sat under the stars, with lanterns hung from the trees. The magical experience imprinted on Marion an entirely new vision of what was possible.

～

AT AVALON, the dogs lived in small social groups and had large grassy fields to run in, contained by eight-foot-tall fences because there would always be those extra-talented greyhounds who could jump ridiculously high. Inside the main building, each pack had its own large room, much like a den. Wothke passionately opposed putting any dog alone in a cage or a pen.

I was peering into one of those rooms now. It seemed like a revolutionary design. Rather than four walls and a floor, the layout was

a system of stepped-up ledges wrapped around the room, except that each ledge was three or four feet deep and covered in earth-colored tile. If you stood in the middle of the floor, you were encircled by dogs, each in its own soft bedding on the ledges stacked halfway up the walls. Above the ledges, the walls were painted a soft yellow, and a hand-stenciled frieze of greyhounds circled the room near the ceiling. It was more like a home than a dog kennel.

I stepped inside with Noreen as my escort. She was a strong-boned woman of middle age who inspired confidence, and yet, when the door closed the behind me, a wave of fear rose in my chest. Noreen stood in the corner and watched.

"I have to be very careful about introducing any new dog to a

Johanna Wothke's daughter Natascha, running with the hounds at Avalon. (Courtesy Pro Animale für Tiere in Not e.V.)

pack," she said. "If one attacks another, then they all will. And they'll kill a dog very quickly, you know."

Six dogs circled round and began jumping on me. One managed to put its paws on my shoulders. The others nearly knocked me off my feet. They were exuberantly curious about me, sniffing my body and licking my hands. There was a wildness to them. They had never been tamed and had astonishing strength. As a pack, they were unified and powerful. Slightly terrified, I sat down on a ledge, thinking it might calm them down, but this only gave them more access. Noses in my ears. A mouth around my hand. Tongues licking my cheeks, noses sniffing. One took my pocketbook and carried it to its bed. Across the room, three dogs remained in their spaces on the ledge—not interested. But the six around me could not have been more intrigued. My heart pounded fast.

Shortly after I came home from Ireland, I had a dream that Lily got out of the house and ran away. The last time I'd seen her was at a neighbor's maple tree, and from there she'd vanished. I kept returning to that tree, looking for her, but she was never there. When I finally realized that she was gone and not coming back, I was overcome with the most excruciating grief—the kind of grief you live in fear of. It was bottomless.

The next day, I was still rattled and felt a shadow over my brain. I told a friend about the dream.

"You do realize that you were dreaming about Gabriel," she said. "Don't you?"

17

—

WINNERS AND LOSERS

In southeast Ireland, about an hour from Cork, there's a small village called Ballyduff. It is one of those postcard Irish places where meadow, farmland, and hedgerow checkerboard the rolling hills, and people at the pub talk about local hurling teams. In the middle of town, a salmon-filled river runs toward the Celtic Sea. I'd come to meet a dogman.

Fechin (pronounced "FeHEEN") Mullen owned that kind of pub in this town, and a friend sent me to talk to him, explaining that he was "deep into the dogs—and a sensitive fellow, too."

Mullen was a youngish man, in his thirties I'd guess, with faint crow's feet around his eyes and an appealingly soft-spoken manner. I followed him out of his pub and we walked five minutes or so until we came to a fence that turned out to be a door, a magical one, blending in so well you'd never know it was there.

Behind the door, we descended a steep staircase to a grassy yard with a row of five homemade dog kennels. Half a dozen greyhounds were observing our entrance, sauntering to their gates in their light-footed and curious way, noses forward—each in its own small pen. Theirs was an outdoor life, in Ireland's wet weather, but Mullen had built them each a little plywood shelter, filled with hay. Plastic muzzles hung neatly on hooks.

A half dozen puppies, about three months old, barked in a nearby pen—yapping frantically in a childish chorus, jumping up and down then falling on top of one another like a slapstick routine, blissfully clueless that though they all came from the same gene pool, not all would be able to run fast.

Mullen was not from one of the families of greyhound royalty that had been in the business for generations. In addition to being a publican, he was a carpenter, and once did a job at a greyhound trainer's house, where he became fascinated by the dogs. That's how he got hooked.

"I loved dogs ever since I was young," Mullen says, emphasizing the word "loved," which sounded like "low-vd" in his soft-spoken brogue.

"That's Tina over there." He gestured to a small black bitch, all stillness and quiet. "She's just won at Thurles a couple of nights ago. She's Taylors Sky's auntie." He laughed. "Do you know who Taylors Sky is? He just won the English Derby a couple of weeks ago."

In the dog-racing world, this was the big show.

"The breeder was Damian Fleming. His family has been in the business for eighty years. He lives just up the road."

Mullen pointed to another. "That's Smoke. I paid 10,000 euro for her and then another 6,000 for her training. Six finals, but no wins. She's only made 6,500." He shrugged it off. "She's paying her way in broods, and we'll be hoping one will make it. See those pups over there? I've sold four of the six already."

Today, anyone can log on and find pedigree lines instantly thanks to the number-crunching and millions of records at greyhounddata

.com. You can trace the percentage of a dog's blood that comes from a particular champion, sometimes back generations, even all the way back to Wilby, Tiney, and Rufus—coursing dogs who ran in the late 1700s, when the aristocracy ruled the sport and events took place on vast private estates.

Breeding has always been a mix of science, mystery, and art. But it no longer has much to do with sexual intercourse. Frozen semen is the thing. Reputable dealers sell it through websites that show photos of virile-looking dogs—a bit like an online dating site, except with prices per vial.

There are no guarantees. Fast dogs bring slow dogs into the world every day, and a loser at the track can sire a winner. So many things can go right or wrong. Do you want to breed from a "fast pacer" (a dog that bolts into the lead right out of the trap) or a long-distance runner that holds something back at first but can pull up from behind? Do you want to cross-breed (cousins, for example), outbreed (bring in new genes), or even bring in a foreign national (say, Australian blood)? There are justifications for each. You will want to give extra thought to the mother. The egg and sperm contribute fifty-fifty, but the mother supplies the placenta and birthing substance, and this tips the scales to give her a slightly greater genetic influence. And then, there is pure luck and the mystery. Who can account for personality? Some dogs are simply born with more heart, more grit, more determination to chase and win.

That day, Mullen told me that a couple of years earlier, he'd taken a big gamble on 1,800 euro worth of frozen semen from an American champion named Flying Penske. It was liquid gold. He'd held onto it for months, thinking long and hard on who the mate should be. He finally inseminated a bitch named Stunning Wilma. She had won seven races. He had a good feeling about her and had the sperm put directly into her fallopian tube at the right time in her cycle.

Flying Penske, I later learned, had died long before this, in 2007.

His spectacular genetic material lived on in frozen sperm that was shipped around the world. According to greyhounddata.com, Flying Penske has sired over nine thousand offspring—and still counting. When I asked an expert how this was even remotely possible, he explained that if you collect semen weekly during a dog's prime, you might get as many as six vials per week. Add that up over a year, and then several years. It makes a lot of vials. Each vial means one breeding, which, if successful, brings an average of six pups—which means thousands of potential puppies. Of course, demand on this scale is rare. You'd only get it for a real champion, which is exactly what Flying Penske was. For the lucky owner, the sperm profit goes on for years after the dog is dead and gone.

Mullen trained his dogs diligently. He showed me his treadmill, which was hooked up to a portable generator, and he hitched up an amber-colored female named Fluff to demonstrate it. He started at a slow speed. Dutifully, she began to plod along. Then he turned it up, and she walked faster and began to pant, soon switching to a modest trot. This was only part of the program. Mullen also conditioned his dogs by taking them swimming every two or three days (the training pool was a forty-minute drive away). A half hour on the walking machine, midweek gallops, weekend runs, plus the basics, of course: food, turnouts from their pens, an evening walk four times a week. It was an enormous effort.

"Over there." He pointed beyond the trees. "I just bought land— seventeen acres." He told me he planned to build proper kennels and a course for training.

I was struck again by how both sides of the greyhound world said they loved the dogs. For animal rescuers, it was all about the act of salvation, one animal after the next, a sort of religion unto itself, a purpose for living. Picking up this or that dog (or cat or horse or pig or badger) meant confronting the darkness of human negligence and cruelty—and, at times, pure evil. The healing and saving gave the rescuer not only victory but the personal power of having conquered suffering and death, if even for only a moment.

The greyhound breeders and trainers achieved their own kind of victory, not just through the heroic winning of races and vanquishing the odds. There was something else, something less obvious, that had to do with the chance to take an animal from birth and train it to work and perform at a high level. The experience seemed to imprint people deeply. You needed not just patience and skill to bring out an animal's talents and will; you needed to cross the line between species and communicate in a nonverbal language. I imagined that this language between animals and humans felt deep and infinite. It was a language that urban people like me could not understand. I imagined that all trainers had a similar experience, whether they were working with dolphins, seals, elephants, or dogs. For some people, the experience created a deep reverence for animals and nature, while for others it was proof of human dominion over all living beings. Whether the outcome was reverence for life or dominance seemed to depend on the individual.

"And what do you do when they're not fast enough?" I asked Mullen. "Or not good enough, or get too old to race, and you can't sire or brood them?"

"Ship Mate is not fast. We'll send him to BAGS at Sheffield, which is a lower-tiered track." Then he added, "I'm a bit of a softie. I can't put a dog down."

Mullen may not have put a dog down personally, but eventually someone else probably would. Selling the dog to a lower-grade track made the dog disappear from his vision.

BAGS stood for Bookmakers Afternoon Greyhound Services. These were daytime races in England, unattended, and designed solely to give bookmakers more betting product. After BAGS, the next step down would be the unregulated "flapping tracks" in England. That was the end of the road in racing. After that there were many possible paths: death (quick, from a vet or a gun), abandonment, a happy adoption, or permanent life in a shelter with other unwanted greyhounds. No one knew. No one had to know.

"Do you make any money at this?"

Mullen laughed. "I'd be afraid to add it up."

But what do you *think*?" I pressed.

"Not even 5 percent."

All that trouble for so little money. All that trouble for dog lives born, injuries, and dog lives gone. Why even bother? Before I could even formulate the words to ask the question, he answered it for me.

"It's all for the dream," he said. "It would mean everything. I put up with the losses for the dream of winning."

The next morning, I stood at the front door of a large house, shaking hands with Damian Fleming, who greeted me with a combination of genuine friendliness and reserve—a facility that the Irish seem to have mastered. I guessed him to be in his late thirties. He had a confident bearing. No wonder: he was on top of the world. Two weeks earlier, his miracle dog Taylors Sky had won the English Derby at odds of 100 to 1. At that moment, he was the hottest breeder in Ireland.

He led me to the kitchen, which was full of windows and sunlight, sleek granite countertops, and new appliances—new Ireland all the way. Mullen, who had set this meeting up, was already sitting at the kitchen table.

Two little tow-headed boys ran about. Fleming gave them toast and affectionate pats on the head, smiling. "First day of summer break," he said. Then he offered scones, baked by his mum. When his cell phone rang, he stepped aside to take it—a business call. He sold filters to pharmaceutical companies and said he had forty accounts.

The greyhound business was in his blood, he explained with

pride. It had begun with his great-grandparents and been passed down father to son, father to son. Fleming had been working at grey-hounds all his life with his dad, Noel. They called their operation Rising Kennels. "Rising" was the prefix for all their dogs.

"We are breeders," he began. "That means we pup them and rear them and get them to their first race. Then we sell them."

I asked him to tell me about Taylors Sky, and Fleming's face brightened. Without hesitating he said the story began back in the Nineties, when Noel bought a bitch they named Rising Dowry. She was a girl of exquisite pedigree; her dad held five track records and her mum's dad won the 1986 English Derby. The Flemings mated Rising Dowry with an English champion, and this brought forth Rising Singer. She was mediocre at the track, but a wonderful mother who bore thirty-one pups, including many stars.

"She was the foundation of everything we had," said Fleming with true gratitude.

Her greatest gift was her daughter Rising Angel, who showed talent right from the start. Somebody offered the Flemings good money for her, but they said no. They knew a prodigy when they saw one. When she went into season they took her home—to Noel's place—and bred her with a dog whose pedigree was nearly royalty, West-mead Hawk, owned by Niki Savva, a renowned English breeder. The pups included a gorgeous white dog with scattered black spots and a big black patch around the right eye. He had a perfect temperament. They named him Rising Hawk.

"He was brilliant from the very first moment," said Fleming.

At Rising Hawk's first trial, when he was barely out of puppy-hood, someone said, "You better watch that fella." But it wasn't until his first official race, when he started galloping those 480 meters, that Fleming knew—really knew—that some incredible spark separated this dog from the hundreds of other dogs he'd known. Rising Hawk had speed and power, but also heart and relentless drive.

"A bomb could go off and nothing would keep that dog from running," he said.

After that first race, a British car dealer named Steve Taylor and his wife, Rebecca, offered the Flemings 20,000 euro for the dog. A deal was made: Rising Hawk was reborn as Taylors Sky. To get him ready for the English Derby, the Taylors hired one of the most successful trainers in England.

Seven months later, at barely two years old, Taylors Sky entered the qualifying rounds. In the quarterfinal, he ran 480 meters in 28.21 seconds, breaking the track record. A few days later came the semifinal. Back in Ireland, Fleming watched the race on the Internet, utterly astonished as Taylors Sky pushed ahead across the finish line.

"My heart pounded so fast I thought I might have a heart attack," he told me.

It's not that Fleming believed the dog would actually win the English Derby; it was miraculous that'd he'd even got that far. The family had to see it. A week later, he and his parents were at Wimbledon Greyhound Stadium.

Fleming positioned himself down at the track by the first bend—in his mind, the first bend was everything. If a dog led at that point, there was a better than fifty-fifty chance he'd win. And so Fleming watched nervously as the handlers walked the six dogs out onto the field, the energy and noise from the crowd rising incrementally each second. Taylor's Sky looked ready and strong as his handler walked him out to Trap 1—the inside slot—tucked him inside, and shut the door. No dog had won the derby from Trap 1 in twenty-six years. Inside the traps, the dogs barked and moaned, knowing exactly what was about to happen. And then, they heard it: the swooshing electric sound as the mechanical rabbit began its taunting journey along the inside rail. Up went the gates and all six dogs exploded forth.

Within a few seconds, Taylors Sky was leading around the bend, legs flying open and shut, open and shut, head pumping up and down in rhythm. As Fleming watched his dog go by in a blur, he knew then what was happening—he knew his dog was going to win the fecking English Derby, and he couldn't believe it. Taylors Sky hurtled across the finish line in 28.17 seconds, a half second in front of the next dog. Fleming screamed and cheered so loud that he lost his voice for days.

Fleming stepped away from the kitchen for a moment, then returned with a photo in his hand. He placed it on the table before me. "Nothing will ever touch this."

Taylors Sky was at the center, eyes shining, tongue out from all the excitement, draped in his "Winner 2011" jacket. The dog was surrounded by an entourage of humans—the British owners Steve Taylor in a tuxedo and his glamorous wife in a black cocktail dress, the trainers and handlers, and the Flemings from Ireland—Damian and his parents—whose "Rising" genetic stock had made it all possible. In the photo, the humans have their arms slung over one another's shoulders, and are grinning wider than seems possible with unfettered joy, while the brilliant white greyhound stands there graciously, having just earned $70,000 for his owners—lifting the boats of all involved that much higher.

"Barring the birth of my two kids, it was the best feeling ever," said Fleming. "Nothing will ever touch it."

As my time with Fleming ran down, I tried to shift the conversation away from winning. I asked how he felt about the dogs.

"They sleep in the bed with us. When I have one who is injured, I send it to my dad, who walks them by the sea because it's good for healing. The brood bitches become pets."

"But what happens to the ones who aren't fast, the ones who can't win?" I pressed.

The smile dropped. Fleming's face clouded over in a second, and his tone changed. An awkward chill settled abruptly between us.

"As far as welfare goes, I can't help you. The Bord makes the regulations and it's my job to follow them."

I persisted in asking about all the dogs that have to be born and discarded in order to get one Taylors Sky.

"There has to be wastage," Fleming finally said, looking at me seriously. "The country has only three or four million people, and half a million of them in Dublin. There just aren't enough homes for all these greyhounds."

Still, he agreed to send me a photo of the night Taylors Sky won and cordially said goodbye.

Mullen was to give me a ride back to Ballyduff, but suggested a detour. Would I like to see where he was rearing some of his pups on a farm? It was only about five miles away.

Rearing was a distinctly Irish practice. When a dog was old enough to leave its mother, at about four months old, it was sent to a farm, where it would spend nearly a year outside in big fields with much more freedom than dogs have in the American or Australian systems, where the young spend this growing phase in the structured confines of commercial kennels.

Of course I said yes.

He took the car twisting and turning along narrow roads through woods into remote countryside, until he turned down a road leading to a farm. He parked at a fenced-in pasture where five fawn-and-white greyhounds lay in various states of repose. When our car doors slammed, they raced toward the fence, competing to sniff us and be petted and lick our hands frantically. They wore no collars, and their only shelter as far as I could see was a cinderblock shed, which had a roof but no walls. They must have huddled on top of one another to stay warm at night. These were the offspring of Stunning Wilma and Flying Penske.

"It toughens them up to be out here for a year," Mullen said. "They don't know nothing from a leash."

After greeting us, the dogs grew bored and returned to their field, lying in the sun. But then a competition between two of them ensued. With a rough pull of the jaws, the larger dog triumphed and carried the treasure a few feet away, then set about gnawing on what appeared to be a pig snout.

Mullen invited me to meet the farmer, whose name was Tom. As we slowly ascended the hill, he informed me that, as well as raising pigs, Tom had a sideline in the dog racing business. I listened only partly, distracted by a ghastly smell that intensified with each passing yard.

"Tom has a very sociable personality," he confided as he parked the car. "If you ever see him at the bar, he'd be meticulously well dressed. He drives a nice car. You'd never know he was a pig farmer."

We got out of the car in front of a compound of warehouse-style buildings. I'd never been to a pig farm before, but I couldn't take in the details because I was overcome by nausea at the smell. It was not the smell of shit, exactly. Well yes, shit, it was that, but there was something else, something far worse than this city person had ever experienced, something like all the suffering and bad doings of the world poured into a vat of sickening stench. My stomach began to churn. I was about to tell Mullen I wanted to leave, but just then a smiling man appeared, tall and slim, in his early fifties, striding toward us in wellies and mud-spattered work clothes. Mullen introduced us and I offered my hand, but Tom did not shake it in the usual way. His right hand remained in his pocket because, as I later learned, he lacked one. He gave me an awkward shake with his left.

When he found out I was a writer, he was delighted and wanted to discuss literature.

"Do you know the work of John Keane?" he asked. "No? He's a playwright who writes about Irish country people. You should see

The Field. It's about what Irish people will do to hold onto a piece of land. Yes, it's very good," he assured me, then moved on to another of Keane's plays, about the long-ago business of matchmaking

Then he paused. "Marriage is still a business." An ironic laugh.

Tom wanted to know where I lived, whether I had kids, and what I did. He was charming and I could have chatted with him all day, though I noticed that when I asked how he came to his line of work, his expression changed just a bit.

He'd planned on forestry, he said, but he took the husbandry test on a lark and passed. So he got a job at this farm some decades ago, back when there were not so many jobs in Ireland. He thought he'd stay just a little while. But he never left. He bought out the owners, got married, and had kids.

He shrugged with midlife reckoning, as if to say, "And that was the end of that."

At this point I was breathing through my mouth so that I wouldn't puke.

"Would you like to hold a baby pig?" he asked me.

I had never touched a pig. I wasn't sure.

"Sure," I replied casually.

"Are you a vegetarian?"

"No." (At that time I wasn't.)

"Do you drink?"

"Yes. But not Guinness."

"Do you eat bacon?"

"Yes, I eat bacon."

Evidently I passed the test.

"Okay, come on." He led the way toward the steel buildings I'd been trying not to look at. I followed along a cement walkway into one. He called it the breeding room.

Inside, I was horrified to realize I was in a steel birthing factory. A long aisle went down the center of an immense warehouse. On each side was a long row of rectangular cells. Inside the cells were sow after sow, huge pink creatures lying in their narrow slots, barely moving except for the rise and fall of their breathing. Pink piglets clustered around each sow's belly, suckling.

Marion had once told me that you could see when an animal has given up on life. I felt that here. The sows lay in complete surrender, powerless mothering machines. The room was filled with their breath. Tom reached into one of the birthing cells to grab a piglet from the litter. They were all wriggling and pink, except one that was noticeably smaller and slower, with transparent bluish skin, barely breathing.

Tom pushed him aside. "That one may not make it," he said, then scooped up a healthy one like a football to give to me.

God no. I did not want to hold a pig. Not. At. All. I didn't want to get closer. I wanted to flee.

Still, I went along as best as I could. With a couple of fingers, I stroked the pig's head as quickly and lightly as possible. My gesture was clear: this was enough, I was done touching the pig.

I accidentally breathed in through my nose and again sensed my stomach rising. We turned to go.

Outside, Tom gestured to the steel buildings around us. "I've got 3,000 pigs there. A truck comes every two weeks and takes pigs to market for slaughtering." And then, after a moment, "Such is a pig's life."

Rueful bitterness, or perhaps disgust, or maybe this was just conviction of the natural order of things. Such was a pig's life . . . I could not parse the tones of a language I did not speak. I did not understand.

Back outside in the not-fresh air, I was desperate to leave, but the men continued chatting. They wanted to talk greyhounds. Tom had an interest in coursing. I mentioned something about the poor hare.

"Yes, yes," he said almost dismissively, waving a hand. "I've heard them squeal. They sound like a baby crying. I know. My wife doesn't like it." He shook his head, with school-of-hard-knocks resignation that there were those who lived and died and those who were strong and those who were weak, and those who wound up with only one hand and went forth anyway breeding pigs because that was how survival worked.

"That's life," he said. "Life is hard."

PART IV

18

—

CHANGES

I felt edgy. Something was prickling me—literally. It happened at night when I lay in bed. There were sharp things getting into my skin. At first I was confused. Were bugs biting me? Was it a rash? Then I realized it was my new feather bed—two inches of soft down added on top of my mattress. The sharp quills of the feathers poked through the cover and the sheet. How disappointing. It was like lying on a bed of needles. Annoyed, I went online and input a search for "painful feathers." Quickly I discovered an easy solution to my problem: another purchase, of course. I just needed a feather bed *cover* to contain all those prickly quills. Credit card. Click. Problem solved.

But now I had a new problem. While searching the Web with the term "painful feathers," I stumbled across some very unfortunate information. I swear I wasn't looking for trouble, but there it was right before me: news and advocacy sites telling me my feather bed might have come from tortured ducks who'd been brutally plucked alive for their down. One click, and there before me in the comfort of my home

I saw footage of workers holding geese and ducks with one hand and violently ripping feathers from the follicles with the other. Afterward, the bloody birds wandered about, dazed, in their cement holding areas. Most down feathers come from animals that are killed for meat. But a small percentage comes from egg-laying ducks which regrow their feathers, so they can be plucked again. The issue of live plucking was first exposed by a Swedish television show that had gone undercover at Hungarian farms in 2009. The practice is now illegal in the United States and Europe. But today the majority of down and feathers come from China, which has stated many times that only a small amount of feathers (less than 1 percent) are live-plucked. PETA (People for Ethical Treatment of Animals) carried out its own investigations, which suggested otherwise. Global brands, from Patagonia and North Face to Ikea, took a look at their supply chains and evidently were not happy with what they found, because they developed new standards and sourcing for the down and feathers in their products. A couple of years later, PETA produced new undercover footage suggesting that live plucking continues. The industry association denied it. How much can the consumer really know? In the global supply chain, it is very difficult to monitor the animals who make our comfortable lives possible.

Because of my exposure to Marion and the animal people, unpleasant revelations like this multiplied. Before I met Marion, I would have been happy to have a "cruelty free" label on my cosmetics, but I never went out of my way. Again, the Internet allowed me to discover that most of my makeup and shampoo brands had been tested on rabbits and guinea pigs that had been strapped down so they couldn't move. Researchers dropped ingredients into their eyes or rubbed creams and lotions into their shaved skin to see which substances caused damage or pain. These experiments didn't happen once to a given animal, but came in series, often for months, until the animal was finally put out of its misery. Had I heard something about all this and blocked it out for twenty years? Absolutely.

But now it was hard to stop. It became overwhelming. I got to thinking about animals in human history and all they'd done for us. They have been at our sides from the beginning, and we have used them for food, clothing, shelter, tools, fuel, and medicine. As farmers, we put them to work, clearing and plowing fields, and carrying our heavy burdens (and ourselves) near and far. We used their pelts as scrolls for sacred texts. We've made them defend, hunt, and messenger for us in peace and wars. They have died, alongside soldiers and sometimes in place of soldiers. For fun, we've had them entertain us by tearing one another to shreds, dancing, singing, and racing. We've made magnificent creatures such as elephants and orcas live in captivity and do tricks. As pets and companions, they've stuck with us when no human would.

There would be no human civilization without animals. And there would be no modern economy without them either.

I began to look at all I wore and ate: wool, leather, dairy, meat, fish, and eggs. And the medicines that kept my family healthy and functioning—tested upon primates. (Not to mention that primates have also died for scientific studies that answered stupid questions, such as, Do baby primates suffer when they are taken away from their mothers and shut in solitary confinement?)

Suddenly, I saw animals everywhere. And then there was Lily, spending most of her life indoors, doing her commissioned job as sister, daughter, and friend and whatever else I needed her to be.

Once I opened this door, it was hard to function. And it was hard to get it shut again. My husband did not always appreciate it. He was an avid outdoorsman who caught trout on a fly and threw them back. Like most hunters and fishers, he feels a spiritual connection with nature when he stands in cold water, acting as a predator and thinking like his prey. I tried to tell him that his catch-and-release mercy might not be what he thought.

"Have you realized that when you catch these trout, you're torturing them with a hook in their mouths, for no reason? If you ate them, that would be one thing. But this! This is just for your entertain—"

"Whoa, whoa. Stop right now, Laura. Don't you dare."

Now that the door was open, a local news story (which normally would not have made a dent) captured my attention. A calf had gotten loose from the halal slaughterhouse in Paterson, two towns away, and ran for his life down River Street. Police tried to corner him with their cars, which must have been terrifying for him. Nonetheless, he outsmarted them and managed to wade into the Passaic River. This standoff went on until animal control officer John De Cando arrived with his dart gun and ketamine. De Cando aimed the tranquilizer perfectly and soon the calf stumbled and went down.

At his office in Paterson, De Cando told me that, in his thirty years on the job, many farm animals had gone running through the streets of Paterson. Sheep, cows, and goats had all escaped from the slaughterhouse. De Cando had to hand it to these animals—the ones who saw their chance and made a run for it. Goats were the easiest to handle, gentler than dogs and usually frightened. Once you held them, they settled down, and they loved to be petted. Sometimes they weren't from the slaughterhouse, but from an Arab or African immigrant's backyard—procured from a farm somewhere—to be slaughtered for a holiday, in the tradition of the old country.

"I've seen crazy things," he told me. "People say I should write a book. But I'm too busy."

De Cando wore a uniform—pants with a stripe down the side and heavy black shoes. His white shirt held an official badge on the chest. From a distance you'd think cop, or firefighter. Only when you got up close did you see the "K-9" on the badge.

I asked him to elaborate on the crazy things he'd seen.

"The worst? Maybe it was the dog with a cherry bomb up its rear end. Or the one that had been set on fire and had its skin falling off. Or the dogs hung by a rope from the neck. Or the house full of snakes. Did these things upset me? *Yes.* Did I take some of it home with me? *Yes.* But on the other hand, I got to see a lot of happy endings. How many jobs give you that? We've saved bears and cats and dogs and deer, and once I went out for two weeks trying to get in a duck with an arrow in his head—we got him to the Raptor Trust. Thirty years ago, we had an adoption rate of 5 percent. Now it's 80 percent. Those are happy endings."

My God, I thought. These animal rescue people are everywhere.

He told me about retrieving the dog of a twenty-year-old man killed in a car accident. The dog had been in the car, but disappeared into the woods after the crash. The young man's traumatized parents desperately wanted their son's dog back. It took days, but De Cando finally found the animal. He was glad that in the darkest possible moment life could offer, he could do this for the parents. Then there was a twelve-year-old girl who had returned home after being hospitalized for depression. The same week, a narcotics bust went down in her building and a cop shot her dog by accident. She was devastated. The dog was severely wounded and De Cando was supposed to put him to sleep. Instead, he took him to the animal hospital, where the vet discovered that all the vital organs were functioning, and so he saved him.

De Cando really loved it when an owner of escaped goats phoned him.

"You have my goats, sir?"

"Yeah, we've got 'em right here."

"Oh, thank God. I'll be right there."

"Great. And then when you get here, I'll give you a whole bunch of tickets for letting them loose."

That's usually when the phone went silent. Another happy ending was on its way. Another life saved. His buddy the retired fire chief had a petting zoo upstate in Sussex County, where the goats could spend the rest of their days in peace.

"All this I get to do for about $65,000 a year."

The runaway cow was a very different story. De Cando couldn't send it to a petting zoo. Once an animal gets away like that, it cannot be used for slaughter, so the owner promised to send it to a farm. De Cando didn't like the sound of it. Neither did the people at the Woodstock Animal Sanctuary in upstate New York, who saw the story on the news. They called De Cando and asked if they could come and get the calf. His answer was yes. Absolutely yes.

⌣

MY YOUNGER son Simon, then aged twelve, and I headed north on the New York State Thruway.

"It looks real," my son said, pointing up ahead.

I strained to look.

"No. Not real. Can't be real." But it was a confusing sight. I sped up to get a better look.

He'd been pointing to a life-sized bear, standing up tall on two legs, riding in the back of a pickup truck.

"If it were just a doll, they would have just thrown it in the back of a truck."

He had a point.

We were silent for a moment as we realized that it was taxidermy.

The pickup sped ahead and soon was gone.

We arrived at Woodstock Farm Animal Sanctuary, where the lucky few who avoided the slaughterhouse got to live out their days in peace and kindness. Its founder, Jenny Brown, was a vegan in her early forties, with movie-star good looks and a prosthetic leg as a result of childhood cancer. She'd been a media producer and got into the animal-saving business after working on a documentary about farm conditions. After a veal calf—removed from his mother, living in an isolated cell—nuzzled her hand, wanting to be petted, she gave up filmmaking and took up advocacy and nonprofit work. She started the sanctuary with her husband, Doug Abel. With vegan cookbooks in the gift shop, her sanctuary existed not just to provide a refuge for animals but also to promote a vegan lifestyle and change the attitude that animals exist for human use.

It was a perfect June day, and the sanctuary was in an idyllic setting on a piece of land with pastures and outbuildings surrounded by the Catskill Mountains. When we arrived, I asked about the Paterson calf.

Her name was Junior. I found her in the barn, lying down in the straw with a white cow named Kayla. The two seemed quite comfortable side by side. Interestingly, Kayla was also an escapee—she'd run from a Philadelphia slaughterhouse. The staff told me that Junior, Kayla, and another cow named Maybelle were usually seen together out in the pasture. They played and groomed one another. They seemed to be friends.

We went on a tour with Sheila, a tall, slim woman with impressive biceps from building barns, hauling rocks, and digging ditches. Her hands were big and strong, and so were her legs, in muck boots.

There were about 180 residents at the sanctuary, she told us, and about half of them were birds. Sheila clearly had a special feeling for them. She spent a long time (what felt perhaps a bit *too* long) telling us the names and stories of all the chickens and ducks. Those over there had been picked up on a street in the Bronx (cockfighting, maybe), while that duck and babies were found on FDR Drive in New York City. See those? They'd fallen off a truck on the way to slaughter. She pointed out their distinct personalities and sociability.

Then she held up a battery cage so we could see the size of the box used to hold multiple birds, with their beaks cut off to prevent them hurting one another.

Chickens are the most intensively farmed animals in the United

States and the world. Whereas cattle and pigs and sheep are slaughtered by the millions, chickens are farmed by the *billions* (more than eight billion), under far lower humane standards than mammals. On small farms, it used to be that the female chickens laid eggs and the males were slaughtered for meat. But in order to maximize production, with cheaper and more profitable birds, the industry developed two distinct strains for the two different jobs. Chickens for the eating market now grow twice as big in half the time as they did in the 1950s. It's hard for them to stand up without toppling over, because of their big, heavy chests. Chickens for the egg business now lay more eggs. But when males are born, they have no market purpose and are bagged up and thrown away or put into a grinder.

Sheila picked up one chicken after the next so we could pet them and feed them, and she invited us into their enclosures so we could watch them scratch about in their natural way. The birds were her friends, she said. She stroked a Red rooster's amber feathers and, before putting him down, kissed him on the back.

My son leaned closer and whispered to me, "If the farmers were to come to get these chickens back, Sheila would *die* to defend them." I had to agree.

Sheila had a gentle manner, and in the most unobtrusive way she offered the suggestion that if we wanted to impact the greatest *number* of lives, we could consider not eating chickens or eggs.

This idea of impacting the *most* lives raised the troublesome question of how you might measure the value of the life you would save.

In the eighteenth century, English philosopher Jeremy Bentham challenged the world when he wrote, "The question is not, Can they *reason*? Nor, can they *talk*? But, can they suffer?"

This proposition, that all beings—animals, children, the sick, and disabled—are due consideration based on their capacity for suffering, rather than on their intelligence, was a revolutionary challenge to the Aristotelian hierarchy. Nearly two hundred years after Bentham

Olive the pig at Woodstock Farm Sanctuary. (Author's collection)

wrote those words, the question of suffering has become a foundation of the modern animal protection movement.

In the pig barn Simon and I met Olive, who, along with several other pigs, was resting in stillness. Obviously Olive had recently rolled about in mud, but now she was cooled down in the straw, eyes closed. Children came and went, taking turns lying down beside her, petting her, and hugging her. The only other time I'd ever touched a pig was in the breeding room of Tom's pig farm in Ireland. I couldn't fathom a more dramatic difference. Olive lay in deep, peaceful repose, her bristly hair caked with mud. She tucked up a hoof, but didn't otherwise move. My son scratched behind her ears, and then her belly and chest. He lay down and hugged her—and for a couple of moments stayed in that position. Later he would tell me that her beating heart was so loud, it sounded like a bass drum.

I had to admit that over the coming days, the image of Olive came back to me frequently; I didn't quite know why. Her peaceful face? Her stillness? But obviously, I was not alone. I got a text from Simon. "Hi mom. Remember Olive? Wasn't she so nice?"

After the tour, Simon and I wandered the property's rolling meadows, past the solar panels and mountain views, and found our way back to the visitor's center and its gift shop. Sheila approached me. She'd noticed that I'd been too nervous to hold the chickens during the tour. Would I like her to help me give it a try?

A few moments later, Sheila was putting a Rhode Island Red in my arms, telling me to hold it close to my body. She was so much lighter than I'd expected, not more than a pound. The mother inside of me came out, and I found my strong hands that had held the babies firmly, so they would feel supported. The hen's coos vibrated against my chest. She felt just like any other gentle creature. Her body was warm, and her feathers softer than I would have imagined. I could have held her for a long time. Mostly I loved her amber eyes, tiny and reptilian, vulnerable, yet dignified, looking out at the world.

⌒

THERE IS a saying that no man is a hero in his own country. I realized that much of what Marion and the women of LAW had started doing back in the Seventies and Eighties was way ahead of their time. Over the last decade in the U.S., the no-kill animal shelter movement has become a mainstream, not a radical proposition. And while there have always been people who have spoken out for animals, human concern for animal protection has dramatically changed for many reasons. One of these is the Internet.

Until quite recently, animal activists and even animal welfare workers were ridiculed, just as Humanity Dick once was. Today, he would have a website and two million Twitter followers, perhaps a million digital signatures from around the world, and video footage of bears and dogs tearing one another to shreds.

According to Alissa Quart in her book *Republic of Outsiders,* animal protection's transition from radical to mainstream is part of a larger trend. She argues that over the last twenty years, technology has made it possible for a rising class of web-powered amateurs and outsiders in the United States—and beyond—to take matters into their own hands and invent new ways of doing things. Technology now provides the tools and the access to information that make it possible to do almost anything yourself—from making movies and becoming a recording star on YouTube, to launching a craft brewery or even starting a charter school. We no longer need big institutions and companies to provide us with all our products and services. Alternatives have always existed, but now they are widely acceptable, so that the line between outsiders and insiders has blurred.

Technology may have provided the means for outsiders to forge new ways of doing things, but the drive and motivation, Quart says, came from the failure of the establishment to do its job well. The incompetence of our experts—from the Hurricane Katrina debacle of 2005, to the bank collapse and bailout of 2008, to the crass commercialization of everything—incited amateurs to take matters into their own hands.

Our government-run animal pounds, our USDA food inspection programs, our entertainment companies, textile manufacturers, and medical labs have failed to protect animals from abuse. Since animals are voiceless, growing numbers of people have taken it upon themselves to step in. They have started smaller family farms that raise animals humanely and find likeminded customers at farmer's markets or via mail order online. Like Marion and the women of LAW, they have started no-kill animal shelters. Animal protectors have developed vegan food and vegan clothing they can market online.

And quite dramatically, in the absence of adequate inspections and law enforcement against crimes of animal cruelty, the amateurs have stepped in to appoint themselves the cops of the livestock that become the food Americans eat.

⁓

HE ASKED to be called Pete—not his real name, but that was typical. Pete had spent much of the last thirteen years on the road, using different identities—always pretending to be someone else. He'd been the shady guy from out of state, or "a dumb redneck" who needed a job and had nowhere to go back to. He'd given off the vibe that he would work hard and was hired to shovel shit out of animal stalls and load dogs and cats onto trucks.

His employer was Martin Creek Kennel, a USDA-certified Class D animal dealer that had sold thousands of dogs and cats to medical laboratories. Unlike Class A dealers, who raised animals for this purpose, Class D dealers did "random sourcing." This meant they got dogs and cats from many places—usually pounds. Pete had been sent on this mission by an organization called Last Chance for Animals, which had discovered that that Martin Creek not only abused animals but also purchased stolen pets.

After five and a half months of undercover work, Pete gathered the evidence needed to call in law enforcement and build a case. When police raided Martin Creek, they seized 125 cats and 600 dogs. The facility was shut down.

Not long after that, Pete met Nathan Runkle, a young animal advocate who had recently started Mercy For Animals, a nonprofit dedicated to ending animal cruelty on factory farms. He told Pete that there were many people working to help cats and dogs. But if he wanted to make a greater impact, he should help farm animals, because there were billions of them and they had the worst lives. Pete was persuaded and became a contractor for Mercy For Animals.

He quickly learned that making an impact on the lives of farm animals was far more difficult than helping cats and dogs. Major food companies have powerful lobbyists and billions at stake.

"When I worked on the Martin Creek case, all of the animals were saved and got into homes. The facility got shut down. I have spent almost thirteen years after that case trying to have that kind of success again. I've had smaller successes but nothing that shut anyone down again. . . . But there was no looking back."

I was struck by all that Pete had sacrificed. He had spent thirteen years alone on the road, witnessing animal slaughter on a daily basis, moving between hotels and friends' couches—a stranger everywhere.

"There were a couple of years when I was homeless, staying with friends or my parents in between jobs and then just going back on the road. That's when you're most productive; you don't have anything to go back to. You don't miss anything."

When I spoke to him in early 2014, he'd recently had a victory. From mid-September to mid-October of the previous year, he'd worked undercover as a farmhand at West Coast Farms in Oklahoma, wearing a microphone and camera. He captured footage of workers kicking and beating sows until they were crying, and docking the tails of baby pigs without euthanasia at conveyor-belt speed. Not just one worker did this, but many. He also captured workers picking up piglets by the feet and slamming their heads on the cement floor to kill them, a method of death called blunt force trauma, legal and accepted in the industry for killing animals who were too sick to survive. However, leaving animals half alive and suffering on the "dead pile" after "failed euthanasia attempts" was *not* legal, and this is what Pete captured.

"Every worker was doing it," said Pete. "The farmer-owner did nothing about it. He talked the talk but didn't walk the walk."

Pete was adamant that though he loves animals—and has since he was a child— his job is focused on basic law enforcement. There were no law enforcement agencies or units investigating animal welfare crimes in Big Agriculture. Food factories were off-limits to the public. Therefore, he reasoned, it fell to civilians like him to do the job. His goal was to protect animals by gathering evidence of crimes and handing it over to the police and the courts—and then the public.

"In thirteen years, every place I've gone into, there have been people committing crimes."

Mercy For Animals gave the footage to the district attorney in Oklahoma and then put it out on its networks. After NBC picked up the story and aired the undercover video, Tyson Foods immediately canceled its contract with West Coast Farms, saying that it would "not tolerate this kind of animal mishandling."

When I asked Pete how he felt about his coworkers in the field, he said that most of the time he didn't hate them. They had no respect for animals to begin with, and they became quickly desensitized to animal cruelty because of the conditions. Many of them had substance abuse problems and were extremely stressed.

"You need to move this damn animal to the pen and why won't the animal cooperate? Why is that animal scared? You start to see that the animal is just trying to frustrate you and give you grief. For the most part, it's not sadism, but people making really bad decisions that cause innocent animals to suffer."

He added that one of the hardest things about his job was how desensitized he became to animal suffering. "You go into a slaughterhouse and at first you're horrified. Then you start working. By the end of the day, your mind is wandering. You're not thinking that this is an animal. It's just something the brain does to survive."

He was far less generous to the farm management and corporations, which blame the abuse on the workers and delegate negligence to the lowest people on the totem pole. According to Pete, the environments in major slaughterhouses keep extreme pressure on workers to meet quotas and achieve production speeds that are unreasonably high—increasing the risk of animal abuse.

In August 2016, the *Chicago Tribune* studied the impact of all known undercover videos of U.S. hog confinement since 1998—a total of twenty films. The reporters found that six of these videos had led to criminal charges against twenty-three workers, eighteen of whom were punished with short jail stints and small fines. Some were forbidden to work with hogs for a period of time. In nine additional cases, workers were fired, or big companies like Tyson cut their ties with the offending food producers.

For Big Ag, the far bigger threat has been the growing public awareness of and interest in how animals are raised and slaughtered. Terms like "free range" for chickens and "gestation crates" for sows were industry jargon fifteen years ago. Now the broader public knows what they mean, and surveys show that a growing number of consumers care.

In Big Ag states, lawmakers have tried to outlaw undercover animal cruelty investigations by passing so-called "Ag-Gag" laws—which make it illegal for people like Pete to take jobs in food farming or factories—in twenty-three states. Five of them have succeeded. One, so far, has been struck down by a federal judge as unconstitutional.

"Fuck the politics," said Pete. "If I meet with a cop it's because I have evidence of people breaking the law. And that means you should not make it illegal for us to do our job."

⁓

A SLEEK new eatery had opened in the neighborhood where I worked: a hamburger joint run by a famous New York City butcher. As I walked to the subway to go home at night, the smell of meat nearly knocked me over. Lunch long gone, my stomach was empty. I was thinking medium rare, with a slice of tomato and onion.

But I couldn't. Each time I thought about stepping across the threshold, I felt a rock in my belly. At first I didn't know what this rock was, but then I paid closer attention and realized, with deep sadness, that it was a full-grown living cow. It was inside of me, and it was also standing on a meadow around Lancaster or maybe Cork County, looking at me with its big eyes, watching.

It was clear that I was totally screwed. I had changed. And it was absolutely awful.

I knew it for sure when one day my cooking buddy Lou showed me a YouTube video of a Cuban Christmas poolside celebration in a Florida backyard. Steel drums and a rumba beat played in the background while a couple of holiday revelers wheeled a rectangular box onto the patio. A man in shorts and flip-flops poured the charcoal in, and then placed a roasting rack on top. Then came the dead pig. Two strong men, each holding a pair of feet, lowered it down to the rack, face turned to the side. They pressed another rack tightly on top and set the fire at a slow burn.

The video showed a time-lapse edit. One hour later, the men returned to flip the pig, now belly side up. All the while it's party time. Cuban music, cocktails, happiness. Lou was laughing as he showed it to me, charmed by the authenticity of it all.

There was a time when I would have found all this wonderfully fun, too, and laughed along with my friend at the charm of a traditional fiesta. As a food writer, I'd spent a great many years engaged in a deep relationship with a family ravioli recipe that was based on veal and pork. And I'd written about sausage-making, prosciutto, pot roast, and more. Foodies—the stupid name for this culture of people who place great importance on growing, cooking, and eating well—were a tribe of which I was a card-carrying member.

Let me be perfectly clear: I cannot say whether they were right or wrong for roasting a pig. But what I can say is that, for me, it is no longer possible to look at this as entertainment or joy—because now I could see the pig as an individual being, its singed hair and crackling skin. I couldn't help but feel sad about the animal's death and, for that matter, all the other animals' deaths, and our own deaths, too.

"Pigs are meant for slaughter," I heard in my head, from Thomas Hardy's *Jude the Obscure.* Jude's miserable wife, Arabella, set her husband straight when he dawdled over killing the pig, "a creature I have fed with my own hands." And we believe her that Jude was too soft-hearted, which is why the world ultimately mowed him down. He recoiled from violence to the innocent, and he was correct to do so because later, though he couldn't know this yet, his own children would be murdered. When he realized that cruelty was unavoidable, he wanted to butcher the animal quickly, to spare the pig any pain. But Arabella objected because she believed a slow kill would make the meat better. "Poor folks must live," she says. Her words stick with me because meat is cheap in this country thanks to the brutality of industrial slaughter lines in factory farms. Humanely produced meat—if it exists—is far more costly, and a privilege.

Suddenly there was nothing to eat no matter where I went. I did not want to be a vegetarian; it left out too many of life's delights. The world was drabber. I struggled to make bolognese sauce for my family, or grill a burger at a summer barbecue. I remembered *boeuf bourguignon* in wintertime and my grandmother's stew. I could not make my favorite chicken piccata or eat Lou's prosciutto.

At a conference of food writers, I mentioned my predicament to Ken Albala, a food historian and colleague in my old network. His reply was simple: "If you don't eat bacon, your life is a waste."

Meanwhile, my kids still wanted to eat meat. Simon, after his time with Olive the pig, was a vegetarian for about six months, but an errant hamburger during spring break sent him back to the carnivore's life. Now, I sometimes cook humanely raised grass-fed beef for them, but I will not buy pork.

Explaining why to Simon, I told him that pigs are as smart as dogs.

"But one is a pet, and one is a food," he replied without missing a beat.

"What's the difference?"

He paused and gave me a you-must-be-out-of-your-mind teenager look.

"Do you actually think that eating a pig is the same thing as eating a dog?"

"I don't know," I answered, a bit mealy-mouthed. "I'm not sure."

"You're doing that journalism thing when you act unbiased. But you really aren't."

"Simon, I really don't know what I think. Do we have the right to take a life we do not need to take?"

That was when the conversation was over for him. He washed his hands of me. "Do you have to have an issue with everything, Mom? You'll never be happy."

Actually, I wasn't telling the whole truth when I said that I don't buy pork anymore. Once a year, I still purchase pork, when I make the family ravioli for the holidays. I am amazed at how easy it is to eat when it is wrapped in pasta, covered in sauce, and generally a part of my favorite dish in the world. I simply shut the door as needed. I can block it out, just like everyone else.

We all want our exceptions.

19

—

MIRACLE WORKER

2013

I took one more visit to Ireland in 2013. This trip, I found Marion looking pale and older, much less comfortable in her body. This was no surprise. She was fighting time, the thing she'd once described jokingly as "my expiration date or whatever you want to call it." We'd been in touch by email so I had a clue.

> I am falling over myself these days . . . Trying to get new horse shelters up before the winter sets in. . . .

> We got a lovely lurcher this morning. I had been trying to catch her for three weeks.

> It's been very hard here. Nobody has money. Everyone is depressed. I don't ever remember such a difficult time in Ireland . . .

It was December, the last month of what had been a wretchedly terrible year. What a contrast to December 2012, when they'd been celebrating deceptively good news. A wealthy woman, Mrs. Elizabeth Burke of Dublin, age seventy—someone they didn't even know—had bequeathed 500,000 euro to the "Limerick branch of the Royal Society for the Prevention of Cruelty to Animals."

Except, no such organization existed.

In such cases, the law said that the money should go to the charity doing the closest kind of work. The government commission in charge of charitable donations said that Limerick Animal Welfare and the Limerick Society for the Prevention of Cruelty to Animals should share the money equally.

"Whoever this wonderful lady was, we'll be praying for her," Marion told the *Limerick Leader*. "We have never received anything like that, [and we are] still pinching ourselves."

But it was not to be—at least not for now—because all year the money had been held up. The LSPCA was insisting that the whole sum—or, at least, more than half—should be theirs.

Marion was visibly stiff and in pain that day. No matter which way she moved, she couldn't get comfortable. The previous month, driving home from the sanctuary one night, she'd fallen asleep at the wheel. When she woke up she found herself in a ditch, with the car wrecked and a fractured disk. She was lucky. She could have been killed.

John had been diagnosed with cancer the previous spring. Thank God it had been contained. Three months of treatment, and it all looked good. But she was worried about him.

She was worried about everything.

Five years after the recession, relief was not yet in sight. Nobody had any money; unemployment was still high. Her thrift shops weren't bringing in what she'd hoped. Donations were down. New animals showed up every day.

Marion at the Field of Dreams sanctuary in progress, Kilfinane. (Courtesy John Mottern)

The main building at the sanctuary had not progressed. It was still just a shell. Her builder had recently informed her that mold had begun to set in and she had to act immediately or there would be major damage.

When I looked at her incredulously, she explained that you can't leave the shell of a building empty for a long period. She had to move ahead with construction, even if it meant another loan, so that she could at least turn on the heat and protect the empty building.

I wondered then, for the first time, if she would ever finish it. Would it be like those developments all over Ireland, unfinished buildings that would eventually have to be torn down?

Yes, an awful year.

Once, when we were talking about Johanna Wothke, Marion said, "I call her the great Johanna. I don't know anyone who can do what she does. She comes in to do a project and within a few months it's done. It's finished down to the paint on the gate, the dog bowls in a row. It's finished. She gets the money and does it. She will go into the most appalling places and get something done. She's not going to have anything to do with SPCA meetings and arguing. She comes on with her bag of money and does it her way. She is an extraordinary person."

I got it in my head that in the midst of my trip to Ireland, I could get to Germany for a day or two to meet the great Johanna, then come back. I had emailed my request in advance to her organization, but getting an audience wasn't going to be easy. She was very busy, opening a new sanctuary and writing the last issue of her magazine for the year. They gave a date, and canceled it. Could I possibly go to Poland instead? Finally, a deal was brokered. Mrs. Wothke would speak with me on December 3 at 11 a.m., if I could keep it to a strict two-hour time limit.

Agreed.

After a long drive across Ireland to Dublin, I took a plane, a train, and a taxi to arrive in Schweinfurt, Germany, late at night. The next morning, I found my way to a grand-looking historic building surrounded by a park. Birds fluttered from one feeder to the next. Pro Animale headquarters was inside.

An administrator greeted me with pleasant formality. "Mrs. Wothke will be with you shortly."

I felt nervous, as though I were going to visit a high priest. To occupy myself, I studied the many photos of Pro Animale's sanctuaries displayed around the room, beneath hand-lettered words painted on the walls: "In Spanien, In Irlande, In Polande, In Russia . . ."

Out in the hallway, footsteps approached, then a whispery conversation took place in German, and finally Johanna Wothke appeared. She wore a loose caftan and sandals, grey hair cropped close to her head, tinted eyeglasses, and not a speck of makeup or jewelry. She reminded me of nuns and monks who renounced the material world. A sense of urgency pressed against the air around her.

"It's a catastrophe!" she said. "If I don't write, there is not coming money. In fact, people are calling wondering where it is."

It took me a moment to realize that *I* was the catastrophe that was taking her away from writing her quarterly magazine. The December issue was always the thickest, with more photos than any other issue, portraying animals rescued and projects completed. It also contained her all-important end-of-year plea, which brought in the largest percentage of Pro Animale's donations for the year. It was December 3 and she still had not finished.

"A catastrophe!" she repeated. "But what can we do? This is when the writer is in Europe," she said, as though I were not there. Then she turned and shook my hand. When she looked me in the eyes, her face softened.

"Come this way."

I followed Johanna down a hallway that was painted black and grey, lined with before-and-after photos that told stories of animal salvation. Pigs, cows, and horses, first found in filth, darkness, or pain, brought into cleanliness, light, and good health. Up near the ceiling were large, hand-lettered German words.

Johanna pointed and translated. "Who is to blame? You I or anyone for the suffering of our helpless fellow creatures?"

Her voice was surprisingly quiet. She sounded almost like a teenage girl when she spoke. And yet everything else about her presence was intimidating, perhaps intentionally so, in order to keep people from interrupting her work. Like Marion, she had much less time ahead than behind her. She couldn't slow down. She had to save more lives.

She led me into an immense room with high ceilings and sweeping windows that brought in winter light. Dozens more photos on the walls portrayed happy pigs rolling in mud, horses running with their manes billowing, dogs at play in the sunshine. The rest of the room was filled with art—large oil paintings, sculpture, religious icons, stained glass. Papers and binders lay neatly stacked on tables. And at the far end of the room, two dogs—one of them a lurcher— lounged like starlets on a small sofa. A constellation of tree limbs hung from the ceiling, threaded with tiny white twinkly lights and ornaments.

We sat at a long, grand table. After several formalities, I began with a simple question. "I'm interested in the idea that someone has a normal life . . . and then everything changes."

I had barely finished before she interrupted.

"I never had a normal life. Never normal. I was born in 1940. My father was not a Jew but he helped Jews. He would not raise his hand and say 'Heil Hitler' and got put in jail for a while. He was a writer, but forbidden to publish. Many writers were forbidden to publish then. Artists were not allowed to paint. His literary circle was always coming to the house discussing the war and the regime and the horrible situation. I was a little girl with my eyes and ears open. No. Not a normal life."

She added, "I have big affinity for Auschwitz and Birkenau." To explain what she meant, she asked if I knew of the Yiddish writer Isaac Bashevis Singer, who wrote that for animals, every day is the Holocaust.

Deep inside of her there was an image of blood. In Berlin, someone had attacked her father because of his anti-Hitler views. He wound up on the ground. It was not a serious injury, but it was very bloody. He got himself to the doctor, who picked up the phone to call the SS, so her father left. She'd carried this story for so many decades that now it was probably as blurry as a dream. But the single image that remained—haunting her, driving her—was her father lying in blood.

Johanna told me that her love of animals was not innate, but something that grew from her empathy for all living things, "seeded in my soul by my father."

Her first contact with the "unjust life of animals" came when she was seven years old and found a pregnant street dog. She took the animal home and kept her in the attic until her mother (of course) arranged for the dog's swift departure. Next there was the pet rabbit she cared for, which, to her utter horror, turned up on a platter one evening at the dinner table. She never got over that. How could you eat a friend? Later, as an art student visiting Florence, she was distraught over the mangy, starving street dogs. She found herself giving them food and water rather than going to the Uffizi Gallery.

At twenty-one Johanna was in Berlin, studying Byzantine art at the free university, when, one August morning in 1961, she woke up to find that all the telephone wires had been cut. In the city center, the East German army was building a wall to separate East from West, Communist from capitalist, free from not free, parents from children, husbands from wives.

At first, Johanna and some other West German students were able to travel back and forth to families on the eastern side, bringing news and getting clothes to bring back to the other students. But this didn't last long.

"Normal life? No. Never a normal life."

When she was at the university, Johanna met a man and married, but it was not a good match, and they divorced. With one young child and a baby, she left Berlin and got a job as an elementary school teacher in North Bavaria. With help from her mother and a bank loan, she built a house in a small village named Uetzing. Her land was on a hill, surrounded by trees and nature. For many years after that, she and her children led a simple rural life that she describes as idyllic and wonderful, a home of art and books—and stray and wild animals, which her children brought home in need of help. She always said yes, and soon animals started to arrive on their own, as if the word had gotten out among them. They came because they were hungry or hurt or sick or needed shelter. This went on for years, until Johanna had become well known throughout the surrounding area as that schoolteacher who took in animals that were in need of care.

One day, the police called her because they were planning to raid a vivisection dealer who lived in her town. He was a small-time operator who bought dogs and cats from farmers or picked up strays in the fields, then sold the animals to larger dealers that supplied laboratories. The police suspected cruelty and asked Johanna if she could come. They needed an animal person there to help. She had no idea what it would entail, but agreed.

When they entered the property, they found dozens of animals living in outbuildings in cages filled with excrement—dogs and cats trembling and trying to hide, fearful of making eye contact. Wothke was beside herself. She took home ten big dogs. They were wild and didn't know the first thing about living in a house, but she felt she had no choice.

The experience struck her deeply. She cleaned up and cared for the first ten, then found them homes. Four months later, she went back and paid the vivisection dealer so that she could take fifteen more. Within six months, she had fifty dogs. Not long after that, she wrote her first newsletter and sent it to her friends, asking for their support. From there, Pro Animale began and grew. She wanted to tell me how passionately she opposed keeping animals in kennels—by this she meant the individual crates and rooms where single animals were kept in isolation. These were prisons, she said.

Her home in Uetzing—where she had lived for thirty years and raised her children—was now one of her sanctuaries.

"Oh, I wish you could see it. What time is your plane back?"

She called in her administrator, who checked train schedules, and then found a Pro Animale staff member to drive me. I'd had different plans for my afternoon but decided to go with the flow. I realized that I'd just experienced the Johanna way. She had an idea and made it happen.

Uetzing is a small Bavarian village with red tile rooftops in a cluster, and little else except pastoral quiet. We entered the house to find the oddest scene. In each room, a cluster of four or five dogs looked at us. They had beds and couches and also some built-in furniture to climb on. We were in a parallel world, in which dogs had taken over the planet and become people. They looked back at me as if it was totally normal for them to be sitting around the breakfast nook together.

In the backyard Johanna had built unusual play structures, designed for dogs, not children, which included stairs that the dogs could climb and look out at the landscape.

After I got over my initial amusement and urge to write this endeavor off as ludicrously impractical, I started to see that it had a brilliance to it. The goal was to find the dogs adoptive homes, so in the meantime, they were socialized with other dogs and living in small groups as close to a wolf pack as possible. They were alert and happy. Yes, it was crazy. But it was an extraordinary vision.

Before I'd left Johanna that afternoon, I asked her the question I continually asked others and myself. "Why animals? How do you decide what to put your energy toward when there is so much suffering in the world? Where do you even begin?"

She answered without hesitation. "Start on the ground on which you stand."

20

—

PARADISE IS FOREVER

2015

Colleen, who is my sister-in-law, and her husband, Filippo, picked me up from the airport at Cancún, and we began the long drive to their jungle home. Signs along the highway advertised snorkeling, swimming with captive dolphins, and "eco tour" expeditions to underwater caves called *cenotes*. We passed one waterfront resort after the next. They had names like El Dorado, Palladium, and Dreams. "All-inclusives," said Colleen, looking out of the window. Her tone held a forced neutrality that recognized the complexity of the world. One creature's joy-filled all-you-can-eat holiday was another creature's habitat destruction.

They had a vested interest in the environment here because they are primatologists. They'd dedicated fifteen years of their lives to the study of spider monkeys here in the Yucatán.

Only forty years earlier, Cancún had been a wild barrier island at the tip of the Yucatán peninsula. In 1975, the Mexican government took out huge loans and financed a resort, luring international hotel companies with deals they couldn't resist. Cancún grew into a vacation mecca for foreigners, with amusement parks, discos, and golf. Three million tourists came each year.

By the 1990s, development began to creep southward to the Mayan ruins of Tulum. This eighty-mile stretch was rebranded as the Riviera Maya, with the slogan "Paradise is Forever," to convey its extraordinary wildlife. But twenty years later, many native species were endangered. Tourism was helping to destroy the natural environment that the slogan advertised.

"When we first starting coming, none of this was here," said Filippo, gesturing with his arm at all of it. At Tulum, Filippo turned inland. It would be another hour's torrid drive.

Despite the many years Colleen and Filippo had been here, it was my first visit. When we arrived at their house, they issued advisories on how to cope with the wildlife. It was the dry season, so scorpions and tarantulas were unlikely, but there could be rats and assassin bugs, which may carry a disease that dissolves your organs. The beds were zipped up inside canopy tents of mosquito netting, not just to protect against bugs, but to keep out other small critters that might emerge in the night.

At present, the pool was unapproachable because killer bees had descended, and I was warned to avoid the army ants, which march on an unstoppable path and give agonizing bites. For those who wonder why humans have crushed and controlled nature, a visit to the jungle may not provide an excuse, but it sure explains a lot.

The next morning, I joined Colleen and Filippo on their regular morning bird walk, where we saw orioles, motmots, an American redstart, red-eyed vireos, green jays, and other standard tropical birds with absurdly bright colors. When a chattery bell-ringing song rose above us, they looked at each other, nodding: Yes, that's it. Simultaneously, they lifted binoculars to their eyes.

It was a Yucatán parrot, hidden with a companion in a nearby tree. We stood still a long while, watching its bright green body, listening.

"They're skittish around humans for good reason," Colleen explained. "Humans steal their babies for the illegal pet trade."

"And they know?"

"You bet they know."

"You'll be safe here," Colleen called up quietly to the trees.

The following week, back home with my husband, I asked how people could be so awful as to stuff parrots into bags, bottles, and tubs to smuggle them across the border.

"Isn't it obvious?" he asked. "Because they don't see the birds as living creatures. They see them as things."

A couple of days later, Colleen and I drove back toward Tulum and passed through a large wooden gate with the sign, "The Jungle Place."

It was a sanctuary for spider monkeys, who lived in an extraordinary human built monkey city that went high up into the trees. The air was kinetic as seventy-two bodies shot about in different directions, climbing, hanging upside down, leaping and swinging in large fast swoops from place to place. They had ladders and ropes, ledges and runways. Though fences are sad for any wild creatures, these were at least twenty feet tall, made of chain-link—perfect for small climbing feet and hands that scaled to the top in less than thirty seconds. It was like I'd come upon a playground on Saturday morning, except instead of children it was teeming with monkeys, which also happened to be acrobats.

Colleen noticed my awe and smiled. "It's a bit overwhelming at first."

A petite woman with short blond hair and high cheekbones emerged through the palm trees. This was Heidi Michlin, who, along with her husband, Joel, had founded this sanctuary for abused and abandoned spider monkeys. She and Colleen embraced like sisters.

Heidi made a sweeping gesture that took in the entire place and she said, with a joyful laugh, "They are my babies," as though this crazy statement could possibly explain what I saw. She introduced her husband, who had two baby monkeys attached to his body.

"This is Aurora," he said, pointing to the one on his shoulder. She was fifteen months old. "And this is Heidilay" (Heidi's childhood nickname). He looked down at the monkey wrapped around his leg. They clung to him as though he were their mother. And really, that's exactly what he was.

The market for illegally poached baby monkeys was brisk in the Yucatán and elsewhere. They are irresistibly cute and vulnerable creatures, with amazing little hands and feet and doll faces—born so small that they could fit inside a coffee mug.

"The poachers shoot the mothers," said Heidi. "Sometimes, the baby stays up in the tree clinging to the mother's dead body, so they take out a chainsaw and cut the tree down."

Since 1975, it has been illegal to import monkeys for the pet trade. Therefore, if you buy a baby monkey in the U.S.—which you can do in about half the states—you most likely will be buying one that was bred in captivity, a descendant of a monkey stolen from the wild some years ago. Though it may be tempting to feel that this might be less harmful, it isn't. Even in captivity, the only way to get a baby monkey is to take it from its mother, which is agonizing cruelty for both.

Of course, monkeys do not make remotely suitable pets. They are adorable as children, difficult as adolescents when their hormones kick in, then downright destructive as adults when confinement becomes unbearable. Just as with backyard tigers, the once-beloved pet gets banished, out of the house to live in the yard—tethered with a rope around its neck, and largely forgotten.

Most of the seventy-two monkeys at Jungle Place were brought in by PROFEPPA, the Mexican environmental protection agency, which had confiscated them from the underground pet trade or squalid zoos.

"It's amazing. In fourteen years, they've only lost four monkeys," said Colleen.

"And what do you attribute that to?" I expected a well-thought-out science-based answer, but Colleen gave a one-word reply.

"Love."

In the wild, spider monkeys live for four or five years with their mothers, learning how to be a monkey and survive. Heidi and Joel undertook the initial job of parenting the orphan babies, allowing them to sleep in their bed at night and stay close during the day, just as they would do with their true parents. As foster parents, they swaddled the babies in blankets, fed them through a bottle, and let them ride on their shoulders. They called themselves the "Mommy and Daddy monkeys."

But the goal was to get the babies to grow up and live with the other monkeys in monkey city. Over the course of many months they went for visits to monkey city—longer and more frequently over time. They watched and learned how to climb and jump, how to behave with the others. Eventually they all left Mom and Dad's house to become full-time, well-adjusted members of the extraordinary community just outside Joel and Heidi's door.

I was mesmerized by their bodies. In the wild, spider monkeys live in the forest canopy. When you see them walking on all fours, with their long spindly limbs, it's clear how they got their name. Their extra-long tails work as a fifth limb.

They have black backs, but when they sit or stand or squat they show their round, silvery bellies. Much of their faces is hairless and light in color, especially around the eyes, so that it looks like they are wearing a pale-colored mask. Their coarse hair tends to spike, punk rocker style, on the top of their heads. I was fascinated by their black four-fingered hands that work like hooks for grabbing when they climb and swing; their black feet are long, with five toes. Most of them glanced at me quickly then looked away, acting as if they hadn't seen me. But several were quite bold, coming right up to the fence and looking at me straight on.

"Look, Laura, you're getting a face greeting," said Colleen. That's when a monkey purses its lips at you, making a kissing face, she explained. I admit that I was flattered.

Heidi walked me through and called out the name and history of each monkey as we went.

"That's Gino. He was chained to a tree in the middle of a garbage dump.

"There's Layla. They filed down her teeth and the rope around her neck was so deeply embedded it needed to be surgically removed.

"Rebecca was chained behind a church.

"Teva arrived with a broken arm hanging off.

"Austin was rescued from an AA group."

"AA?" I echoed.

"Yes, Alcoholics Anonymous. You know. They thought that holding a baby monkey would help people with their recovery."

As Heidi walked past each enclosure, the monkeys acted like she was the Pope, or the president, or at least a rock star. They came racing to the fence. One after the next, arms emerged, reaching and straining to touch Heidi or even just try to touch a bit of her clothing. After they touched her, the monkeys sniffed their fingers for Heidi's smell. She greeted each one by name, touched their hands, patted them, kissed cheeks. At one point, she stepped up close to the fence and let three monkeys take turns grooming her. With laser focus, they inspected her scalp for foreign objects, running their fingers through her hair, one section at a time.

All the while, Heidi told me to stay back out of reach. At one point she gestured to a large monkey, letting me know that "he could beat the shit out of you."

"We didn't plan this," said Joel, when I asked how all of this came to be. He explained that he and Heidi arrived in the Yucatán in 1999, with plans to buy land on the beach, build a house, and retire. They'd both been married before, and Heidi was quite wealthy.

One day, a friend of a friend asked them if they would take a baby monkey in for the night. It didn't take them but an hour or so to realize that the baby had a very high fever and was gravely ill and dehydrated. They took him immediately to a vet, who said he probably wouldn't live forty-eight hours.

"That made me mad," says Heidi. "I told him to do everything he could to save the monkey, and we'd pay whatever it took."

For three weeks, they nursed the baby and gave him medicine throughout the day. The baby lived, and they named him Chaac, after the Maya rain god. (And no, they never gave him back.)

After that, word spread and people started bringing monkeys, rescued from lives in chains, who could never return to the wild. That house on the beach slipped out of reach day by day. When it became clear that another life was taking hold of them, they built this place in the jungle and expanded, one enclosure after the next.

Heidi had long ago run out of money. She'd spent it all on the monkey city. She told me that she wished she had more so that she could remove all fences and build a dome of forest so they could be free.

⁓

IN RECENT years, we have learned about the extraordinary intelligence of numerous animals—great apes, marine mammals, birds, and elephants in particular. There has been a movement, led by scientists, policy people, and lawyers, to reconsider how we think about them. A conference at Yale in 2013 brought together some of the greatest researchers to consider whether or not these animals should be considered as nonhuman persons. This didn't mean that animals would suddenly get the right to vote or drive cars. The idea of "nonhuman persons" simply meant that they would be respected as individuals, not things. Presently animals exist in two legal categories: they are wild or they are property. A dolphin in captivity has no more rights than your kitchen table.

Attorney Steven Wise of the Nonhuman Animal Rights (NhAR) project has been helping to lead this quest. He's gone about it through the unique approach of filing legal suits on behalf of chimpanzees that have been held in awful circumstances—as pets or in research laboratories. Each time, he argues that they deserve freedom based on habeas corpus, the legal concept that you cannot be detained and imprisoned without your day in court.

Through a lawsuit, he asked the court to agree that a primate named Kiko—held alone in a cell all her life—was a "legal person" for the purposes of a common-law writ of habeas corpus. The argument was that she possessed a right to bodily liberty. He requested that the court free her so that she could live her life in a primate sanctuary.

He made the same argument for two chimpanzees, Hercules and Leo, who were kept for years at Stony Brook University for studies on human locomotion; in other words, researchers studied the chimps to help them understand evolutionary aspects of human gait. For this they had spent years living indoors, in cells.

Wise thought he had his best shot with these two chimps. Studies of how humans came to walk were not about life and death (for humans, that is). He had an amazing sanctuary lined up for them, where they could live on an island in an environment close to their natural habitat, free of charge. He finally got a judge to hear the case. And though Wise did not prevail, just getting her to hear the case was a breakthrough.

Jane Goodall has stood up for Wise's clients, urging the judge to let these animals go to a sanctuary. So far, they are still waiting.

⌒

FILIPPO BROUGHT me to Punta Laguna, which sat at the edge of a forest filled with hundreds of spider monkeys. It was a small village comprised of about thirty families who still spoke Mayan. They were subsistence farmers when Colleen and Filippo had first arrived, but in 2002, after many years of lobbying, they persuaded the government to declare Punta Laguna a National Protected Area. This paved for the way for them to start an ecotourism business, which was their long-held dream. Colleen and Filippo built a mutually beneficial partnership with the villagers, who allowed them, and the other founding researchers, to set up a field site.

The village was more like a street than a village, and most homes were built of sticks and thatch. In the forest, our Punta Lagunan tour guide pointed out the different trees and wildlife that had provided food and sustenance to the Maya for generations. He took us past crumbling ruins, and enormous guanacaste and fig trees with bromeliad flowers growing on their branches. Then we hiked over dry leaves down into a ravine, as he and Filippo talked about where the monkeys might be.

Suddenly our guide stood still, and so did we—heads tilted back, looking way up. Yes, there was movement in the canopy. Two monkeys leapt from branch to branch. I gasped so loudly that I surprised myself and Filippo. I had no idea! As lovely as Heidi's sanctuary was, there was no comparison, no comparison at all, to seeing monkeys living in the wild. Soon mother monkeys appeared with babies clinging to them tightly; we watched another pair eat fruit from the treetops; we saw them lazing in the branches. I felt a great and wondrous sense of all I did not know.

Mother spider monkey leaping with a baby monkey wrapped around her waist.
(Courtesy Filippo Aurelli)

There was one image that stood out most, an image I cannot for-get: an adult male and a juvenile, perhaps his son, were moving easily above, rattling the leaves, making a gentle clatter. The adult male leapt from branch to branch, and the younger one followed. Then they came to a big gap between trees, and the adult took a huge flying jump across the void, landing neatly on a limb. The juvenile began to follow, but then stopped. We could see the hesitation, some kind of caution or uncertainty as to whether he could jump that far. We waited in the silence, wondering what he would do. Seconds later, his little body swung out into the air and flew across a bit of sky, landing safely. It was at that moment that I understood habeas corpus. I asked myself, Do we have the right to detain these fellow creatures and take possession of their amazing bodies? Shouldn't they have the right to be free?

21

—

SANCTUARY

2016

It had been two years since the mysterious Elizabeth Burke of Dublin left 550,000 euro to the nonexistent "Limerick Branch of the Royal Society for the Prevention of Cruelty to Animals." In 2015, the High Court finally came to the same conclusion as the original commission had: the two Limerick-based animal charities should share the funds equally.

"Wait," I said to Marion, over the phone. "Do you mean LAW will be getting half the money? You're going to be getting a quarter million euro?"

"Well, a bit less because of the court fees. It's 220,000 euro."

"So you can finish the sanctuary? Or get close?"

"Yes," she said with a laugh, and I heard a scrap of joy in her voice.

But before I could say anything more about finishing the sanctuary, she moved on to the next thing.

"Some land has come up for sale next to the sanctuary. I wanted to use some of the money to buy even a few acres. We really need more pasture for the horses, but they are all telling me no. We'll be overleveraged."

I could tell from her tone that she had still not fully accepted this, and was wondering if there was some way she could make it happen.

Marion went ahead and completed the main building—well, almost completed. When we spoke in late 2016, the animal quarters were finished and now held 120 dogs and cats. This was the first winter with the under-floor heating turned on. "You should see the dogs and cats lay about. It's like they're in heaven." The kitchen was finished, and so was the presentation room. Adoptions were going well. People loved to visit the sanctuary. The total population of animals now exceeded two hundred. Yes, it was great, she agreed. But as always, there was a strangling worry in her voice. Elizabeth Burke's generous bequest had run out before Marion could complete the veterinary clinic—and for that she'd have to find eighty thousand euro more. Plus, the original building needed a new roof—it was ten years old now—and of course this was all on top of her regular overhead. Well, at least she'd put up five horse shelters the previous winter, so now all the horses—twenty-seven at the moment—had a place at night. (Previously she'd had to put some of them outside with blankets on them.) "That's a big accomplishment," she admitted. And then she added, "It will never be all done." I heard a bit of acceptance in her voice.

Before I got off the phone, I asked her about the greyhounds. The Irish system had been hit hard by the recession. Between 2007 and 2014, the industry's income fell by nearly half. English tracks were closing, and that meant less demand for dogs and a serious loss of profit to Irish breeders. Meanwhile, new greyhound activism groups had started in Ireland and all around Europe, and many were on alert. In recent years, when the Bord had made moves to export dogs to places like China and Macau, activists arrived from everywhere and marched in the streets of Dublin to stop them. Wasn't this progress? I asked her. Did she feel she'd made a difference?

*Greyhound racing protesters in Dublin, 2015. Louise Coleman holds a flag.
(Courtesy John Mottern)*

"I feel that we have success that the greyhound tracks are closing in Europe and America—and especially the decline of the English trade," she said. "Ireland is like no place else because the government gives the business so much money. The Bord got almost fifteen million in taxpayer money in 2016, and they're going to get sixteen million in 2017. It keeps going up. Until that stops, there will be a lot of death and suffering."

We discussed her latest project. A few months earlier, she and some animal welfare colleagues had announced the establishment of a new political party, the Irish Animal Welfare Party. Its mission was to fight the abuse of animals, and they were going to take on puppy farming first.

For the animal protector it never would end. Nothing would ever be enough.

To change the subject to something brighter, I asked her if she'd be having a grand opening for the main building. After all, this was the centerpiece of her sanctuary.

"Not until I have the veterinary clinic complete. And," she quickly added, "the Garden of Remembrance" —a place where people could bury the ashes of their beloved pets. "I can't die until I have the garden." She laughed. "Then you can sprinkle me up and put me there, too."

~

TIME PASSES. On my older son's sixteenth birthday, my husband took him and his group of longtime friends camping; there is a photo of all of them beneath autumn's changing leaves—one of those landmark images that marks the dizzying passage of time. I was happy that he was more settled in life and had friends.

But not long after that, things changed. He developed questions we couldn't answer for him—questions that the majority of high school students weren't interested in. On the Internet, he discovered that there were people who shared his views about the world and, in particular, his interest in social justice, and he was driven to find them. Perhaps he was influenced by the Occupy movement, as these were the days when protesters were camped out in Zuccotti Park and frequently made the news. Perhaps he would have gone down this path no matter what.

One day he told us he wanted to go to the Bronx to be part of a march against the stop-and-frisk laws that allowed police to carry out racial profiling. He was too young, but he was passionate and that was hard to deny. We drove him into New York City and hung around a couple of blocks away, in case he needed us. (He did not.) Later, he told us that at the end of the march that some parents stood up and spoke about how their unarmed children had been shot by police and died. I believe that day changed him. A few months later, he wanted to go to the May Day parade in New York City. It was a legally permitted march in support of the labor movement—quite tame compared to the stuff he'd been talking about. We agreed, but with conditions for where he could and couldn't go. Later that night, he came home needing a couple of stitches in his face.

He started talking about anarchism, Marx, and capital. While this would have been par for the course in a college student, Gabriel was still in high school, and he stuck out. His group of friends didn't know what to make of him. They backed away for a time.

I secretly worried that I had somehow helped to make him this way. I'd been born with some sort of questioning gene. Had I passed it on to him? How strange that I could celebrate nonconformity in others, but I was continually pushing my older son toward the middle. Yes, I agreed with the fight for justice. But he was my son, and I wanted him to be safe. He didn't understand yet the price he might have to pay.

Of course, it was his life, and he had his own choices to make.

Since meeting Marion and the other animal protectors, I have given a lot of thought to the human desire to save others from harm—how love makes us want to reduce pain and suffering. It is the root of compassion, and I believe it is worth the effort. But in my dark moments I do wonder, have always wondered: Can anybody save anybody? And if salvation is not possible, is there some kind of saving grace in the struggle?

Saving animals is surely easier than saving humans. I have noticed similarities among the people who do this work. They come from backgrounds of childhood loneliness and trauma, loss, and injury, often soothed by the friendship of an animal that could, without words, meet them at the borderline and bring not only comfort but also joy. Others seemed convinced that compassion was something they'd been born with, implanted in their genetic code. And there were those who got into the rescue business for the simple reason that they could not bear to see the powerful take advantage of the weak.

This was Johanna Wothke, who told me about her father helping Jews during the Holocaust. It was Finbarr Heslin, the veterinarian, and Mike Butcher, the defender of pit bulls, who both told me, separately and emphatically, "I don't like bullies."

I understood that I'd been attracted to Marion because of her belief that the sufferings of all voiceless beings are similar. And by the same token, all forms of oppression come from the same root. Helping animals was her preference; but she did not care to sort through who might be the truly innocent.

"If I saw someone on the ground, I'd get down and help," she once said to me, "whether it was a person or an animal. Others would walk by and say it's someone else's business. But I think that human beings should look after everything."

"Why animals?" I'd asked her more than once, until she finally gave me an answer in a way I could at least somewhat understand.

"I don't see any difference. We are them. They are us. We all come from the same place."

When Marion had asked her builder to make a corral, on top of everything else he was doing, he said to her, "Now Marion, you can't put your arms around the world."

"But that's *exactly* what we're trying to do," she later said to me. "We want the world to be a better, more compassionate place."

⁓

WE NOW know that animals not only are more intelligent than we'd thought, they also have more types of intelligence than we'd ever considered because we were so busy comparing them to ourselves. We know that elephants weep for their dead and comfort one another, that primates understand inequity, that some birds understand the passage of time and can form simple sentences. Many species take care of one another, work cooperatively, and feel something that looks a lot like empathy or even love. We also now have proof of the most inconvenient thing—that animals suffer emotional and physical pain more than we'd ever wanted to believe.

Just as we find in the earliest religious texts, animals continue to be sacrificed for human sins on factory farms, in laboratories, and in the wild. And yet, in the ten years since Lily was brought to Rosie's doorstep, there has been major change. Each decade, national polling reveals Americans' rising concern for animal welfare. Ringling Brothers announced that it would end the use of elephants in its performances and a year later shut down. SeaWorld, the largest marine mammal park, is phasing out its orca program after the excoriating documentary *Blackfish* shone a light on its awful treatment of these animals. California has made it illegal to use cetaceans such as dolphins in entertainment. Industrial food companies are eliminating battery cages for hens and gestation crates for sows because of consumer outcry. In 1970, according to the Humane Society, Americans put fifteen million dogs to death; today, that number has declined to just under three million. Pope Francis, evoking his namesake St. Francis, refers to animals as our brothers and sisters. The European Union has outlawed sales of cosmetics tested on animals. Animal welfare activists are raising their voices in Asia. The animal welfare movement has gone mainstream.

Charles Darwin believed that sympathy evolved as an instinct in animals because it helped species evolve. In *The Descent of Man,* he wrote that "communities which included the greatest number of the most sympathetic members, would flourish best and rear the greatest number of offspring." Competing instincts of selfishness and greed would, at times, prevail, but humans, because of their intellectual power to reflect, have the capacity to look back at their selfish actions and feel regret, then do better in the future.

It seems that in many ways humans have evolved over time to become a more compassionate species. But clearly progress is not linear, and we have a long way to go. If our love for pets inspires compassion for other animals with whom we share this planet, I would not be surprised.

People like Marion and those of her tribe help pave the way, though the doing comes at a high price.

As for Lily, my sight hound, she is eleven or twelve years old now. She is still slim, beautiful, graceful as a ballerina. But her eyes are cloudy with cataracts, and she is far less interested in running than she used to be. She is always at my side. I long ago realized, of course, that she was never Gabriel's dog, but mine.

The little boy I wanted her to befriend is now grown and gone. I send him texts with videos of her—simple things. Sleepy dog barely able to get up at night to go out. Leaping dog. Spiraling in the air dog. And every once in a while: Running dog. Flying.

Marion at the Field of Dreams with her dog Harley, 2010. (Courtesy Joe Fitzgibbon)

EPILOGUE

Where they are today

Since delivering Stafford Taylor's tigers to California, wildlife veterinarian **Simon Adams** has continued to investigate abuses, provide testimony, and assist in transport and rescue of zoo and wildlife animals of all kinds. He was an advisor to landmark cases of elephant abuse—Tuli in South Africa and Arna in Australia. He is currently campaigning in the UK and internationally for legislation to end the use of wild animals in circuses, and to promote better standards for wild and captive elephant management.

The **Bord na gCon** has received significant criticism in recent years for its level of debt ($20 million for its new Limerick Stadium), dog doping, inadequate management, and dependence on government subsidies to maintain a surplus on its balance sheet. A 2014 study by the independent Indecon Consultants made 27 recommendations to reform the industry. Nonetheless, the Irish government continues to increase funding to the greyhound industry. In 2017, it allocated 16 million euro to the Bord na gCon, up from 11 million euro in 2013. The Bord na gCon remains a self-regulating agency.

In 2013, an estimated 16,400 greyhounds were bred in Ireland. Approximately 8,600 were exported to Britain or sent to the coursing pool. Of the remaining 7,800, some are certainly among the estimated 3,500 greyhounds racing at Irish tracks now. Greyhound welfare advocates continue to suggest that numbers like these indicate that thousands of dogs go missing each year. In reply, Bord na gCon Welfare and Track Support Manager Barry Coleman says that the advocates do not have sufficient information or understanding of the business to draw conclusions. Nor does the Bord have precise figures relating to the fate of all greyhounds. However, he points out that many can be accounted for as follows: Ten percent of greyhound puppies do not survive due to illness or injury; some are being reared and schooled for racing; some are exported to race in other countries; some are adopted; some are in kennels awaiting adoption; some retired racers are surrendered at pounds; some are retained for breeding; some are kept at home by owners. It is unknown how many retire each year. Coleman says that complete numbers are unknowable. To date, the Bord has no registry that makes all greyhounds traceable from birth to death.

Since the protest against the industry began, the Bord na gCon has taken steps to improve greyhound welfare. A veterinarian is now present at all races, and a new welfare bill in 2011 raised standards of care and regulation. An increasing number of owners seek adoptive homes for retired racers. In addition, each year the Bord na gCon holds retired greyhound shows in Irish communities and donates money (usually an amount between 1 and 2 percent of its government subsidies) to the Irish Retired Greyhound Trust (IRGT). In 2016, the IRGT reported finding homes for 517 Irish greyhounds and funding several Irish animal welfare groups that rehomed 374. Almost all of these dogs had to be sent to Europe or North America because they are still unwanted as pets in Ireland. Limerick Animal Welfare does not participate with or accept money from the Bord na gCon.

After the closure of the Barcelona greyhound track, **Anna Clements** and her husband, the vet Alberto Sorde, founded SOS Galgos to promote adoption of greyhounds (especially those used by hunters), thousands of which are abused and abandoned every year throughout Spain. SOS Galgos educates young children about animal welfare and recently opened an educational center in Barcelona.

Since his undercover work in Spain with the ISPCA, investigations carried out by **Mike Butcher** and his unit at the RSPCA have sent more than three hundred people to jail for dogfighting.

Louise Coleman has continued to find homes for greyhounds and other dogs through her organization Greyhound Friends in Hopkinton, Massachusetts. She also advocates for greyhounds internationally.

Christine Dorchak, **Cary Theil**, and their organization GREY2K USA Worldwide continue to press for the end of greyhound racing in the U.S., a battle that focuses on Florida, home to the majority of remaining tracks. In 2016, they successfully lobbied Florida lawmakers to pass a new regulation that will require greyhound tracks to report all greyhound injuries—a measure that the industry fought for many years. Internationally, the organization has worked with animal welfare advocates in Australia, Argentina, Ireland, Macau, the UK, and other nations to end greyhound racing.

Demi the Graveyard Dog became more confident and settled in as the years passed. She went to work with Jill Hopfenbeck every day and enjoyed catching balls in the backyard and running around with Jill's other sight hounds. She had a good life until her death at age fourteen.

Due to health matters, Greyhounds in Need founders **Anne Finch** and her husband, Arthur, retired after more than twenty years rescuing and rehoming greyhounds from Spain. The organization continues their work (with the help of patrons Jilly Cooper, Judi

Dench, Peter Egan, and Ricky Gervais). Finch estimates that, to date, Greyhounds in Need has been involved in the rescue and homing of 18,000 dogs from Spain. Many other organizations in Europe are now also dedicated to the Spanish greyhound

Veterinarian **Finbarr Heslin** runs a busy small animal veterinary hospital in County Kildare. Since working with the ISPCA on behalf of Irish greyhounds in Spain, he has continued to collaborate with many national and international welfare groups. After he investigated a criminal dogfighting ring and testified in a successful prosecution, his practice was petrol-bombed. (The hospital suffered significant damage but no animals were hurt.) As chair of a government committee aimed at ending puppy mills, his investigations and report led to legislation in 2010 that raised standards for all dog-breeding operations in the country. Most recently, he has helped push forward new regulations for microchipping and registration of dogs.

After the **McCarthy family** of Castletroy moved into the six-acre halting site allocated to them by Limerick County Council in accordance with the Irish High Court decision, the land became very valuable. Nearby settled people continued to object to the presence of the Travellers, complaining about the caravans, animals, noise, campfires, fear of crime, and atmosphere of poverty that the halting site had brought into their midst. The council considered a number of solutions, including the development of a new mixed housing complex for Travellers and others, but ultimately decided to give the McCarthy family a different, much smaller site down the road including several new "half homes" that featured a modern indoor kitchen, a bathroom, and a small sitting area. Instead of bedrooms, these cottages had a bay for a caravan to park, which is where the Travellers were expected to sleep. When I visited with them in 2013, they told me that the site is too small for the families and includes no area for horses to graze, and they'd been waiting for years for real bedrooms to be completed. As of early 2017 they are still waiting.

Molly the Bear is now thirty-one years old and still living at Bear With Us sanctuary in Canada. Though the mission of Bear With Us is to rehabilitate bears and return them to the wild, Molly was unlikely to survive due to the fact that she has no fear of humans. Since 1995, she and another former circus bear named Yogi have shared a 40,000-square-foot forested enclosure with a pond.

Brendan Price and his wife, Mary, have rehabilitated and rescued more than 800 seals through the Irish Seal Sanctuary. Today, he no longer handles seals but continues to work as a wildlife advocate and to advance the role of wildlife rehabilitators. In 2016, he published his first book, *In Search of Sanctuary: Wildlife, My Teacher*. "I believe ordinary people with extraordinary and empathic experience and stories are the fulcrum on which the world will turn in favor of wildlife," he writes.

The tigers from Stafford Taylor's farm lived in a large enclosure with trees and grasses and an open top at Wildlife WayStation in the hills outside San Diego, surrounded by wildlife and peace. They received regular enrichment activities to create an interesting life in captivity, and always had food and medical care. Because of their difficulties in early life, they were never as strong as other Siberian tigers and struggled to retain weight. After many years, the male died first, then the adult female and the baby female. The young male, Maddrass, lived to be more than twenty years old.

Two years after returning to the U.S. from Ireland, Semon Wolf passed away. **Beverly Wolf** now lives in a beautiful part of South Carolina, where I found her sharing her home with a lovely lurcher named Luke. When I asked her if she was proud of saving thousands of dogs during her years in Ireland, she said she was not: "It just needed to be done." Beverly's home is filled with furnishings from Fedamore, including many photos of her and Semon and their hunting life at Scarteen. She still has her Irish horse, Simba, the last foal she bred at Fedamore. She is eighty now and rides him often.

Johanna Wothke remains at the helm of Pro Animale für Tiere in Not e.V., along with her daughter Natascha. Pro Animale now has thirty sanctuaries in Europe which collectively shelter more than 3,000 animals, including dogs, cats, horses, cows, sheep, pigs, and donkeys. Since purchasing the land in Galway and building the original site in 1998, Pro Animale has invested 3.1 million euro in Avalon Greyhound and Horse Sanctuaries, with funds raised from German donors and others around the world. Johanna still publishes her magazine *Der Troppen* (*The Drop*) to report on Pro Animale's work.

ACKNOWLEDGMENTS

Above all, my deepest thanks to Marion Fitzgibbon, who gave me, over the course of many years, hours of her precious time. She answered hundreds of questions in person, by phone, and by email, and shared old documents and photographs. She surely had no idea what she was getting into when she agreed to participate in this project. I am forever indebted to her for her honesty and for sharing her story.

My tremendous thanks to Beverly Wolf, who welcomed me into her home in South Carolina, shared photos, told me her incredible Irish story, and answered many follow-up questions by phone over the years.

I thank all of the people who gave me interviews (listed in the bibliography) and especially the following people who went above and beyond, answering repeated queries and reviewing the manuscript: Simon Adams, Clarissa Baldwin, Anna Clements, Louise Coleman, Christine Dorchak, Anne Finch, Joe Fitzgibbon, Finbarr Heslin,

Heidi Michlin and Joel Rangel of the Jungle Place, Fechin Mullen, Brendan Price, Rosemary Warren, and Johanna Wothke, who made time for me at a very inconvenient moment and shared photos for this book. My thanks also to the photographer John Mottern for his generosity.

Gratitude to David and Jamie Monaghan, who gave me hospitality, guidance, and friendship when I was in Cork and Ballyduff. I also thank Pattie Punch at the Limerick University Library for finding Judge Barron's legal decision.

My thanks to the MacDowell Colony where, for three inspiring and silent weeks, I wrote part of this book.

All books require help from many people, but this one especially came at a difficult time and I received extraordinary help and support.

Amy Cherry at W. W. Norton, brilliant and kind, has been a calm and steady force in my writing life for a long time now. I am more grateful than words can ever say for the exceptional editor and human being she is. I was very late in delivering this book. I thank her for waiting for it, and I frequently count my lucky stars to be with her and W. W. Norton for three books.

At Norton, I also thank Nancy Palmquist and her team who were kind, tolerant, and exceptional professionals in the production of this book. And I thank Remy Cawley for the same.

Allegra Huston, in the eleventh hour, brought elegant and skillful copyediting that went above and beyond all other copyeditors I have known. She made this book significantly better, thanks to her grace with language and her firsthand knowledge of Ireland. She saved me from many mistakes, and I am very grateful.

James Levine and Lindsay Edgecomb at Levine Greenberg Rostan Literary Agency in New York were the kindest and most supportive agents on earth, and had faith in the project from the beginning when others did not. They are beacons of publishing wisdom and generosity.

A very special thanks to the writer and animal person Alice Elliot Dark, who spoke with me very early on and shared her advanced understanding about animal rights when I was still ignorant on the subject. I also thank the writers Lisa Gornick, for giving feedback on the first chapters, and Anne Burt, Christina Baker Kline, Jill Smolowe, and Nancy Star, who listened and provided many forms of encouragement. They and the rest of the Montclair Writers Group have offered wisdom and practical guidance for more than sixteen years. I treasure them all. Thank you to artist and friend Nancy Ring for repeatedly asking, "What is your essential question?"

Thank you, Colleen Schaffner and Filippo Aurelli, my brilliant primatologist family members, who provided scientific perspective, shelter, and friendship, and took me to places in Mexico I could never otherwise have dreamed of going. Special thanks to the amazing Colleen for her review and added help on the final manuscript.

I don't know how to thank the Book Doctors, a.k.a. Arielle Eckstut, David Sterry, and their daughter Olive Sterry. This book would not have been written without the extraordinary lengths of friendship they gave, which included scenes of creative improvisation, forceful deadlines, optimism, boundless kindness, tactical assistance, and an absurdly extended period of physical shelter, so that I could write. Special thanks to Olive for sharing her art room with me, and Joann Eckstut for her positive encouragement.

My sons, animal lovers and independent, clear-eyed thinkers, gave me countless insights over the years that I was writing and thinking about animals. They were the inspiration for this book, and I am grateful that they allowed me to share their voices, spanning the time from childhood to young adulthood. They would have had easier childhoods if I had not been a writer, but they never complained. They are the light of my life and part of all I do. I thank them for their patience and support.

My thanks to Elizabeth Rush Marsden, to whom this book is dedicated, and who, along with her daughter Bree Marsden, happened to be at Saffron Hill (the greyhound sanctuary at Rosemary Warren's home) the day Lily was found and delivered. Elizabeth's guidance and friendship opened the door to this world. I thank her for this, but most of all I thank her for bringing Lily into our lives.

Gratitude to my mother, Marcia Schenone, to whom this book is also dedicated because of the extraordinary compassionate example she showed from my earliest moments of life.

Above all, I thank my husband, Herb Schaffner. He has been my number one champion since we met decades ago. He is a brilliant and generous editor, lover of Yeats, center of my life, writing and otherwise, the morning to my night, the believer against my doubts. Nothing would have been possible without him.

SELECT BIBLIOGRAPHY

Items marked with an asterisk were especially influential.

BOOKS

Beers, Diane L. *For the Prevention of Cruelty: The History and Legacy of Animal Rights Activism in the United States*. Athens, OH: Swallow Press/ Ohio University Press, 2006.

Bekoff, Marc. *The Emotional Lives of Animals: A Leading Scientist Explores Animal Joy, Sorrow, and Empathy—and Why They Matter*. New York: New World Library, 2008.

Berns, Gregory. *How Dogs Love Us: A Neuroscientist and His Adopted Dog Decode the Canine Brain*. Seattle: Lake Union, 2013.

Darwin, Charles. *The Descent of Man, and Selection in Relation to Sex*. London: John Murray, 1871.

De Waal, Frans. *Are We Smart Enough to Know How Smart Animals Are?* New York: W. W. Norton, 2016.

Duffy, Seán, ed. *Atlas of Irish History*. 2nd ed. Dublin: Gill & Macmillan, 2000.

Faruqi, Sonia. *Project Animal Farm*. New York: Pegasus Books, 2015.

Gmelch, George. *The Irish Tinkers: The Urbanization of an Itinerant People*. 2nd ed. Prospect Heights, IL: Waveland Press, 1985.

Gmelch, Sharon. *Nan: The Life of an Irish Travelling Woman*. Long Grove, IL: Waveland Press, 1991.

Kolbert, Elizabeth. *The Sixth Extinction: An Unnatural History*. New York: Henry Holt, 2014.

*Linzey, Andrew. *Animal Theology*. Urbana, IL: University of Illinois Press, 1995.

———, ed. *The Global Guide to Animal Protection*. Urbana–Champaign: University of Illinois Press, 2014.

Lynam, Shevawn. *Humanity Dick: A Biography of Richard Martin, M.P., 1754–1834*. London: Hamish Hamilton,1975.

MacWeeney, Alen. *Irish Travellers: Tinkers No More*. Los Angeles: Alan Ward Fine Art Photographs, 2011.

Monagan, David. *Ireland Unhinged: Encounters With a Wildly Changing Country*. San Francisco: Council Oak Books, 2011.

Morell, Virginia. *Animal Wise: How We Know Animals Think and Feel*. New York: Crown Publishers, 2013.

Pachirat, Timothy. *Every 12 Seconds: Industrialized Slaughter and the Politics of Sight*. New Haven: Yale University Press, 2011.

Phillips, A. A., ed., and M. M. Willcock, trans. *Xenophon and Arrian on Hunting*. Aris and Phillips Classical Texts. Liverpool: Liverpool University Press, 1999.

Quart, Alissa. *Republic of Outsiders: The Power of Amateurs, Dreamers, and Rebels*. New York: New Press, 2013.

Ryan, Thaddeus. *My Privileged Life: With the Scarteen Black and Tans*. New York: Derrydale Press, 2002.

*Shevelow, Kathryn, *For the Love of Animals: The Rise of the Animal Protection Movement*. New York: Henry Holt, 2008.

Singer, Peter. *Animal Liberation*. New York: Avon, 1976.

*Thayer, Gwyneth Anne. *Going to the Dogs: Greyhound Racing, Animal Activism, and American Popular Culture*. Lawrence, KS: University Press of Kansas, 2013.

*Thompson, Laura. *The Dogs: A Personal History of Greyhound Racing*. 2nd ed. London: High Stakes, 2003.

Wise, Steven M. *Rattling the Cage: Toward Legal Rights for Animals*. New York: Perseus, 2000.

PERIODICALS

Abrahamson, Alan. "Ailing Tigers Get New Start in Life." *Los Angeles Times*, December 12, 1994.

Bracken, Dymphna. "Greyhound tied to a tombstone." *Limerick Leader*, November 16, 1994.

Brady, Ray. "Hiberians Away!" *Town and Country*. Accessed at www.lasthunt.com/hib1.html, November 1, 2016.

"A Brutal Sport Hounded to Extinction." *The Daily Mirror*, July 19, 2009. (Includes citation for 1905 Los Angeles Times article about coursing.)

Crist, Steven. Sports World Specials; Home for Greyhounds, *New York Times*, February 3, 1986.

Dillon, Joan. "Early Adoption Pioneers, 1956–98." Greyhound Articles Online, https://greytarticles.wordpress.com/adoptionrescue/early-greyhound-adoption-pioneers. Accessed January 23, 2017.

Dodd, Stephen. "The real beast is lurking in us." *Irish Independent*, September 3, 2000.

Fortune, Michael. "IGB unveils €700,000 industry support plan." *Irish Independent*, May, 4, 2016.

Greene, John. "Funding increase flew in the face of all evidence." *Sunday Independent*, November 2, 2014.

Halbfinger, David M. "Dismal End for Race Dogs, Alabama Authorities Say." *New York Times,* May 23, 2002.

Jackson, David, and Madison Hopkins. "Pork Industry, Activists Debate Cruelty Recorded in Undercover Videos." *Chicago Tribune*, August 3, 2016.

Lane, Mark. "Mercy mission rescues Irish greyhounds." *Irish Independent*, September 26, 1991.

Macintyre, Donald. "Not all dogs go to heaven, it seems." *Irish Times*, October 24,1994.

Marino, Lori, and Michael Mountain. "Denial of Death and the Relationship between Humans and Other Animals." *Anthrozoos*, March 2015.

Myung-Ok Lee, Marie. "Your down coat could be the product of cruelty." Salon, December 15, 2013, http://www.salon.com/2013/12/15/your_down_coat_could_be_the_product_of_cruelty.

O'Neil, Siobhan. "Tigers not facing death." *Irish Press,* October 18, 1994.

"Opposition to blood sports restated by ISPCA." *Irish Times*, November 11, 1996.

Phalon, Richard. "Becoming One's Own Man (Semon Wolf breeds horses in Ireland)." *Forbes,* November 26, 1990.

Phelan, Eugene. "Animal aid rivals clash over funds." *Limerick Leader,* July 1, 1989.

———. "Dogs hounded out of Ireland, but are petted in Germany." *Limerick Leader*, August 14, 1995.

———. "Welfare group and Bord na gCon in clash on greyhound track record." *Limerick Leader*, January 11, 1997.

"Plains Meet a Classic for Coursing Men." *San Francisco Call*, December 6, 1902.

Prendiville, Norma. "Castlemahon tigers' farewell." *Limerick Leader*, December 17, 1994.

———. "Looking after the underdog." *Limerick Leader,* March 15, 2003.

Romano, Robin. "A Trans-Atlantic Rescue." *Boston Globe*, February 12, 1995.

Rosen, Judy. "Animal Traffic." *New York Times Magazine*, September 5, 2014.

Rosenberg, Howard. "Greyhounds' Bleak Fate: 'Running for Their Lives.'" *Los Angeles Times*, January 2, 1993.

Schecter, Anna, Monica Alba, and Lindsay Perez. "Tyson Foods Dumps Pig Farm after NBC Shows Company Video of Alleged Abuse." *NBC News*, November 20, 2013.

Sulzberger, A. G. "Greyhound Races Face Extinction at the Hands of Casinos They Fostered." *New York Times*, March 8, 2012.

"Travellers Halt at College Row." *Irish Independent*, January 30, 1991.

"When the Race is Over." *Irish Times*, July 20, 1999.

Reports and Government Documents

British Greyhound Racing Board, National Greyhound Racing Club, Lord Donoughue of Ashton. *Independent Review of the Greyhound Industry in Great Britain*. November 27, 2007.

Department of Agriculture, Food, and the Marine (Ireland). Indecon International Consultants. *Review of Certain Matters Relating to Bord na gCon*. July 7, 2014.

GREY2K USA Worldwide. *High Stakes: Greyhound Racing in the United States*. February 2015.

Heslin, Finbarr. "Report Commissioned by the ISPCA on the Greyhound Industry in Spain and the Part Played in It by Irish Greyhounds." 1997 (unpublished).

John Ryan, Charles O'Reilly, John McCarthy, Martin McCarthy, and Nora McCarthy vs. The University of Limerick [1991], 66 MCA (High Court).

S.I. No. 657/2011 – Welfare of Greyhounds Act 2011. Accessed at https://www.oireachtas.ie/documents/bills28/acts/2011/a2911.pdf.

Websites Used for Research

GREY2K USA Worldwide. www.grey2kusa.org. Information from the leading anti-greyhound racing advocate.

Houses of the Oireachtas. https://www.oireachtas.ie/parliament. Records of Irish lawmakers' debates on the importance of greyhound racing to the Irish economy,and public subsidies of Bord na gCon.

Irish Greyhound Racing Board/Bord na gCon. www.igbe.org.

*The Last Hunt. www.thelasthunt.com. Damon Sinclair's website for his film about the Ryan family and the Scarteen Hunt.

National Greyhound Association (United States). www.ngagreyhounds.com.

Nonhuman Rights Project. www.nonhumanrightsproject.org. Information about Steven Wise's efforts to change the common law status of some animals from "things" which are owned to "persons" who possess fundamental rights.

Stanford Encyclopedia of Philosophy. www.plato.stanford.edu. For Aristotle and other philosophers' writings on animals.

Websites of Charitable Organizations

Bear With Us Sanctuary and Rehabilitation Centre for Bears. www.bearwithus.org.

GRAI, Greyhound Rescue Association Ireland, which leads the annual walk for greyhounds in Dublin each year. http://www.grai.ie.

Greyhound Friends. www.greyhoundfds.org.

Greyhounds in Need. www.greyhoundsinneed.co.uk (founded by Anne Finch).

ISPCA. www.ispca.ie.

The Jungle Place, a sanctuary for the endangered spider monkey in Quintana Roo, Mexico. http://www.thejungleplace.com.

Limerick Animal Welfare. www.limerickanimalwelfare.ie.

Pro Animale. www.pro-animale.de.

SOS Galgos. www.sosgalgos.com.

Wildlife Waystation. www.wildlifewaystation.org.

Video

"Greyhounds/Connections." Metropolitan Museum of Art. n.d. Accessed at http://www.metmuseum.org/connections/greyhounds.

Reynolds, Gerry. "Tigers Are Not Just For Christmas." *RTE News*, November 29, 1991. Accessed at http://www.rte.ie/archives/2016/1128/834975-limerick-girl-gets-two-tigers/

Author Interviews

Baldwin, Clarissa
Bent, Barbara
Beumer, Johanna
Butcher, Mike
Clements, Anna
Coleman, Barry
Coleman, Louise
Colette, Martine
Conroy, Noreen
Cooke, Mary
Dorchak, Christine
Dynan, Anne
Finch, Anne
Fitzgibbon, Marion
Fleming, Damian

Fox, Mary Jane
Guccione, Gary
Gunning, Geraldine
Heslin, Finbarr
Hopfenbeck, Jill
Hyde, John
McCarthy family: Bridget, John, Mary, Olive, Tina
Mullen, Fechin
O'Halloran, Rita
Price, Brendan
Shannon, Ann
Sharp Bolster, Melanie
Warren, Rosemary
Wolf, Beverly
Wothke, Johanna